THE 52 ATTRIBUTES OF GOD

Produced by Raymond Creed,
Director of *'Rebuild Christianity Publications'* and the *'Rebuild Christianity'* web site at www.rebuildchristianity.com

Author of: -

'Facing the Unthinkable'

'The Leeds Liturgy'

'The Phantom Conflict'

Storefront
http://stores.lulu.com/rebuildchristianity or
http://stores.lulu.com/store.php?fAcctID=976144

Soft cover editions may also be available through Amazon and other International Book Distributors.

THE 52 ATTRIBUTES OF GOD

(Bible teaching on divine attributes and the challenge of deification in Patristic Literature, Medieval Mysticism and Contemporary Christian Spirituality)

Ecclesiastes 12:1
"Remember now your Creator in the days of your youth, while the evil days come not, nor the years draw near when you shall say, 'I have no pleasure in them.'"

Thought Starter: Any Fool
"Any fool can deny the existence of God, but it takes an even bigger fool to claim to be God!"

Raymond Creed

Rebuild Christianity Publications
www.rebuildchristianity.com

Produced by Raymond Creed,
Director of *'Rebuild Christianity Publications'* and the *'Rebuild Christianity'* web site at www.rebuildchristianity.com

Published by Rebuild Christianity Publications

Copyright © the Author 2011
(Backdated to cover all material produced by the author before 2011)

All Rights Reserved,
The Moral Right of the author has been asserted.

First (Pilot) Edition 2009, is now out of print

Second (International) Edition 2011

ISBN: 978-1-907910-05-0

Contents

Introduction X

Preface: A Thankless Task XI

THE 52 KNOWN ATTRIBUTES OF GOD 1

Dedication 2

Prologue: Colours 3

C1: Introducing the Attributes 5

S1: Aims 7

S2: A Practical Approach 10

S3: Explanation of Terminology 12

C2: The Twenty Three Largely Shared Attributes ... 15

LS1: Complexity (Diversity) 17

LS2: Creativity (Originality) 20

LS3: Emotion (Sensitivity) 23

LS4: Enlightenment (Illumination) 27

LS5: Eternity (Everlasting Existence) 30

LS6: Faithfulness (Trustworthiness) 33

LS7: Greatness (Majesty) 37

LS8: Heroism (Courage) 40

LS9: Humanity (Personality) 43

LS10: Humour (Witty Irony) 47

LS11: Intelligence (Reason) ... 51

LS12: Jealousy (Protective Possessiveness) ... 54

LS13: Joy (Gladness) ... 58

LS14: Judgement (Condemnation) ... 61

LS15: Mystery (Hidden Invisibility) ... 65

LS16: Self-Revealing (Communicative) ... 69

LS17: Suffering (Endurance) ... 73

LS18: Unity (Indivisible Oneness) ... 76

LS19: Will (Total Determination) ... 80

LS20: Wonder (Total Beauty) ... 83

LS21: Worthiness (Unlimited Value) ... 86

LS22: Wrath (Furious Anger) ... 90

LS23: Zeal (Enthusiastic Fervour) ... 94

Summary ... 98

C3: The Fourteen Potentially Shared Attributes ... **105**

PS1: Generosity (Abundance) ... 107

PS2: Goodness (Benevolence) ... 110

PS3: Grace (Unmerited Favour) ... 113

PS4: Holiness (Total Purity) ... 116

PS5: Humility (Modesty) ... 120

PS6: Justice (Impartial Fairness) ... 123

PS7: Law-Giving (Rule-Making) 127

PS8: Love (Benevolent Compassion) 131

PS9: Mercy (Forgiveness) 134

PS10: Patience (Persevering Self-Restraint) 137

PS11: Peacefulness (Total Harmony) 141

PS12: Righteousness (Correctness) 144

PS13: Simplicity (Straightforwardness) 148

PS14: Uprightness (Infallible Truthfulness) 152

Summary 156

C4: The Fifteen Barely Shared Attributes of God **161**

BS1: Absolute Being (Independent Self-Existence) 163

BS2: Adequacy (Competence) 166

BS3: Glory (Renown) 170

BS4: Immanence (Total Involvement) 173

BS5: Immutability (Stability) 177

BS6: Infinity (Unlimited Extent) 180

BS7: Omnipotence (Total Power) 183

BS8: Omnipresence (Total Presence) 187

BS9: Omniscience (Total Knowledge) 190

BS10: Omniwisdom (Total Shrewdness) 194

BS11: Perfection (Faultlessness) 197

BS12: Self-Sufficiency (Total Independence) 200

BS13: Sovereignty (Lordship) 204

BS14: Transcendence (Lofty Detachment) 207

BS15: Tri-Unity (Pluralistic Oneness) 211

Summary 214

C5: The Oldest Lie 219

Definitions 221

Prologue: The Self-Glorifiers 223

5.1 A Deadly Ascent 225

5.2 A Secure and Lasting Friendship 236

5.3 Becoming a Friend of God 252

Overview 273

Appendices: Tables and Bible Summaries 281

A1: Biblical Summary 283

A2: The Eighty-Eight Names of God 289

A3: Different Views of Deification 292

Selective Bibliography 295

S1: Book List 297

S2: Reference Works 300

S3: Media Sources 301

S4: Other Information Sources 302

Other Titles by the Author ... **303**

Facing the Unthinkable ... 305

The Leeds Liturgy ... 306

The Phantom Conflict ... 308

Notes ... 309

Key

A: Appendix

C: Chapter

S: Section

Su: Summary

BS: Barely shared attribute

LS: Largely shared attribute

PS: Potentially shared attribute

Introduction

'The 52 Attributes of God' explores God's unique character. It uses ancient Jewish methods of bible interpretation (*'Midrash'*) along with prayerful meditations, proverbial sayings and simple summaries. Each chapter combines both analytical with devotional material and readers are encouraged to progress at their own pace. *'The 52 Attributes of God'* is readily accessible for both private and group use and employs a stimulating variety of questions to aid reflection and to encourage practical application. It shows how all 52 of the divine attributes were displayed during Christ's death and it helps rebuild Christianity by using *'Midrash'* to provide a clearer picture of God's nature. Great care is taken to answer such questions as: -
1) Who is God?
2) What is He like?
3) How did He react to the death of His Son Jesus?
4) How does He react to the corruption found within much of today's Church?
5) To what extent can we become like God?

'The 52 Attributes of God' should prove particularly useful to religious ministers (of all denominational backgrounds), local church elders, Christian teachers, evangelists and theological students. The Messianic Jewish community and those wishing to delve deeper into theology would especially benefit. Any public or academic library with a theological section will find it a rich resource. It should also be of assistance to those confused or troubled by particular *'spiritualities'* which alluringly offer the chance to become divine.

This book ends by warning that those choosing to ignore the clear distinction between God and Man (by presuming they have a right to become mini-gods) often end up behaving like devils.

Readers who do not wish to know how this book came to be written should skip the Preface. To purchase a download, hard or soft cover edition please visit: -

http://stores.lulu.com/rebuildchristianity or

http://stores.lulu.com/store.php?fAcctID=976144

Soft cover editions may also be available through Amazon and other International Book Distributors.

Preface: A Thankless Task!

In the stirring Preface to his book *'The Knowledge of the Holy'*[1] the great Christian writer A. W. Tozer gave a warning which is proving to be of greater relevance today than when it was first penned in the middle of the Twentieth Century. He stated that, *"The low view of God entertained almost universally among Christians is the cause of a hundred lesser evils elsewhere among us. A whole new philosophy of the Christian life has resulted from this one basic error in our religious thinking."*

An Indifference to Truth

Now a generation later, *"the hundred lesser evils"* he mentioned have mushroomed and become even greater evils. Beliefs and practices which would have been unacceptable when I[2] suddenly became a Christian at the age of nineteen on October 18th 1975 have now become the norm. These include the widespread acceptance of homosexual practice within Anglicanism, the *'interfaith'* ceremonies practiced by liberal forms of Christianity and the *'devils dance'* of the Toronto Experience which spread across much of the Evangelical Sector during the 1990s. Meanwhile, much of the Eastern Orthodox Church continues to give the impression of being little more than a nest of anti-Semites, whilst Roman Catholicism appears to be a religious mafia offering sheltered employment for child molesters. Yet these are only a few instances of a widespread turning away from God in all of the Christian Traditions. Alongside the disintegration of traditional Christian faith and morality is a stupefying indifference to truth. Sadly present in many Churches is a lazy *'so what?'* attitude to even the most important Biblical teachings. The writer can personally vouch for the fact that all too often, many within the Church[3] dismiss Christian doctrine as *'boring,' 'dull', 'heavy'* or *'irrelevant.'* With a yawn and a shrug of the shoulders they negate those very truths which could give them eternal life. Where there is zeal for doctrine, it is usually a zeal for <u>false</u> doctrine and when challenged about this the result is

---

[1] The Knowledge of the Holy p.6; first read by the writer in late 1978.
[2] The designation *'the writer'* will more often be used in place of personal pronouns like *'I'* or *'me.'* The latter's overuse can convey the impression of an opinionated egotism.
[3] The word *'Church'* is used in its broadest sense to mean the visible Church, represented by such Traditions as Eastern Orthodoxy, Roman Catholicism, Liberal and Evangelical Protestantism, Pentecostalism and Messianic Judaism.

anger or even worse, a smug *'you haven't got what I've got'* pride. Amongst the writer's contemporaries are those who would give a thousand excuses over why they couldn't attend a local Bible Course and then go on to waste money and time, travelling hundreds of miles to attend a convention given by a charlatan preacher whose sermons consist only of disjointed anecdotes. In most of the Churches encountered by the writer a real love of the truth has been a rare commodity. Indeed, this state of affairs has applied throughout a variety of cultural and social settings. Now it seems that anything is acceptable as long as it *'feels good,'* and it is this factor which dominates most Churches today. Entertainment, the desire for social acceptability and the lust for personal success are all idols which have largely Christ. The chief desire has consisted mainly of *'a form of religion,'* bringing psychological comfort but offering no real challenge, (2 Timothy 3:5). Anything not meeting this desire has been rejected and this rejection has included Jesus Christ Himself!

God has, in effect, been sidestepped and ignored – something which would simply not have happened in the Victorian era, where a crisis of faith or unbelief will have been proclaimed with a noisy fanfare and a roll of drums. Now unbelief is taken for granted and to such a degree that it is those with a genuine faith in Jesus who are regarded as being abnormal or politically incorrect.[4] In many Churches, truth has crept out by the back door whilst even the most absurd lies of Satan have been given a public welcome.[5] It is this mixture of spiritual apathy (amongst the majority) and irrational religious fanaticism (amongst a noisy minority) which makes writing *'The 52 Attributes of God'* such a thankless task. The writer has few illusions about the appalling state of most Churches in the Western World. From a business viewpoint, the task is sheer folly, as the market for the Christian God has largely collapsed and is likely to remain that way for the foreseeable future. Why waste time trying to promote a product for which there exists no demand? Moreover, it's a product with a tarnished image; in part created by the excesses of those claiming to follow the Christian God. Common sense observation would suggest that Christianity is all but *'played out'* and all that

---

[4] The Christian Institute provides thorough documentation of the increasing harassment Christians within the United Kingdom are coming under. For further details please refer to http://www.christian.org.uk/

[5] An example in 2003 was the welcome which greeted the appointment and enthronement of the pro-homosexual Hegelian Druid, Doctor Rowan Williams. His tenure has been characterized by deep moral corruption and the further disintegration of the Anglican Communion. Under Williams, it's tempting to wonder whether the Church of England in particular, got the leadership it deserved.

Church leaders can do is to find a comfortable niche as accredited social workers of the *'New World Order.'* However, the growing intolerance toward even moderate forms of Christianity in the West makes even this option unlikely. In the area of social work, faithful Christians are being squeezed out on the grounds of political correctness – one recent example being Catholic adoption agencies which may have to close because of their unwillingness to hand children over for adoption by homosexual parents.

The picture only worsens when Biblical warnings are considered. In Luke 18:8b, Jesus Himself asked, *"When the Son of Man comes shall He find faith on the earth?"* Judging by today's world the answer is a resounding *'no!'* Christ has been spurned and with Him the God He claimed to follow. Adding to this gloomy picture are the other portions of scripture like 1Timothy 4:1 which warn of a menacing worldwide apostasy. At this moment in time (December 2010), the writer seems to have little incentive to publish anything about God. Possibly the best thing he could do is to stroke a soothing cat to calm his troubled nerves!

Motives for Writing This Book

So why is the writer bothering to release this book if all appears lost? The answer assuredly goes back to scripture, where a whole array of prophets persevered in witnessing to the one true God when everything around them seemed hopeless. A particularly striking example was Jeremiah (who didn't appear to own a cat to soothe his troubled nerves)! As a true prophet, he knew that the Kingdom of Judah was doomed and that judgement would come upon his contemporaries. Nevertheless, he still continued his ministry until the end of his life – for which he also got very little thanks. His was a model of perseverance to inspire any believer. Another example was Christ Himself who knew that His own work would end in an agonising death and public disgrace. He was very aware that the old religious system in which He'd been brought up was doomed and, foreseeing the destruction of Jerusalem by the Romans in AD70, he wept for it, (Luke 19:41). In addition, there was the apostle Paul who continued to preach the Gospel in seasons of great blessing <u>and</u> also when it seemed to produce nothing but persecution. Towards the end of his life he had to face the permanent rejection of his message by the Jewish people, whom he'd loved so dearly (Acts 28:17f & Romans 10:1-3).[6]

These and other Biblical examples (such as Noah who only made eight converts) show that <u>it is precisely at those times when everything seems lost that believers in the one true God need to persevere in their own respective vocations.</u> Giving up on the faith is <u>not</u> the response scripture recommends. Instead, we are to continue witnessing to the faith even when the World and the Church are busily rejecting it. The command is *to 'hold fast'* until Christ intervenes in His own unique way and time, (Revelation 2:25). As followers of God, we are engaged in a long distance marathon, not a short sprint. If we give up we will be absorbed into a deceptive world system, hurtling toward destruction. Mercifully, we do not persevere using our own inner resources but are imbued with Christ's strength and so we continue, remaining open and willing to receive that strength. Christians are like the players in a football team, giving their all to play the game, even though the score against them is five-nil. They have no right to quit the playing field just because the match isn't going their way.

Exactly how believers will persevere in their witness depends very much upon their individual calling and circumstances. For some, their witness to Christianity will primarily be through their character and manner of living; for others it will be through having an established ministerial position in the Church and for still others it may be through the writing of endless tomes via the Internet! Furthermore, a persevering witness is one that will continue in the face of mass global deception and apostasy by the Church itself. In this context, what really matters is <u>not</u> whether we are successful in terms of gaining large numbers or a *'big name;'* but whether <u>there is a faithful and constant witness, achieved in the power and love of God's Holy Spirit.</u> Only this sort of witness will bear the right fruit, both in our own lives and in the lives of those receptive to our sharing of Christ, (Galatians 5:23).

---

[6] In my own case I've spent three and a half decades living though the prolonged and protracted death of English Christianity. I regard it as the most tragic development in my life. Christianities perceived irrelevance has helped to create a spiritual vacuum that's being filled by militant forms of Atheism, Islam and Paganism.

A Simple Explanation

The simplest explanation over why I'm engaged in reminding a largely faithless people of their God is that the good Lord is supremely worth writing about. As Creator, He is to be honoured by even the tiniest spark of creativity. Indeed, the act of writing about the Deity can become an act of worship. Through tapping the keyboard of my personal computer, I am paying homage to His Holy Name. I write to glorify God. If the rest of the Church chooses to ignore what is written, then in one sense, that is not my problem. My job is to be faithful to my calling; the results of which must be left to judge.[7]

The very real hope is that at least a handful of readers will be encouraged to persevere in the Christian Faith. Learning about God's awesome character should fire their enthusiasm, paving the way for them to receive His holy love – which will last for all of eternity. *'The 52 Attributes of God'* is also meant to encourage believers who have become despairing about the deteriorating spiritual condition apparent in all branches of Christianity. Sometimes, it's only by being reminded of who God is that the temptation to relinquish the faith is overcome. For those influenced by false teaching *'The 52 Attributes of God'* clearly point to those truths which should robustly oust the false teaching in question.[8]

Due to its no-nonsense portrayal of scriptural truth, *'The 52 Attributes of God'* may legitimately act as a source of condemnation for those who are spiritually lazy, intoxicated by false spiritual influences or who are blindly pursuing their own agendas. Whether this book performs a redemptive or a retributive function will depend largely upon the response of the reader. It can act either as a prompt for those wishing to know the truth or as an opportunity for others to knowingly reject it.

---

[7] This does not preclude following a very active approach in terms of marketing and promotion but it does mean that once I've done my best in these areas I have to accept that it is God who will give the growth that's needed to fulfil a ministry, (1 Corinthians 3:6). At this stage of my work, I would prefer steady rather than explosive growth which could produce severe problems of control.
[8] One such teaching is belief in the possibility of becoming a mini-god through the practise of certain spiritual techniques. The growing acceptance of this delusion meant that (from March-July 2010) the writer needed to prepare a whole new chapter in order to refute it. (See Chapter Five *'The Oldest Lie.'*)

By this stage, it should be apparent that my approach to the task of writing about God's character is being undertaken in a mood of sober realism. The writer has no illusions about the World or about the Church, (which is thundering at an ever-faster rate toward full-scale apostasy).[9] Many tragic developments are waiting to take place. However (and very thankfully) no problem exists concerning the subject of God Himself which the writer has always found to be of considerable personal interest. If the resources provided here help readers to resolve some of their personal problems all well and good, but this has not been the primary intention. The central purpose has always been to remind a faithless Church of what the real God is like. The writer will briefly recount how he came to be engaged upon this particular task.

How This Book Came to Be Written

The material for chapters 2-4 based upon notes previously compiled for private study (from February-April 1986.) They were subsequently used as part of a Church Bible Exposition Course in 1987 and then adapted for a weekend theological workshop, given at this same Church in October 1988. Details about the names of God were inserted during mid-1999.

However the real beginning can be traced back to a meditation that first came to mind on Thursday, 11 November 1999 whilst walking towards a certain City Centre through a thick grey mist. (Entitled *'Make Known'* it was word processed that very same day.) Its theme was the need to accept the challenge to make God's ways known in an age of great spiritual darkness.

"Make known
The way of the Lord
Make known
This way to others
Make known
This way in a manner that can be blessed,
Make known
This way in a manner that can last,
So there remains a vivid witness to
Christ in this age of grave spiritual darkness."

---

[9] This will be the subject of two books due for release sometime in 2012 at the latest. Details will be announced on the rebuildchristianity.com web site in due time.

At the time I perceived that, in the Western World much of the Church had erred by treating God as if He were dependent upon them for success in spreading His Kingdom. This point was reflected in a second meditation (entitled, *'Is God a Beggar?'*) also written on Thursday, 11 November 1999.

"Is God a beggar who depends upon human ingenuity to accomplish His plans?

Is the Lord of Creation an abject failure who needs man-made schemes in order to succeed?

Is the Almighty so ineffective that He can do nothing without human permission?

Of course not!
Yet, this is how many in the Church perceive Him."

Much re-working of *'The 52 Attributes of God'* followed, but growing work pressures and a close personal bereavement in April 1999 imposed a delay of eighteen months. Even then things were left to ferment quietly and unobtrusively until something drastic took place which was to get me out of what had become a wilderness period in my life. Any impact (if any) I was having upon the church at this time was negligible.

Sadly, that *'something'* was the tragic events of September 11th 2001, when the twin towers of the New York Trade Centre were destroyed by terrorist action. Like many others at the time, the writer was plunged into turmoil by the horrific scenes of that dreadful day, coupled with the haunting thought that this atrocity could be a prelude to even worse acts of mass destruction. However, one thing did become clear; namely that a four-year *'hiatus,'* (which had lasted from September 1997-September 2001) was now coming to an end. I was, with very mixed feelings, being called back into the front line of God's purposes. Over subsequent months, an abundance of events would confirm that this was indeed the case. During Tuesday and Wednesday 13-14th November 2001, the writer undertook some limited fasting and it seemed as if the Holy Spirit was saying three things: -

"Remind my people of who I am and what I am like."

"Make a start by using the resources you already have."

"Your time in the wilderness is at an end. I am calling you back to exercise a 'watchman's ministry,'[10] which will confront the many evils done in My Name."

Upon subsequent reflection the writer decided the wisest way forward would be to: -
1) Prepare this book for some form of Internet publishing.
2) Be committed to publishing only those works where much of the background research had already been done.
3) Accept that God was renewing His call to confront apostate forms of Christianity.

'The 52 Attributes of God' represents an implementation of the first two points. Should these result in producing good fruit in people's lives then I would consider implementing the third and far more difficult instruction.[11]

Further confirmation came when I referred to various scripture passages like Hebrews 11 which highlighted the need for perseverance. There was a dovetailing between the whole pattern of Biblical teaching and what the Holy Spirit appeared to be saying to me directly. It was <u>not</u> a case of picking one or two passages at random in order to justify a prior revelation – a procedure often

---

[10] Meaning a ministry which specialises in: -
- Exposing deception in the Church
- Warning Christians about any specific dangers facing them
- Providing information about relevant social and spiritual developments
- Discerning what God may be doing (or saying) in a particular situation or a period of history

Although they can have a reputation for *'fault finding'* such ministries can provide an invaluable service. However, they do require an awful lot of emotional stamina, determined perseverance and spiritual grace. (A dry sense of humour also helps.)

[11] It first began to be implemented in June 2004, when the writer accidentally came across a certain Liberal Christian discussion forum. It was then subsequently implemented on two Anglican discussion forums where he spent four years confronting the growing darkness within Western forms of Anglicanism (which climaxed in the disgraceful manipulation present at the 2008 Lambeth Conference). The depravity associated with Lambeth is described in the writer's polemical article *'United to what?'* After it the writer withdrew from the Anglican scene in order to concentrate upon rebuilding the Christian Faith through the production of good teaching literature. There remains only a tenuous contact with the Virtue Online forum in order to obtain feedback for some of his ideas on church governance.

followed by false prophets. The result of this was an extensive drafting and re-drafting of materials (over the late 2001 and 2002 period) – until the need to address the crisis of Anglicanism (from December 2002) onwards delayed further progress. However, another draft of *'The 52 Attributes of God'* (then under the working title *'About God'*) was completed by Saturday, 30th October 2004, with minor improvements in June 2005. Matters then finally rested until August 2006 when a Sunday Times newspaper article by Martin Wroe (2006) suggested the option of *'print-by-demand.'*[12] Here was the very real possibility of getting a book published without having recourse to book agents or conventional publishers. This prospect appeared most attractive and in early December of that year the further draft work on *'About God'* was begun. A study of Grudem (1994 pp.156-160) in late February 2007 clarified my understanding of how different attributes related to one another and the concept of *'mutual referencing'* was introduced. Release for limited distribution took place early in the following May.

In October 2009, at the suggestion of a family friend, *'About God'* was split into two. **Part A** became *'The 52 Attributes of God'* and **Part B** *'The Phantom Conflict,'* with the original title *'About God'* being abandoned. A further review of each of these chapters (in November-December 2009) removed most remaining minor errors with some additional alterations made to some of the Appendices. However, the need to prepare a new chapter on *'The Oldest Lie'* in March 2010 delayed matters again. Final editing began in December 2010 and involved the introduction of new summaries and some minor restructuring and updating of information. Finally, in April 2011, *'The 52 Attributes of God'* was ready for international distribution.[13]

Date references in the footnotes will designate when the original drafts of *'The 52 Attributes of God'* were produced. This is done in order to show the reader how it was built up over a period of time. On a final very pedantic note, it's worth mentioning that line spaces on numbered lists are regarded as being the equivalent of a full stop. Consequently, this symbol will be omitted unless the point being listed amounts to more than one sentence.

The Author, Saturday, 30th April 2011

---

[12] Sunday Times, News Review 13.8.2006 p.4.3
[13] *'The Phantom Conflict'* had been released for International Distribution in December 2010.

XX

THE 52 KNOWN[14] ATTRIBUTES OF GOD

"Indifference to God leads to indifference to other people, shown by the small compassionate acts that are <u>not</u> done to help others."[15]

---

[14] The adjective *'noble'* could be used in place of *'known'* in order to highlight the illustrious, grand and wholly moral qualities of every single divine attribute.
[15] The author, Thursday, 11th November 1999

Dedication

This book is dedicated to the late Doctor Michael Woodhouse (1934-2007) with warm thanks for the helpful encouragement, teaching and prayer support he provided during the crucial period from late 2001 until early 2007.

PROLOGUE: COLOURS [16]

<u>White</u> is for God's purity
His freedom from sin

<u>Red</u> is for Christ's blood
Shed freely to save

<u>Orange</u> is for God's anger
Glowing hot like a coal

<u>Yellow</u> is for God's light
Giving us truth

<u>Green</u> is for God's creativity
Abundant in its lush fertility

<u>Blue</u> is for God's mystery
Deep and unfathomable

<u>Purple</u> is for God's royalty
One King and Lord of all

---

[16] This meditation was written in January 1984 and expresses the vibrant array of God's divine attributes.

C1:
INTRODUCING THE ATTRIBUTES

S1: AIMS

'The 52 Attributes of God' aims to answer the following questions; *'Who is God?'* and *'What is He like?'* by: -
1) Providing a basic outline of the Deity, as revealed in scripture
2) Emphasising the sheer greatness of God
3) Leaving no excuses on the Judgement Day for those determined to depart from His way

The answers hope to be as comprehensive as possible, or at least to prove of sufficient use in helping people to know and to enjoy God for themselves.

'The 52 Attributes of God' has been written not only to inform the expert theologian or to present evidence (bolstered by complex arguments) proving God's existence;[17] but to clearly describe to the reader the characteristics of God. In addition, it hopes to correct any dangerous overemphasis upon either the attribute of holiness or of love. Furthermore, it is intended to provoke worship and to inspire prayer – devotional material having been inserted to facilitate this. The following verse provides the backdrop to this whole work: -
"The more holy a person becomes
The more loving they are;
The more loving a person becomes
The more holy they are."
Another intention has been to settle the question; *"To what degree, if any, can human beings become like God?"* An attempt is made to show that, whilst some divine characteristics are (or can be) shared with humanity, many others are reserved for God alone. This fact should make nonsense of the *'deification'*[18] claims made certain eastern religions or by those with New Age and/or mystical Christian leanings.

---

[17] In part, this is because some of the arguments posed by Christians in order to prove God's existence are often naïve and unconvincing, *'Intelligent Design,'* being just one example. It poses that the presence of orderly design requires the presence of an intelligent designer. Unfortunately, this argument underplays the very pertinent element of random chaos which entered creation because of sin. There is also the problem of subjectivity, for a particular design may exist only in the eye of the beholder. Moreover, such arguments tend to distract from gospel preaching which is the only method of public evangelism commended by scripture. Although I believe in Intelligent Design I still think it's a waste of time arguing the point with unbelievers. Doing so is the equivalent of trying to explain the difference between the colour red and the colour green to a person blind from birth.

[18] *'Deification'* is the process whereby people think they can become like God. (A fuller definition will be found in the definition list at the beginning of **C5**.)

An attempt has also been made to draw a sharp contrast between an idol and the one true God of scripture. An idol is a false god, occupying a place within the human heart that should be reserved for God alone. Many different types of idols exist;[19] but, in essence, they comprise of a dependence upon any person, place, object or idea in place of God. Idolatry is simply the worship of an idol.

'The 52 Attributes of God' is aimed at the lay reader as well as *'the religious professional'* and is not meant as a purely academic study. Where logical argument and specialised terminology are deemed, useful they're made easier to follow in the glossaries and summaries. It should be ideally suited for students, lay people and overworked ministers (who may simply need a *'refresher'* on key points). It has also been designed for small group work and rests upon the following assumptions: -
1) A divine name often reveals a personal characteristic of God
2) Human beings and God have some characteristics in common, but not enough for the former to become mini-god's in their own right
3) An understanding of the divine attributes is an absolute prerequisite for effective Christian living

A conscious attempt has been made to build upon the exceptionally solid theological foundations laid by some of the writers listed in the bibliography. A particular debt is owed to J. I. Packer and A. W. Tozer who first fired an interest in the divine attributes when the writer was a young (and very muddled) believer during the late 1970s. They provided an excellent foundation upon which to build. Indeed, one aim of *'The 52 Attributes of God'* has been to develop the insights provided by these men and to apply them in today's worsened spiritual climate, where much of the Church appears increasingly poised to embrace a major global deception. Another intention is to re-state (in simpler terms) the points made by such sixteenth century Puritan writers as Stephen Charnock. For all of their many virtues, the Puritans tended to hide important theological insights behind a superfluity of words.[20] Other, more recent writers (*e.g.* Herman Bavinck) although more concise, frequently wrote in such an abstract manner as to distance their readers from the God whom they more-or-less accurately portrayed. Should the writer be able to repeat what these authors said but with a greater clarity, then an important service will have been rendered. The intention is <u>not</u> to

---

[19] These can range from the crude Totem Poles of tribal religions to the sophisticated goods of Western Civilization.
[20] All too often their style served to irritate rather than to inform the reader.

be an unthinking traditionalist, merely *'parroting'* what has been said before but to modify and improve upon accepted tradition. Quite emphatically the writer does not accept that, in their understanding of God, the Church Fathers, the Puritans or any other group of thinkers managed to grasp the whole picture with nothing more needing to be added. To assume so would be to commit the sin of intellectual laziness. However, the writer is still extremely thankful for the many insights gained from such authors. What is of lasting importance from their work is now (alongside other contemporary and equally valid insights) being brought to light, right here in the twenty-first century. Theirs is a very pertinent voice which needs to resonate once more.

Where the writer does attempt to be original is not so much in what he says but in the way he says it. He hopes to blend the best parts of his formal theological training with devotional material; with such a combination appealing to the heart as well as to the head. The devotional material includes wise sayings, prayers and meditations, with added humour where appropriate.[21] Questions are also posed to encourage readers to interact with the contents – either as individuals or in groups. *'The 52 Attributes of God'* is best used in a lively interactive manner – it was never intended solely as an academic textbook.

This work can also act as a basis for further study. *'The 52 Attributes of God'* would constitute a good foundation from which to tackle the more exacting works of Bavinck, Charnock and Packer. It can just as readily be used as a logical next step from Tozer's more foundational yet profound approach in his treatment of the Almighty in his book *'The Knowledge of the Holy.'*

Questions

1) What questions does this book address?

2) What are its key assumptions?

3) How does this book attempt to be original?

---

[21] The writer is keenly aware that one person's good joke is another person's offensive joke. His intention has always been to avoid the latter style.

S2: A PRACTICAL APPROACH

A practical approach is adopted throughout *'The 52 Attributes of God.'* This involves firstly a brief definition followed by a description of each one the 52 known attributes of God. In application of Deuteronomy 19:15 three Biblical authors are employed to reveal the particular truths concerning each divine attribute.[22] The intention is to encourage the reader to behave like the *'noble'* Bereans of Acts 17:11 and to *'search the scriptures'* in order to establish the validity of any given teaching. This explains why the reader is frequently encouraged to refer to a Bible Concordance. To simply *'force feed'* scripture passages would do a disservice – far more is learnt when individuals look up the word of God for themselves. Many of the key points are divided by sub-headings and line spacing. Information is presented in readily digestible chunks with the meditations and questions adding a refreshing interactive element. Readers are continually encouraged to actively engage with its contents.

Given the rapid spiritual decline embarrassingly visible throughout most of the Church in the Western World today, it was deemed appropriate to show how each divine attribute explains the Lord's view concerning apostasy.[23] This divine viewpoint needs to be taken into account if believers are to remain faithful to Him.[24]

The writer has also focused upon how each attribute was demonstrated during the death of Jesus. It is assumed that this event acted as a *'shop window'* into the very nature of God. In one sense, Christ (when upon the cross) had been completely abandoned by God and yet God was always present in that He was manifesting all 52 of His attributes at precisely that pivotal point in history. Resolving this apparent paradox between divine absence and divine presence at the cross of Jesus is just the sort of subject upon which theologians have spent hours of speculation and which this study hopes to resolve, at least in part.

'The 52 Attributes of God' assumes that what is true of God is also true of Jesus because Jesus Himself is <u>fully</u> divine, possessing <u>all</u> of the attributes of Deity; as it is written in Colossians 2:9 *"For in Him*

---

[22] This was judged as sufficient to establish the main points. Any further citation of Biblical authors would have made this study far too long.
[23] The term *'apostasy'* means a deliberate *'turning aside from God'*
[24] However, no attempt is made here to provide a wider analysis of apostasy. The writer hopes to deal with this subject in later books.

dwells all the fullness of the Godhead bodily." This means that Jesus possesses (and manifests) all of the unique attributes of God to an unlimited degree. Just as God is eternal, infinite and absolutely perfect so too is Jesus. He is in no sense any lesser than God and, as God, we can pray to Him with a confidence given by God. Admittedly, all of this can sound very dogmatic, but in a work of this modest size any doctrinal assumptions need to be succinctly stated. At this point the writer feels compelled to confess his deeply held belief that *"Jesus Christ has come in the flesh,"* (1 John 4:2). Holding this belief for over the course of three-and-a-half decades has allowed him to come to a greater understanding of *"the known attributes of God."*

Summary Tables listing relevant bible passages pertaining to some of the divine attributes and the divine names are provided in **Appendix 1** and **2**. In contrast **Appendix 3** uses diagrams to illustrate the different views of how people wish to become like God. These Summaries are a good reference tool, focussing upon the various truths concerning the character of God. They should prove most useful to those wishing to establish new Christian Fellowships upon a sound doctrinal basis.[25]

The Selective Bibliography is useful to those wishing to engage in further research. It also points to those sources which have influenced the writer throughout the course of his Christian life.

Questions

1) Why is it important to *'search the scriptures'* in order to establish the validity of a theological teaching?

2) Why do Christians need to know how God may react to the sin of apostasy?

3) What do Christians mean when they claim that *'Christ is divine?'*

---

[25] It is envisaged that most of these newer assemblies will be in the undeveloped world where there still exists some hunger for the truth. In addition, it is felt that the expression of divine truth in a confessional format has value in its own right. The Church has successfully used such a format for many centuries and the writer is simply perpetuating this tried and tested traditional style of teaching.

S3: EXPLANATION OF TERMINOLOGY

The word *'God,*' refers to <u>the completely perfect, personal, supreme spiritual Being who possesses an unlimited number of interrelated, non-conflicting attributes.</u> In John 4:24, Jesus Himself stated, *"<u>God is Spirit</u> and they that worship Him must worship Him in <u>spirit</u> and in <u>truth</u>."* Scripture reveals that God is both infinite and personal. This means that, to an unlimited degree, He can think, feel, decide and relate to others in a highly sociable way.

Like scripture, this study uses the term *'God'* interchangeably with *'Lord.'* The term *'Lord'* means *'revered (or sovereign) master'* and has connotations of *'ownership,'* emphasising the fact that God owns and rules over everything.

The term *'Divine Being,'* is that description of God as a largely invisible presence, capable of existing regardless of humanity's perception of Him. His existence is <u>not</u> dependent upon us. Akin to Genesis 1:1, *'The 52 Attributes of God'* acknowledges the self-existence of God.

The divine attributes <u>are those impressively excellent characteristics or qualities that belong to God and which constitute His divine nature.</u> The term *'divine nature'* can be used interchangeably with *'divine essence'* and refers to the sum total of attributes possessed by God. Together these attributes answer the question *'What is God like?'*

God has 52 attributes which can be known to humanity because each one has been revealed in a number of different scripture passages. However, God also has an unlimited number of attributes which He has chosen <u>not</u> to reveal in scripture and which <u>cannot</u> be known to humanity. The Apostle Paul in 1 Corinthians 13:9a highlighted this point when he admitted, *"we know in part."*

Found throughout scripture are three main *'groupings'* of the 52 known attributes: -
1) The Largely Shared Attributes: these are particular divine attributes held in common and shared by both God <u>and</u> humanity – the difference being one of quantity. *Example:* both God and humanity have power but God's power is unlimited and always used perfectly. Human power is limited and liable to be abused.

2) The Potentially Shared Attributes: God – and only those in a right relationship with Him through Jesus Christ – share these attributes. *Example*: the attribute of holiness which begins to develop only after an individual has received spiritual regeneration.

3) The Barely Shared Attributes: these attributes belong largely to God alone. They can never be shared by anything within His Creation to any significant degree. The difference is one of both quantity and quality. *Example:* God's ability to be everywhere at once, (His omnipresence).

The advantage of the above classification is that it recognises that divine qualities cannot be placed in separate water-tight compartments.[26] There is a gradation from a barely shared attribute (which people can possess only to a small degree, if at all) to a potentially shared attribute (which faithful Christians can enjoy more and more should they continue to grow in their relationship with God) and lastly a largely shared attribute (which anyone can display to a significant degree, assuming the possession of normal human faculties.)[27] It must be borne in mind that many other (perhaps an unlimited number of) attributes exist, but God has chosen not to reveal them to us – certainly not on this side of eternity.

Each divine attribute is linked by a system of *'mutual referencing'* whereby when one divine attribute us touched upon (*'referenced'*) so is another. Close linguistic and logical connections exist between each one with scripture providing both a *'backward'* and a *'forward referencing'* between different attributes. This can be seen in the benediction given at the end of Jude's Epistle which states, *"to the only wise God our Saviour, be glory and majesty, dominion and power both now and ever, Amen"* (Jude 25). Here, the abstract nouns *'glory'* and *'power'* mutually refer to one another; with a *'forward reference'* taking place from *'glory'* to *'dominion'* and a *'backward reference'* from *'power'* to *'glory.'*

This linguistic connection also suggests an underlying logical connection wherein the existence of one divine attribute either confirms or implies the existence of another. Take again the examples of *'glory'* and *'power'* in Jude 25. In this context the

---

[26] However, the writer does not claim that his classification of divine attributes is the only valid one. Other forms of classification used by some of the books listed in the Selective Bibliography are equally helpful.

[27] This classification of attributes and subsequent discussion of them is indebted to points made by Grudem (1994) pp.156-160.

existence of glory, rapidly suggests the existence of power. The without the other would be tantamount to expecting sunlight to exist without the sun! Where there is glory there simply must be power – for glory is the expression and manifestation of power. Furthermore, divine power must have some visible expression if it is not to remain hidden from Creation. Without displays of divine glory through both natural and supernatural phenomena how would anyone know that God was worthy of respect? The attributes of divine glory and power stand or fall with one another. A bible-based logic can be very helpful in uncovering the various kinds of relationships existing within the Deity.[28]

Questions

1) Explain (in your own words) what is meant by such terms as 'God,' 'Divine Being' and 'divine attribute?'

2) Why is it important to have a good understanding of Christian terminology?

3) Why is it helpful to place the divine attributes into different categories?

4) Explain in your own words the concept of 'mutual referencing.'

---

[28] Further examples of the linguistic and logical connections between the different divine attributes can be found in the footnotes accompanying the analysis of divine uprightness (Attribute **PS14**)

C2:
THE TWENTY THREE LARGELY SHARED ATTRIBUTES

LS1: COMPLEXITY

(Known also as *'Diversity'*)

LS1.1 Prelude

Three reasons explain why God's nature is difficult to understand,
Two come from us and one is from the Lord!
Firstly, *we are too sinful to completely comprehend the Divine*
Secondly, *our minds are too weak to survey God's unlimited depths*
*But **thirdly,** there are things which the Lord Himself has chosen to hide*

LS1.2 Definition

The <u>largely shared</u> attribute of *'complexity'* refers to God's ability to possess many <u>apparently</u> diverse attributes, with no conflict or inner tension.

Divine diversity is implied by the name **Echad** – meaning *'complex'* or *'compound oneness.'* An example of this name being used in scripture occurs in Deuteronomy 6:4 which states *"Hear O Israel; the Lord God is one* (Echad) *Lord."* It demonstrates that God can exist as a Trinity of three Persons.

LS1.3 Bible Exposition

Two further Bible passages demonstrating the existence of this attribute are Psalm 22:1 and Romans 9:18.

Psalm 22:1
"My God, my God why hast you forsaken me? Why are you so far from helping me and the words of my roaring?"

This cry of desolation confirms that even the godliest of people knows what it is to be puzzled by God's complexity during times of great affliction when He appears alarmingly absent. Indeed, this was the passage that Jesus Himself quoted when dying upon the cross, (Matthew 27:46). Here He was confronted by the seemingly irreconcilable paradox between divine love and the apparent indifference of God to what was a truly terrible degree of suffering. Far from being an all-powerful deliverer, the Lord appeared to be totally distant and uncaring. When divine intervention seemed of absolute necessity it did not happen – at least not in the way that was expected. The natural response to this situation was the kind of unbelief expressed in the harsh mockery recorded in Matthew 27:39-44. In reality, that unbelief only demonstrated that the people concerned had an over-simplified view of God. They expected instant miracles and when they were not forthcoming they turned away in scornful unbelief. Real faith is shown by a continued trust in God even when His complexity is a source of bewilderment. This was a point that Christ amply demonstrated upon the cross. Through His continued trust He opened the way for us to receive salvation.

Romans 9:18
"Therefore He has mercy on whom He will have mercy and whom He will He hardens."

Theological conundrums (including the relationship between divine sovereignty and human responsibility) also display the complexity of God. Rather like the experience of suffering, such puzzles may provoke those weak in faith to find fault with the Almighty, (Romans 9:19-20). However, this problem is reduced when it's realized that, <u>in this world we will never understand everything about God.</u> The Supreme Being is too great for human comprehension; indeed, if we understood everything about God then this God would not be the God of Scripture, for by definition He is someone beyond the grasp of the greatest of human minds. Theological difficulties are simply the inevitable outcome of this situation. Sometimes, the best response to an insurmountable theological difficulty is to get on with praising God until the time comes when He chooses to ease that difficulty or to give the strength to accept that, in this world, some questions will never be resolved. The policy of praising God amidst a theological difficulty was one followed by Paul in Romans 11:32f.

When viewed alongside Deuteronomy 6:4, these two passages show that: -

1) The complexity of God is more keenly felt during times of suffering and the theological perplexity caused by such doctrines as *'election'*

2) God may appear indifferent to our plight simply because He is working in ways beyond our limited comprehension

3) The paradoxical nature of God may serve to provoke a hearty form of worship

LS1.4 Application

In response to God's *'diversity'* believers would be wise to: -

1) Accept that there are things about God that are just not possible to know in this life

2) Ask God to provide the faith to continue to believe in Him during times of darkness and perplexity

3) Avoid finding fault with the Lord just because we do not understand His ways

At the close of this study it's reasonable to conclude that God can work in ways which transcend (rise above) human comprehension

LS1.5 Conclusion

1) Divine *'complexity'* shows that God may react to the sin of apostasy in ways which perplex those who have turned against Him

2) At His death Jesus demonstrated this attribute by accomplishing an unlimited number of things – only a few of which can be known in this life

For further study please refer to the words *'suffering,' 'elect'* or *'election'* in any Bible Concordance or Dictionary

LS1.6 Epilogue

Heavenly Father, grant me the grace
To understand those biblical teachings that I should understand
Whilst accepting those that I can't

Help me also to know exactly
What teachings I am being called upon to understand
At this present time
Please hear my prayer Amen.[29]

---

[29] This prayer was first made on Tuesday, 16 November 1999. It expresses the need to depend upon God in order to understand those biblical teachings which promote spiritual growth.

LS1.7 Questions

1) What is the best way to react to a particular scriptural teaching which may be difficult to understand or accept?

2) Why do God's ways of working in people's lives seem impossible to understand?

3) How would you comfort someone tempted to find fault with God after suffering a series of tragedies – none of which were of their own making?

LS2: CREATIVITY

(Known also as *'Originality'*)

LS2.1 Prelude

In the beginning there was nothing but God, but God commanded and everything came into being.

LS2.2 Definition

The <u>largely shared</u> attribute of *'creativity'* refers to God's ability to plan, originate and construct things, either from nothing or by using existing raw materials.

Divine originality is implied by the name **Yahweh Tsebha 'oth** – meaning *'the Lord of vast (angelic and human) hosts'* or *'the stars in heaven.'* An example of this name being used in scripture occurs in Isaiah 48:2 which states *"For they call themselves the holy city and stay* (wait) *upon the God of Israel; the Lord of Hosts* (Yahweh Tsebha 'oth) *is His name."* It demonstrates that God can send angels to protect people.

LS2.3 Bible Exposition

Two further Bible passages demonstrating the existence of this attribute are Psalm 33:6 and Hebrews 11:3.

Psalm 33:6
"By the word of the Lord were the Heavens made and all the host of them by the breath of His mouth."

These words occur in a Psalm exhorting the people of Israel to *"praise the Lord"* with a variety of musical instruments. The writer assumes that Creation originally came about as a result of a divine command. In light of recent cosmological theory, it is interesting to note that the word *'Heavens'* does allow for the possibility that God created more than one Universe. Yet God exists distinctly apart from His Creation. The Universe may comprise of awe-inspiring immensities but the Lord is still infinitely larger. To Him, even the biggest galactic clusters are no more than tiny sparks dancing in the night. Incredibly, the creative power that made those massive objects may operate in the hearts and minds of those who believe in Jesus. All that is required is a willing heart and an open mind. Often, those believers marginalised on the fringes of society manifest this very same power. Sometimes it is comforting to realise that the Lord chooses to begin a fresh creative work with those having little status in either the Church or the world. As the ministry of Jesus showed, a new work often begins with social outcasts. No individual or group of people are too insignificant for His attention.

Hebrews 11:3
"Through faith we understand that the worlds were framed by the word of God, so that things which are seen were made of things which do appear."

In these few words, the writer shows that faith rather than doubt is the true basis of knowledge. He thus contradicts over three centuries of western philosophical tradition. Commencing with the seventeenth century mathematician Descartes (1596-1650), this tradition believed that knowledge was advanced through a process of radical doubt. Hence, one doubted everything so that the things surviving this sceptical approach could then be regarded as being more-or-less valid. Although useful as a means of pruning out obviously bad ideas, when carried too far this approach has led to radical scepticism which doubts everything, including the existence of doubt itself! Akin to today's Post-Modern philosophy, the pursuit of knowledge has become a pointless exercise because doubt remains over whether there is any real knowledge out there to pursue. What passes for knowledge is merely an ideologically determined, socio-psychological construction which need not correspond to any objective truth. In contrast, scripture teaches that a correct understanding of Creation can only be valid from a basis of faith. One needs to believe in a creative God who has made everything that exists. Such a belief can be further built upon and also act as a basis for healthy scientific enquiry. It is time for western philosophy to place faith rather than doubt at the centre of its various schemes of thought.

When viewed alongside Isaiah 48:2, these two passages show that: -

1) The Cosmos is not eternal – it had a definite beginning in time

2) The creativity of God may provoke congregational praise

3) God's Son, Jesus Christ, played a major role in the formation and shaping of Creation

LS2.4 Application

In response to God's *'originality'* believers would be wise to: -

1) Allow the vast starry hosts of Heaven to testify to God's power

2) Accept that faith rather than intellectual speculation is the way to understand God's work in Creation

3) Avoid focussing upon only the material side of reality

At the close of this study it's reasonable to conclude that God is the author of everything that is beautiful

LS2.5 Conclusion

1) Divine *'creativity'* shows that God may deal with the sin of apostasy by regarding it as a grievous violation of His created order – especially where sexual immorality is involved

2) At His death, Jesus demonstrated this attribute by confirming that God had devised a totally original solution to the problem of human sin

For further study please refer to the words *'create,' 'created' 'creator'* or *'made'* in any Bible Concordance or Dictionary

LS2.6 Epilogue

Lord of angelic and human hosts
For the sake of your son, Jesus
Fill me with your awesome creative power
Fill me to an unlimited degree so that I may be effective
In your work of witnessing to others about your love, Amen[30]

LS2.7 Questions

1) What motivated God to create everything even though He had no need to do such a work?

2) Why is faith required to understand that God created the planets? What consequences may arise if such a faith is absent?

3) How would you convince a sceptic that the Universe resulted from an act of divine Creativity? List those arguments to which the sceptic may be clinging before attempting to answer them.

LS3: EMOTION

(Known also as *'sensitivity'*)

LS3.1 Prelude

If the Lord has no feeling, why did He send His son to die for us?

LS3.2 Definition

The <u>largely shared</u> attribute of *'emotion'* refers to God's ability to feel, be moved by, empathise with, sensitively relate to and freely identify with His Creation.

Divine sensitivity is implied by the name **Elohim Rachum** – meaning *'merciful and compassionate God'* or *'Gods.'* An example of this name being used in scripture occurs in Deuteronomy 4:31 which states, *"For the Lord your God is a merciful God, (Elohim Rachum) He will not forsake you neither will He destroy you, nor forget the*

---

[30] This prayer was first made on Thursday, 17 November 1999. It expresses the need to receive divine power in order to be effective in God's service.

covenant of your fathers which He swore to them." It demonstrates that God can still feel a strong sense of compassion toward His people even when they are being very badly behaved.

LS3.3 Bible Exposition

Two further Bible passages demonstrating the existence of this attribute are Psalm 149:4 and Luke 12:32.

Psalm 149:4
"For the Lord take's pleasure in His people, He will beautify the meek with salvation."

This psalm of praise shows the Lord's response to genuine worship. Motivated by a perfect love, the Lord has graciously condescended to allow our feeble praises to fill Him with pleasure. He has chosen to be moved by human worship. This is a great privilege – one that we often do not realise exists. It is a two way process whereby we worship the Lord, who is then moved with pleasure before deciding to bestow those blessings which beautify our own salvation. Such blessings excite further human praise to God and the whole process is then repeated. However, for praise to be effective there must first be a right relationship with God through Jesus Christ. In addition, praise must be directed to the right source – namely God Himself. Finally, praise must be undertaken in the right attitude of meekness. Never must we feel that we are doing God a favour by granting Him our worship. Quite the contrary, all the favours come from Him. Once this fact is accepted then our relationship with Him can become a thing of continued heartfelt thanks and praise.

Luke 12:32
"Fear not little flock for it is your Father's good pleasure to give you the kingdom."

Represented here is a word of comfort given to some insecure disciples who doubted whether their heavenly Father could indeed provide for their needs. Like many first century Jews, they perhaps had a view of the Lord as some remote and forbidding figure, quick to punish but slow to reward. Their faith would also have been shaken by the humiliations associated with the Roman occupation of their land. They needed to see that <u>the Lord was very happy to give eternal life to those who believed in Him.</u> Contrary to the forbidding image generated by Calvinism, the Lord is not some arbitrary despot who coldly decides in advance to save the few whilst damning the many. Such a caricature has done much to undermine the credibility of the Christian faith across the ages. Admittedly, in Matthew 7:13-14 Jesus does warn that only a few will find the narrow way to eternal life; but in part this is so because *'the many'* have decided to be wilfully blind to the generosity of the Lord's offer of salvation. It is not the Lord's fault if people find themselves in a condition of eternal ruin. Let us be sensitive to God, so that we can enjoy his company forever. We may also find that our sensitivity to God will give us sensitivity toward those in real need. However, as further exploration of the other attributes will show, God can be grieved and angered by human sinfulness. He is keenly aware of all our sins and may choose to react to them in a deeply emotional way.

When viewed alongside Deuteronomy 4:31, these two passages show that: -

1) God is emotionally involved with His people; their actions can provoke feelings of divine displeasure or pleasure

2) True worship is a means of exciting divine pleasure

3) God's emotional identification with His people causes Him to meet their spiritual, psychological and physical needs

LS3.4 Application

In response to God's *'sensitivity'* believers would be wise to: -

1) Allow the Holy Spirit to instil a warm-hearted sense of gratitude for the Lord's emotional identification with His people

2) Ensure their worship takes place in the right attitude of humility

3) Avoid viewing God as being a cold despot, randomly choosing to save or to damn whomever He wishes

At the close of this study it's reasonable to conclude that God has freely chosen to be excited by the praises and actions of His people

LS3.5 Conclusion

1) Divine *'emotion'* shows that God may react to the sin of apostasy (especially if violence is perpetuated in His name) with keenly felt repugnance, anger, sadness and grief

2) At His death Jesus demonstrated this attribute by being so moved by the plight of sinners that He chose to die an agonising death on their behalf

For further study please refer to the words *'delight'* *'grieve'* or *'pleasure'* in any Bible Concordance or Dictionary

LS3.6 Epilogue

Abba Father,
May the word of our lips and
The attitude of our hearts
Be a source of pleasure
To You,
To your son Jesus and
To your Holy Spirit,
Amen[31]

LS3.7 Questions

1) What three factors make our praises a source of divine pleasure?

2) Why do you think the Lord has chosen to allow our worship to excite feelings of divine pleasure?

3) How is worship likely to be affected by the belief that God is beyond any form of emotion? Suggest ways to help someone whose life has been blighted by viewing God as an unemotional despot, randomly choosing to give or withhold eternal life. What problems are such people likely to suffer and how may these be overcome?

---

[31] This prayer was first made on Thursday, 18 November 1999. It expresses the need to take account of God's feelings just before a time of worship.

LS4: ENLIGHTENMENT

(Known also as *'Illumination'*)

LS4.1 Prelude

Being enlightened by God can be a painful process. This is because we actively resist the light He wants to shed upon our lives.

LS4.2 Definition

This <u>largely shared</u> attribute of *'enlightenment'* refers to God's ability to bestow understanding, to guide, to mentally inspire, to show the truth to and to teach, using a variety of methods.

Divine illumination is implied by the name **El Yahweh Vayya'er Ianu** – meaning *'God is the Lord who shows us the light.'* An example of this name being used in scripture occurs in Psalm 118:27a which states *"God is the Lord who has shown us light,* (El Yahweh Vayya'er lanu); *bind the sacrifice with cords, even unto the horns of the altar."* It demonstrates that God can use formal religious ceremonies to enlighten us about what Jesus, His Son, accomplished for us on the cross.

LS4.3 Bible Exposition

Two further Bible passages demonstrating the existence of this attribute are Micah 7:8 and John 16:25.

Micah 7:8
"Rejoice [gloat] not against me, O my enemy. When I fall, I shall arise; when I sit in darkness the Lord shall be a light for me."

Faced by massive social corruption, the prophet Micah puts his faith in God. His understanding has been sufficiently enlightened for him to realise that the Lord <u>can</u> overcome the spiritual darkness lurking within each one of us. To be shown the truth can be an illuminating yet hurtful experience, but it may bring comfort and peace too. It is inspiring to imagine a bearded prophet sitting in the darkness of a prison cell, gasping in amazement at some wonderful spiritual insight. All believers can be encouraged by the fact that, even in the most difficult of circumstances, the Lord is still there both to guide and to illuminate. Times of darkness may appear to last forever but for a true believer they are only for a limited period. Our enemies often gloat prematurely. This is because they fail to discern the supernatural resilience that the Almighty can give to even the weakest of believers.

John 16:25
"These things I have spoken to you in proverbs, but the time comes when I shall no more speak to you in proverbs, but I will show you the Father."

With great wisdom the Messiah is preparing His disciples to face serious troubles. They were obviously in a very fretful, unsettled state of mind; now was the time for plain speaking. Like all great dispensers of knowledge, Jesus varied His teaching methods according to the needs of His audience. In the case of His disciples the need was for a very direct approach. The time for speaking to them in parables was over. There is an implicit claim to deity in the words *"I will show you the Father."* This is because only God is capable of showing God plainly, without any error or confusion. Unless aided by the Holy Spirit no one can know anything about the Lord. This is because that which is limited cannot plainly see that which is unlimited. Thankfully, the One who is completely unlimited can show Himself to limited human beings in ways that can be both understood and accepted. The Lord does not speak like a vague eastern guru, full of contradictory sayings and obscure riddles – quite the opposite – the Lord who enlightens speaks in ways that may be rather too specific for our liking! Indeed, He often speaks to confound our prejudices; He also speaks to save our souls.

When viewed alongside Psalm 118:27, these two passages show that: -

1) Divine enlightenment can inspire a selfless attitude toward others

2) Divine enlightenment can be a source of joy in times of difficulty

3) Divine enlightenment can use a variety of teaching methods, specific to the needs of the audience

LS4.4 Application

In response to God's *'illumination'* believers would be wise to: -

1) Actively expect the Lord to provide the illumination needed to make difficult decisions

2) Adopt a very direct approach when conveying divine truth, when this is needed

3) Avoid being enticed by any false enlightenment, emanating from the wrong spiritual sources

At the close of this study it's reasonable to conclude that believers are usually called to make an active and practical response to any divine enlightenment they may have received. Such a response is often designed to promote the well-being of others.

LS4.5 Conclusion

1) Divine *'enlightenment'* shows that God may deal with the sin of apostasy by giving more than enough truth to those who have turned against Him so that they will be without excuse on the Day of Judgement

2) At His death, Jesus demonstrated this attribute by enlightening the repentant thief over where his destination would be in the afterlife, (Luke 23:43)

For further study please refer to the words *'illumine, light, teach* or *teacher'* in any Bible Concordance or Dictionary

LS4.6 Epilogue

Lord, in this time of darkness
When you seem so very distant
Show me the truth so that I may praise you, Amen[32]

---

[32] This prayer was first made on Thursday, 25 November 1999. It expresses the need to ask for divine enlightenment when we do not see any way forward in our lives.

LS4.7 Questions

1) What help can divine illumination give to believers who are grievously distressed by the evils in society?

2) Why is it sometimes necessary to convey truth through the use of parables and stories? When would a more direct approach be appropriate?

3) Which is the best way to handle someone who claims to have enjoyed life-changing spiritual enlightenment, yet cannot give a coherent account of this experience? Suggest ways to probe the possible spiritual, psychological and cultural sources of such an experience.

LS5: ETERNITY

(Known also as *'Everlasting Existence'*)

LS5.1 Prelude

Good things can last forever, but first we must trust Jesus to be our Saviour

LS5.2 Definition

This largely shared attribute of *'eternity'* refers to God's unceasing, timeless, everlasting and perpetual existence. He always has existed and will always continue to exist.

Divine everlasting existence is implied by the name **El Olam** – meaning *'everlasting God'* or *'God from everlasting.'* An example of this name being used in scripture occurs in Genesis 21:33 which states *"And Abraham planted a grove in Beersheba and called on the name of the Lord, the everlasting God (El Olam)."* It demonstrates that God can be called upon in times of need.

LS5.3 Bible Exposition

Two further Bible passages demonstrating the existence of this attribute are Isaiah 60:20 and Revelation 4:8.

Isaiah 60:20
"Your sun shall no more go down, neither shall your moon withdraw itself; for the Lord shall be your everlasting light and the days of your mourning shall be ended."

This is a prophecy denoting the eternal life believers will enjoy in *"a New Heaven and Earth"* (Revelation 21:1) where the sun and moon will no longer need to exist because God Himself will provide the light. All those who love God will see Him clearly and any experience of suffering will be ended. One can imagine a vast crowd of people joyfully worshipping the Lord under a pure white sky whose very light denotes His presence. Mourning shall have ceased and the trials of this world will have long since been forgotten. Particular encouragement can be drawn from the fact that this is an unconditional promise, applicable to every follower of Jesus. Seeing our sufferings in the light of eternity can give us the strength to endure them. It was this perspective that helped Christian martyrs to face their suffering with a courage that astounded their persecutors.

Revelation 4:8
"And the four beasts [high ranking Seraphim or Angelic Beings] *had each of them six wings about him. They were full of eyes; and they rest not day or night, saying 'Holy, Holy, Holy, is the Lord God Almighty, who was and is and is to come.'"*

In this incredible vision God stands outside of time, enjoying the worship of glorious Angelic Beings. Entwined together in this triune God is an unlimited diversity of attributes; these include everlasting existence, divine holiness, divine unity and sovereignty and total power. Each attribute reinforces the splendid glory of the Lord. In their worship the Seraphim loudly proclaim that God has had (and will continue to have) an eternal existence from before His Creation; during the existence of His Creation and after this Creation has been destroyed in order to make way for a new heaven and earth, (Isaiah 66:22f & Revelation 21:1f). His *'being'* does not depend upon the health of the universe, when it ceases to exist God will still be present in all of His glory. With regard to human affairs, He works inside of history to prepare those who know Him for an eternity spent in a new creation. This He does in order that we may enjoy a loving relationship with Him that lasts forever. From God's perspective, Creation represents only a tiny beginning of His work. It is the brief overture before the main concert begins.

When viewed alongside Genesis 21:33, these two passages show that: -

1) God has always existed

2) God's radiant life will fill a new Creation – free from all forms of suffering

3) Every attribute of God has an eternal existence

LS5.4 Application

In response to God's *'everlasting existence'* believers would be wise to: -

1) Acknowledge that (for believers in Christ) no suffering lasts forever

2) Actively join the Angels in worshipping God for all of His positive attributes

3) Avoid believing that God's existence is dependent upon His Creation

At the close of this study it's reasonable to conclude that God is a Being with an endless array of positive attributes. These enable Him to create new things from nothing and to be the subject of endless Angelic worship

LS5.5 Conclusion

1) Divine *'eternity'* shows that God will react to the sin of apostasy by consigning to an eternal Hell those who stubbornly remain faithless toward His son Jesus

2) At His death, Jesus demonstrated this attribute by giving eternal life to those remaining faithful to Him, (Matthew 24:13)

For further study please refer to the words *'everlasting'* or *'eternal'* in any Bible Concordance or Dictionary

LS5.6 Epilogue

*Everlasting God, please give everlasting life to X
A person I love
Please also give it to Y
A person whom I find profoundly irritating, Amen*[33]

LS5.7 Questions

1) What characteristics will feature in God's new Creation? Why will it be necessary to destroy this present Creation in order to make way for the new one?

2) Why is it helpful to celebrate the attributes of God? How may this kind of celebration determine the wording of any prayers or worship songs?

3) How would you comfort people who have just lost a loved one? What scripture passages, if any, would you use to help them? How would you judge when it's appropriate to use them?

LS6: FAITHFULNESS

(Known also as *'Trustworthiness'*)

LS6.1 Prelude

God is faithful, even when His people are not

LS6.2 Definition

This <u>largely shared</u> attribute of *'faithfulness'* refers to God's consistent and loyal trustworthiness, meaning that He never acts out of character. He will keep and honour <u>all</u> of His promises.

Divine trustworthiness is implied by the name **El Emeth** – meaning *'God of truth'* or *'faithful God.'* An example of this name being used in scripture occurs in Psalm 31:5 which states *"Into your hand I commit my spirit; you have redeemed me, O God of truth* (El Meth).*"* It demonstrates that God can be trusted even at the point of death.

---

[33] This prayer was first made on Thursday, 25 November 1999. It expresses the need to ask the Lord to grant everlasting life to all sorts of people. To employ this prayer effectively, it will be necessary to place specific names in place of X and Y.

LS6.3 Bible Exposition

Two further Bible passages demonstrating the existence of this attribute are Deuteronomy 7:9 and 1 Corinthians 10:13.

Deuteronomy 7:9
"Know that the Lord your God He is God, the faithful God who keeps covenant and mercy with them who love Him and keep His commandments to a thousand generations."

Here the Israelites were being reminded of important spiritual priorities before entering the land promised to them. Their personal and corporate fellowship with the Lord was assured <u>as long as they continued to love and obey Him.</u> This has remained so, right up to the present day. Admittedly, He might not display His faithfulness in ways we would necessarily like or appreciate, but such displays will always be for our good and they will always honour the teaching of scripture. On a more practical note His faithfulness toward us should engender faithfulness in us toward Him. This faithfulness can be shown by a serious willingness on our part to obey the doctrinal and moral standards of God's Word. This should preclude any casual attitude to matters of truth. Individuals may make all sorts of grandiose spiritual claims about themselves but unless there is a fundamental willingness to obey God's Word, such claims can be dismissed. However, should individuals faithfully obey biblical teaching (as best as they understand it) then God's mercy to them will last forever. Furthermore, those who are faithful to the light they have may benefit future generations in ways they could never have imagined. This was the case with the Sixteenth Century Puritans, who played a major role in the moral and economic development of western civilisation.[34] Faithfulness to God can bless people in many unexpected ways.

1 Corinthians 10:13
"There is no temptation taken you but such as is common to man. But God is faithful and will not allow you to be tempted above your endurance, but will, with the temptation make a way of escape that you may be able to bear it."

These encouraging words were addressed to a congregation buffeted by internal division as well as many other problems. Paul

---

[34] Evidence for this point is provided in Adair (1998) chapter twelve

was aware that every believer, without exception, was caught up in an unremitting spiritual war. Simply by professing Christ they had made themselves a target for the evil one. (This is as true today as it was then; the devil uses many methods to lure Christians into evil ways.) At Corinth he provoked many to *'fall out'* over petty issues, whilst others fell into a smug overbearing spiritual pride and not a few were intoxicated with false visionary experiences. Backbiting and a love of novelty were also rife. For those genuinely eager for the things of God, Satan reserved the temptation of spiritual depression. The desire to give up must, at times, have been overwhelming. For them, although they may not have been aware of it at the time, their most pressing need was to realise that God puts a limit upon all temptation. Believers are given either the strength to endure temptation or shown a way of escape.[35] It is as simple as that. Also, it's in the very nature of temptation to present us with a choice – either of <u>faithfulness</u> or <u>faithlessness</u> to God's will. We must choose to be faithful even when the temptation is at its most fierce. The Lord, will enable us to endure or will (in His own time and way) provide a means of escape. In the meantime, let us continue doing the good we can achieve.

When viewed alongside Psalm 31:5, these two passages show that:

1) God's faithfulness can be trusted, even at the point of death

2) God's blessing will be upon those who are faithful to Him

3) God's faithfulness is apparent through even the worst temptations of Satan

LS6.4 Application

In response to God's *'trustworthiness'* believers would be wise to: -

1) Avoid giving up on God during times of trial

2) Continually hope in divine mercy

3) Commend their souls to God at the point of death

---

[35] On a personal note, the writer has lost count of how many times the atrocious apostasy within much of English Christianity had almost provoked him to give up on the Christian Faith; yet God gave him the grace to endure.

At the close of this study it's reasonable to conclude that God is able to award obedience and to limit temptation

LS6.5 Conclusion

1) Divine *'faithfulness'* shows that God may deal with the sin of apostasy by keeping His promise to inflict many curses upon those who cease to follow Him or to obey His teaching, (Leviticus 26:14-45)

2) At His death, Jesus demonstrated this attribute by fulfilling every Biblical prophecy which had predicted this event, (Psalm 22:1 & Matthew 27:46)

For further study please refer to the words *'faithful,' 'faithfulness,' 'obey'* or *'obedience'* in any Bible Concordance or Dictionary

LS6.6 Epilogue

God of all mercies, thank you for getting me through this trial. Please use it as a means to bless others, Amen[36]

LS6.7 Questions

1) What are the likely rewards of showing a consistent faithfulness to God's will?

2) Why does temptation come in many guises? What is the best way to resist it?

3) How would you comfort someone who is grievously tempted to despair and feels that God has broken His promise to bless their faithfulness?

---

[36] This prayer was first made on Thursday, 25 November 1999. It expresses the need to specifically thank the Lord for having brought us through a particularly unpleasant temptation.

LS7: GREATNESS

(Known also as *'Majesty'*)

LS7.1 Prelude

There is only one appropriate response to the greatness of God – and that is to worship Him!

LS7.2 Definition

This <u>largely shared</u> attribute of *'greatness'* refers to God's awe-inspiring depth of character, immensity of being and dignified stateliness, embodied in the outstanding qualities of His moral character.

Divine majesty is implied by the name **El Gadol Venora** – meaning *'the great and terrible God.'* An example of this name being used in scripture occurs in Deuteronomy 7:21 which states *"You shall not be frightened at them; for the Lord your God is among you, a mighty and terrible God* (El Gadol Venora).*"* It demonstrates that God will express His greatness to provide fortitude and to encourage His people before a time of conflict.

LS7.3 Bible Exposition

Two further Bible passages demonstrating the existence of this attribute are 2 Samuel 7:22 and Titus 2:13.

2 Samuel 7:22
"Wherefore you are great, O Lord God; for there is none like you, neither is there any God beside you – according to all that we have heard."

These are words of praise and thanksgiving for a Deity whose greatness establishes His fame even in an indifferent world. It is easy to imagine King David's excitement as he uttered this prayer. Indeed, the best of prayers manage to inspire feelings of awe and love. At the theological level, David's prayer evokes an implicit denial of the polytheism which, at that time, dominated the surrounding nations. Moreover, the God whom David follows <u>is</u> a communicating God who does not hide Himself behind some strange silence unless He's decided (for our own good) to put us through a time of trial or that sin on our part has imposed a blockage. Prayer for David (and for us) is a two way process, whereby we not only <u>speak</u> but also <u>listen</u> to the Lord, whose greatness is unlimited. In short, God can communicate with the human race precisely because He is great and has an infinite capacity to relate directly to people.

Titus 2:13
"Looking for that blessed hope and the glorious appearing of the great God and our saviour Jesus Christ."

In a church situation degraded by much false teaching, the Apostle Paul directs attention to the glorious return of Jesus. He is keen for believers to look away from destructive errors in order to focus upon the wonderful truth of Christ's return. However, as Revelation 19:11f shows, the Second Coming will be a truly dreadful event for the wicked because it's at this point that they will be forcibly removed from the face of the Earth. Divine majesty will be fully displayed and this will strike terror into the hearts of those who've militantly opposed God's purposes. However, as well as the severity of judgement, mercy will also be shown at Christ's return when this event will save the human race from extinction (Matthew 24:22). The Second Coming will highlight the inter-connectedness of Christ's Deity and Humanity. Just as God is great, so Jesus is great.[37] On a more specific note, this passage shows that believers should look forward in time to Jesus who will, at His second coming, appear in His complete glory to put right the many wrongs in this world. Divine greatness is shown by the fact that God actively intervenes in world affairs – either as Judge or Deliverer.

When viewed alongside Deuteronomy 7:21, these two passages show that: -

1) There is no need for believers to allow fear of opposition to deter them from following God's will

2) Believers should pay homage in prayer to God's greatness

3) Divine greatness will be manifested at the return of Jesus

---

[37] Exactly the same could readily be said of all of the other divine attributes; that which applies to God also applies to Jesus.

LS7.4 Application

In response to God's *'majesty'* believers would be wise to: -

1) Begin prayer with an acknowledgement of divine greatness

2) Acknowledge that God's greatness is supremely manifested in Christ.

3) Avoid a flippant or disrespectful attitude toward the Lord

At the close of this study it's reasonable to conclude that God is a focus of awe and an inspirer of hope

LS7.5 Conclusion

1) Divine *'greatness'* shows that God may deal with the sin of apostasy by publicly humbling those who've chosen to turn against Him (*e.g.* by allowing their names to be linked to scandalous behaviour)

2) At His death, Jesus demonstrated this attribute by suffering the worst forms of abuse without retaliation

For further study please refer to the words *'great'* or *'majesty'* in any Bible Concordance or Dictionary

LS7.6 Epilogue

Majestic God of Israel
In abject desperation and
Turbulence of mind
I call upon you, the High King
To employ your greatness to deliver me
From the dreaded 'FLOP' of
F̲ailure, L̲oneliness, O̲bscurity and P̲overty

In the name of Jesus
Please answer this prayer
As quickly as possible, Amen [38]

---

[38] This prayer was made on Monday, 10th January 2000 and expresses the need to appeal to God to grant victory in the Christian life. Its title was *'The Failure's Prayer.'*

LS7.7 Questions

1) What are the best ways to acknowledge God's greatness in our prayers and daily lives?

2) How can divine majesty be a source of comfort to believers undergoing a severe trial?

3) How can divine greatness be portrayed to a mixed audience? (Some of whom may be disdainful or even dismissive of God, whilst others may lack the confidence to believe in His ability to relieve them of their personal suffering and poverty.)

LS8: HEROISM

(Known also as *'Courage'*)

LS8.1 Prelude

The trouble with most prosperous societies is that they lose sight of the idea of heroism. Firm principles becomes a thing to be scorned rather than admired

LS8.2 Definition

This <u>largely shared</u> attribute of *'heroism'* refers to God's ability to perform great deeds and to confront evil, whilst Himself accepting great suffering, pain and grief.

Divine courage is implied by the name **Tsur** – meaning *'rock,'* which indicates that heroism can have a solid, rocklike quality about it. An example of this name being used in scripture occurs in Deuteronomy 32:15 which states *"But Jeshurun waxed fat and kicked, you are waxen fat, you are grown thick, you are covered with fatness. Then he forsook God which made him and lightly esteemed the <u>rock</u>* (Tsur) *of his salvation."* It demonstrates that God can directly challenge the spiritual complacency caused by living in a wealthy society.[39]

---

[39] The prosperity of the Western World has been under increasing strain since the banking crisis of September 2008. (By early 2011, planned reductions in government expenditure, severe disturbances in the Middle East and a terrible earthquake in Japan were adding further pressure.)

LS8.3 Bible Exposition

Two further Bible passages demonstrating the existence of this attribute are Isaiah 53:7 and Matthew 26:39.

Isaiah 53:7
"He was oppressed and He was afflicted, yet He opened not his mouth. He was brought as a lamb to the slaughter and as a sheep before her shearers is dumb, so He opened not His mouth."

These words form part of the Messianic prophecies which largely make up this section of Isaiah; here presenting a stark prediction of the trial, torture and death of Jesus. As a fully divine Person Jesus could have scattered all of His enemies but He forsook that right in order to redeem humanity from sin. Here was a truly heroic humility. The above passage also shows that all true prophecy is centred upon the Person and work of Jesus – both are exalted. Of particular relevance is the example which Jesus gave of self-control. During His tortures He displayed an awesome degree of courage – retaining a truly divine calm amidst an avalanche of abuse. Amidst the severest of physical beatings He remained silent. He showed that the best remedy to counter evil is not verbal abuse or physical force but rather humble submission to God's will in what may be a very harrowing situation. Shouting back at the devil or his emissaries only adds to the level of evil in the world. We need to know when to keep silent in the face of provocation and when to act forcefully as Jesus did when He took a whip to clear the moneychangers from the Temple precincts, (John 2:13-16).

Matthew 26:39
"And He went a little farther and fell on His face and prayed, saying, 'O my Father, if it be possible, let this cup pass from me – nevertheless not as I will, but as you will.'"

These words highlight the heroism of God still further. He who had created billions of galaxies had freely chosen to become a frail Jewish man who, understandably, wanted desperately to avoid the awful horror of crucifixion. Indeed, the temptation to shrink back from the cross must have been almost overwhelming for Christ knew full well He would be cut off from His Father's love, which hitherto He'd known from all eternity. As a result, He would endure a dreadful separation from God's blessings. His Deity would be repelled by any possible contact with sin, whilst His humanity would be repelled by all of the many horrors that a Roman crucifixion would mean. The tragic sadness of this moment is not difficult to imagine. Yet knowing full well what lay ahead of Him Christ humbly submitted to His Father's will. The very words *"not as I will, but as you will"* speak of a breath-taking heroism. They are words that have since been repeated by many Christian martyrs and saints. They are likely to be repeated again as the tide of anti-Christian sentiment grows and spreads throughout the world at large. Even in the hitherto tolerant Western World martyrdom is a distinct possibility for Christians living in this present age.

When viewed alongside Deuteronomy 32:15, these two passages show that: -

1) The heroism of God can generate a solid rock-like faith

2) The courage of God was most vividly shown in the death of Jesus

3) True courage is shown in humble submission to God's will

LS8.4 Application

In response to God's *'courage'* believers would be wise to: -

1) Acknowledge that the Lord is still with us in the midst of our sufferings.

2) Actively submit to the Lord during times of affliction

3) Avoid any self-willed rebelliousness

At the close of this study it's reasonable to conclude that God grants self-control to those in submission to His will

LS8.5 Conclusion

1) Divine *'heroism'* shows that God may deal with the sin of apostasy by empowering people to confront it in a bold and decisive manner

2) At His death, Jesus demonstrated this attribute by showing how He, as a mortal human being, was willing to die an agonising death in order to save people from their sins

For further study please refer to the words *'courage'* or *'rock'* in any Bible Concordance or Dictionary

LS8.6 Epilogue

Two types of courage I ask for Lord;
The courage to know when to stay in a difficult situation and
The courage to know when to withdraw from a difficult situation

A third type of courage I need Father;
The courage to submit my will to yours
Even when I know that in so doing
I will experience rejection and suffering[40]

LS8.7 Questions

1) What problems may arise when a nation becomes too comfortable in its affluence?

2) How could prosperity diminish a nation's courage?

3) Why did Jesus still decide to go to the cross, knowing full well it would involve awful suffering?

4) How may self-control be maintained in a situation where evil is rife and God seems remote?

LS9: HUMANITY

(Known also as *'Personality'*)

LS9.1 Prelude

There is one thing the devil loves to rob us of; our humanity

LS9.2 Definition

This largely shared attribute of *'humanity'* refers to God's personality and His capacity to become a limited human being – having all of the traits associated with humanity, but without sin.

---

[40] This prayer was first made on Monday, 10th January 2000. It expresses the need to go to God in order to receive the courage to obey His will.

Divine personality is implied by the name **Yahweh Raah** – meaning *'The Lord is my shepherd.'* An example of this name being used in scripture occurs in Psalm 23:1 which states *"The Lord is my shepherd* (Yahweh Raah), *I shall not want."* It demonstrates that God can perform a very human role.

LS9.3 Bible Exposition

Two further Bible passages demonstrating the existence of this attribute are Isaiah 53:2 and John 4:6.

Isaiah 53:2
"For He shall grow up before him as a tender plant and as a root out of dry ground; He shall have no form or comeliness and when we shall see him there is no beauty that we should desire him."

This prophecy shows that Christ was no charismatic celebrity whose striking looks would be enough to win audience attention. In appearance He was ordinary and not readily noticed. Yet in His ordinariness God was present. Jesus was (as John 1:14 pointed out) *"the Word made Flesh."* In contradiction to Eastern Philosophy, Man was not ascending to *'Godhood,'* but rather God was descending to Manhood in the person of Jesus. The gulf of sin lying between God and humanity was being bridged solely from God's side. How could this be possible? Part of the answer lies in Genesis 1:27a which states that, *"God created Man in His own image."* This meant that God bestowed *'personality'* upon Man because He too is personal; He has within Himself the capacity and motive to accept certain limitations upon His divine nature in order to identify with the whole of Mankind by become a living human being. The God Christians are called to follow is not the abstract entity of philosophical speculation; instead, He's the personable and gracious Father of the Lord Jesus Christ. [41]

---

[41] Incidentally, none of this would be possible if God was an impersonal *'it.'* Should He somehow have been an impersonal *'it'* then we too would be an impersonal *'it,'* because we are created in His likeness. Alternatively, we could have been given a personality but then not have been made in His likeness. It is far more logical to assume that the statement in Genesis 1:27a refers to a personal God who created human beings who show a resemblance to His own personality. Lastly, it's difficult to see how an impersonal *'it'* could possess either the ability or the motivation to reach out to the human race in love. Any claim that God is an *'it'* is perhaps one of the most grievous slanders that can be made about Him.

John 4:6
"Now Jacob's well was there and Jesus, being wearied with His journey, sat thus on the well and it was about the sixth hour."

God's ability to accept human limitations is shown in this description of Jesus (who was tired and sweaty from a long journey). Here, the very embodiment of Deity is seen to be suffering from the all too human complaint of tiredness. <u>God was identifying with human frailty by experiencing that frailty for Himself.</u> This close identification with the human condition is a source of hope. Like Him, we need to have the wisdom to know when to rest and when to take refreshment.[42] Sometimes, when we are at our most weary, God may provide an unexpected blessing or open up some avenue of service. He may do this to improve our morale and to make us more sympathetic to those to whom we minister. In the case of Jesus, His weariness provided an opportunity to witness the truth to a despised Samaritan woman with a less than pure personal life. Amidst human exhaustion, God can still act.

When viewed alongside Psalm 23:1, these two passages show that:

1) The Lord has both the ability and the will to *'take on'* human nature

2) The personality of God makes it far easier to accept His humanity – as fully portrayed in Christ

3) In Jesus, God had first-hand experience of personal rejection, exhaustion and temptation

LS9.4 Application

In response to God's *'personality'* believers would be wise to: -

1) Accept that God is supremely qualified to be our shepherd because He knows our limitations

2) Acknowledge that the Lord may do a powerful work through apparently insignificant people

---

[42] The writer perhaps took this advice a little too literally when typing this exposition during the afternoon of January 13th 2000 when he *'nodded off'* at the keyboard! He hoped he hadn't disturbed the clientele of a certain Computer Centre!

3) Avoid adopting the view that God is an impersonal *'it'*

At the close of this study it's reasonable to conclude that God is a Being who possesses all of the attributes of personality. These include the ability to think, feel, decide, communicate and love

LS9.5 Conclusion

1) Divine *'humanity'* shows that God may deal with the sin of apostasy by displaying human emotions like anger, grief and sorrow

2) At His death, Jesus demonstrated this attribute by suffering such human needs as thirst, whilst hanging upon the cross, (John 19:28)

For further study please refer to the words *'person'* or *'spoken'* in any Bible Concordance or Dictionary

LS9.6 Epilogue

In you Lord is the highest attribute of personality – LOVE!
Please pour out that love in my heart and in the hearts of those you lead me to pray for. For the sake of your great name, please answer this prayer, Amen[43]

LS9.7 Questions

1) What attracted people to Jesus even though He had no striking physical appearance?

2) Why do you think God created people *'in His own image,'* (Genesis 1:26)? To what extent does human personality reflect divine personality? What are the ways in which God's personality differs from human personality?

3) How would you respond to an intelligent but argumentative person who regularly refers to God as *'it?'*

---

[43] This prayer was first made on Thursday, 13 January 2000. It expresses the need to acknowledge God's love when praying for others.

LS10: HUMOUR

(Known also as 'Witty Irony')

LS10.1 Prelude

God needs a sense of humour because He has the likes of you and me to deal with!

LS10.2 Definition

This <u>largely shared</u> attribute of *'humour'* refers to God's ability both to amuse and to be amused by a lively combination of unexpected ideas or expressions. Any proud human pretensions are deflated and exposed as absurd.

Divine irony is implied by the name **El Chai** – meaning *'the living God.'* An example of this name being used in scripture occurs in Hosea 1:10 which states *"Yet the number of the children of Israel shall be as the sand of the sea which cannot be measured nor numbered; and it shall come to pass, that in the place where it was said unto them, 'You are not my people,' there it shall be said unto them, 'You are the sons of the living God* (El Chai).*"* It demonstrates that God can deflate human value judgements by using circumstances to prove them are wrong.

LS10.3 Bible Exposition

Two further Bible passages demonstrating the existence of this attribute are Job 40:2 and John 9:27.

Job 40:2
"Shall he that contends with the Almighty instruct Him? He that reproves God let him answer for it."

In this dialogue between God and Job, the idea of arguing with the Lord is exposed in all of its foolish absurdity. Job had felt justified in putting his case before the Lord because he'd endured sufferings which would have destroyed a lesser man. He had felt the need to express his innermost self and his case in its entirety before the Lord. However, if there's one thing to be learnt from his example it's *'never to get into unnecessary arguments with the Almighty because there is only ever one loser – us!'* On a more practical note, such arguments are a waste time and energy that could be better spent on more fruitful activities. However, it could well be argued that at certain times, adverse circumstances may press us into a more contentious mood and a good row with the Lord may help *'clear the air'* but even then the end result of such conflict should always be submission to His will. In addition, it should also be acknowledged (from Job's prior example) that the Lord might well respond to our criticisms of Him by asking us pointed questions that expose our own foolishness. Arguing with the Almighty may cost us our dignity and should only be done sparingly, if done at all. Psalm 2:4 reinforces this, showing that even when the world's rulers plot and scheme against God and His Messiah the response is always one of derisory laughter. This is because the Lord clearly sees the absurdity of human pretensions.

John 9:27

"*He* [the recently healed blind man] *answered them* [Christ's religious enemies] *'I have told you already and you did not hear it. Would you hear it again? Will you also be His disciples?'*"

The scene is the interrogation of a miraculously healed blind man. He evidently could not gauge the *'body language'* of his audience who were united by a jealous hatred of the Messiah – the very person who had cured this man's blindness. Consequently, he reacted to their harsh questioning with a blundering naivety which was both comical and moving. Its effect was to place the Pharisees in an extremely foolish light. The whole conversation between them and this man was at complete cross-purposes. It was a comedy of errors, exposing the pompous self-importance of his questioners. By asking *'Will you also be His disciples?'* this formerly blind man could not have posed a more infuriating question! One could only wish to have been there! No wonder we hear that in verse 34c *"they cast him out"* for, quite unintentionally, he had violated the most fervently held religious prejudices of his audience. This whole incident confirms that God may use the most humble and unlikely of people to correct the proud. Sometimes the effects of this are very amusing. Moreover a deeper irony is present in this passage. The blind man, an essentially simple character, could now *'see'* whereas those Pharisees who had been set in authority over him were inflicting upon themselves a most terrible spiritual *'blindness.'* Like many contemporary Church leaders, the Pharisees were getting to the point where they could no longer see the truth because they did not

<u>want to see the truth.</u> To quote an old saying, *'there's none as blind as those who will not see.*[44]

When viewed alongside Hosea 1:10, these two passages show that:

1) The Lord displays an ironical sense of humour, often manifested through wordplay

2) The Lord uses pointed questions to show the utter absurdity of arguing with Him

3) The Lord uses irony to expose the folly of religious pretentiousness

LS10.4 Application

In response to God's *'irony'* believers would be wise to: -

1) Appreciate the fact that scripture encourages believers to display a sense of humour

2) Employ pointed questions, irony and humorous stories to deal with religious pretence

3) Avoid being unduly solemn concerning spiritual matters[45]

At the close of this study it's reasonable to conclude that God uses questions, irony and wit to deflate the pretensions of proud *'religious'* people who may have become intoxicated with their own self-importance

---

[44] Having seen church leaders and ministers in this state, the writer would request anyone reading these words never to reach this point otherwise the consequences can be truly awful.

[45] This obviously depends upon the seriousness of the matter in hand. To be light-hearted about something of great import would not be right at all.

LS10.5 Conclusion

1) Divine *'humour'* shows that God may deal with the sin of apostasy by using irony to expose the pompous hypocrisy most often seen in those leaders who have hardened their hearts against the truth

2) At Christ's death, a sense of irony was present in that the heathen Roman Centurion was able to show respect – even when his supposedly God-fearing compatriots could not, (Luke 23:47)

For further study please refer to the words *'proverbs'* or *'parables'* in any Bible Concordance or Dictionary

LS10.6 Epilogue

Father, thank you for your gift of humour but let me be wise in its use, Amen[46]

LS10.7 Questions

1) What are the best ways to curb undue solemnity on the one hand and undue frivolity on the other in matters pertaining to God?

2) Why do you think God employs humour when dealing with the human race? How effective is humour as a means of divine communication? Give reasons for your answer.

3) How can irony be employed to undermine religious pretentiousness? In which situations could humour be helpful and in which could it be harmful?

---

[46] This prayer was first made on Monday, 17th January 2000.

LS11: INTELLIGENCE

(Known also as *'Reason'*)

LS11.1 Prelude

To acknowledge divine intelligence is to learn humility

LS11.2 Definition

This <u>largely shared</u> attribute of God's *'intelligence'* refers to His ability to reason, think and perceive so that He works in a logical and orderly way.

Divine reason is implied by the name **Logos** – meaning *'intelligent word'* or *'creative expression of divine wisdom.'* An example of this name being used in scripture occurs in John 1:1 which states *"In the beginning was the Word* (Logos) *and the Word was with God and the Word was God."* It demonstrates that God can express His will in a manner that's simultaneously creative, intelligent and meaningful.

LS11.3 Bible Exposition

Two further Bible passages demonstrating the existence of this attribute are Isaiah 1:18 and Mark 12:25.

Isaiah 1:18
"'Come now and let us reason together' says the Lord, 'although your sins be scarlet they shall be as white as snow; although they be red like crimson they shall be white as wool.'"

These words are a prophetic plea to a wayward people who have strayed from the things of God. With incredible condescension, the Lord is making an appeal to reason, treating people as rational human beings with the power of inner motivation and free will. This glorious God, *'maker of Heaven and Earth'* is freely choosing to engage in an intelligent dialogue with a portion of His humanity. Present is a note of compassion with a gentle call for a response. Sin, for its part, is shown to be irrational and pointless. From God's perspective wilful sin is a sign of a lack of intelligence. It's also interesting to note that when God chooses to communicate He does <u>not</u> blank out the human mind but He sharpens and strengthens it. Consequently, we are to beware of any demand to sacrifice our mind or intelligence for a religious or political cause. Also, we are to avoid meditative practices which encourage mental passivity. It is this very passivity which may lead to a greater vulnerability to deceiving spirits. When God does speak, the mind should be alert and ready to carefully discern what is being said. In spiritual matters believers in Christ are to be alive and attentive to whatever issue is at hand. They can't afford to leave their brains outside the church door. If they are to remain faithful to Isaiah 1:18, Christians must reject any teaching which says, *"You are not in faith if you use your mind"* or *"Don't analyse – just receive this blessing."*[47] Any movement or experience which propagates such an erroneous teaching is operating under a false spirit; it is not of God.

Mark 12:25
"For they shall rise from the dead, they neither marry nor are they given in marriage – but they are like the Angels in Heaven."

Very shrewdly, Jesus employs a mixture of revelation and common sense logic to defeat the intellectually arrogant Sadducees (who were perhaps scowling in fury). He does this by simply stating that a different order of social relationships exists in the afterlife. Marriage is precluded, but this does not mean that the departed are not capable of enjoying good relationships with one another. In many ways, life is very different from that on Earth but one thing we do not lose is our individual personality. This was shown by the example of the rich man, Abraham and Lazarus in Luke 16:19f. All three parties retained their individuality in the afterlife even though they were in very different places. Through these words the Saviour uses scripture with great effect to parry His opponents' prejudices. In full public view, these prejudices were shown to be an utter nonsense. Arguing with Jesus can be dangerous; we may end up making fools of ourselves. Divine intelligence may be used to expose the folly of human pride and any hypocrisy deriving from it.

When viewed alongside John 1:1, these two passages show that: -

1) The intelligence of the Lord was manifested in the ministry of Jesus

2) The Lord employs reason when pleading with stubborn people

---

[47] This was often said when people were being pressurised into receiving *'The Toronto Experience.'*

3) Divine intelligence is very effective in demolishing intellectual pride

LS11.4 Application

In response to God's *'reason'* believers would be wise to: -

1) Use their intelligence in matters of faith and practice

2) Appreciate that social relationships in the afterlife will differ from those experienced now upon the earth

3) Avoid those meditative techniques which render people passive (often by *'blanking out'* the human mind)

At the close of this study it's reasonable to conclude that God is a God of reason – acutely discerning in all of His dealings

LS11.5 Conclusion

1) Divine *'intelligence'* shows that God may deal with the sin of apostasy by devising clever ways to thwart the proud schemes of apostates

2) At His death, Jesus demonstrated this attribute by showing that God had an intelligent plan to thwart the wiles of Satan and to undo the harm caused by human sin

For further study please refer to the words *'reason'* or *'thoughts'* in any Bible Concordance or Dictionary

LS11.6 Epilogue

Dear Lord, please help those in your Church to display a healthy intelligence in religious matters[48]

---

[48] This prayer was first made on Thursday, 20th January 2000. It expresses the wisdom of praying for believers to show a much needed healthy intelligence in the conduct of their affairs.

LS11.7 Questions

1) What are the dangers posed when people stop using their minds in matters of religious faith and practice? How can such dangers be avoided?

2) Why did Jesus adopt such a firm stance toward the Sadducees? In what circumstances would a firm stance be needed today?

3) How would you answer a theologian who held a sceptical attitude toward belief in the afterlife? What arguments would you use?

LS12: JEALOUSY

(Known also as *'Protective Possessiveness'*)

LS12.1 Prelude

To provoke a woman's jealousy is to risk humiliation but to provoke divine jealousy is to risk eternal destruction

LS12.2 Definition

This <u>largely shared</u> attribute of God's *'jealousy'* refers to the protective possessiveness He displays toward all of His people. This leads Him to demand their total loyalty and abstention from all forms of evil.

Divine possessiveness is implied by the name **Elohim Qanna** – meaning *'jealous God or Gods.'* An example of this name being used in scripture occurs in Exodus 20:5 which states *"You shall not bow down to them nor serve them* [idols]; *for I the Lord your God am a jealous God* (Elohim Qanna), *visiting the iniquity of the fathers upon the children unto the third or fourth generation of them that hate me."* It demonstrates that God wants the undivided loyalty of His people.

LS12.3 Bible Exposition

Two further Bible passages demonstrating the existence of this attribute are Deuteronomy 5:9 and 2 Corinthians 11:2.

Deuteronomy 5:9
"You shall not bow down to them nor serve them; for I the Lord your God am a jealous God, visiting the iniquity of the fathers upon the children unto the third or fourth generation of them that hate me."

Moses is delivering the Holy Law of God and he is stressing that there is one unique focus of loyalty in the spiritual area – God alone. Fiercely rejected is the view that the Lord wishes to manifest Himself through religious images (called *'icons'*) and statues. Such things represent God through the filter of limited, sinful human imagination and are therefore fallible and prone to misinterpretation. The Lord is implacable in His opposition to the use of such images in worship which over the centuries has had devastating consequences, spanning the generations. In the case of the Eastern Orthodox Church the adoption of icons has led to judgement, first by Islam and then by Communism. Within twenty years of the outbreak of World War One in August 1914, many Russian peasants who had bowed before images of Christ and the Virgin Mary found themselves being forced to revere the images of Marx, Lenin and Stalin. Those who wanted image worship were given image worship – but not in the form they initially desired. In pointing out that the iniquity of the fathers is visited upon the third and fourth generation, the Lord is warning that sin spreads and can have long lasting effects across generations.[49] The writer shudders to think what long-term consequences the current apostasy of the Church will inflict upon those who are as yet unborn. His own view is that the ultimate result may well prove to be a global holocaust. May he not live to see such a time!

2 Corinthians 11:2
"For I am jealous over you with a godly jealousy, for I have espoused you to one husband that I may present you as a chaste virgin to Christ;"

---

[49] A modern day social worker's report would confirm that the same destructive behaviour patterns are readily and often subconsciously handed down from parents to children.

Divine jealousy is reflected in the words of the Apostle Paul writing very much from his heart. Passionate concern is portrayed in his words to the Corinthian Church and Paul is determined that they should remain pure in their devotion to Christ. He hates false apostles who have infiltrated the Corinthian Church (and are even popular there) precisely because they have compromised that purity. In Paul's case, his jealousy was a sign of his personal care for the welfare of those who'd been linked to his ministry. His attitude was not a display of outraged pride but rather a firm and determined love, utterly committed to seeing holiness manifested amongst God's people. Their standards were not to be those of the world. His example challenges us to ask whether we are jealous for the welfare of God's Church or apathetically indifferent. If the latter, may the Lord have mercy on our souls, for indifference is a sin He really hates.[50] To commit this sin leads directly to divine jealousy – eventually the apathetic will learn the hard way that outraging God is no light matter. Many lazy, self-indulgent Churches in the Western World quickly need to recall this fact.

When viewed alongside Exodus 20:5, these two passages show that: -

1) God hates any attempt to worship Him through man-made images

2) The effects of sin can last for generations

3) The presence of jealousy could be a sign of great care and concern about a person or group of people

LS12.4 Application

In response to God's *'possessiveness'* believers would be wise to: -

1) Appreciate the fact that God demands undivided loyalty from those who serve Him

---

[50] This was confirmed by the harsh warning given to the Laodicean Church in Revelation 3:14f. Over the period of 1975-2011, the writer saw how indifference to truth virtually destroyed the indigenous Churches of the United Kingdom. Spiritually, they died from within and the warning of Revelation 3:14f was amply fulfilled. Theirs was *'the death of English Christianity.'* The writer regards this as the most tragic development he's ever witnessed in his life. It's resulted in a spiritual and moral vacuum that's now (April 2011) being filled by all manner of evil.

2) Avoid the use of images (icons) in worship or flirtation with any type of false teaching

3) Acknowledge that jealousy might be a more appropriate emotional response in some situations

At the close of this study it's reasonable to conclude that God is implacable in His determination to purify His people and to destroy evil; in particular, He hates the sin of apathetic indifference.

LS12.5 Conclusion

1) Divine *'jealousy'* shows that God may deal with the sin of apostasy by letting people reap the consequences of their own actions. He may allow them to be cruelly oppressed by an idolatrous religion they had wished to follow

2) At His death, Jesus demonstrated this attribute when the temple veil was torn from top to bottom, clearly indicating that He would not allow <u>any</u> priestly hierarchy to obstruct this new relationship He'd established with His people

For further study please refer to the words *'jealous'* or *'jealousy'* in any Bible Concordance or Dictionary

LS12.6 Epilogue

Lord, grant us the wisdom to distinguish between a godly and an ungodly jealousy, Amen[51]

LS12.7 Questions

1) What is the best way to avoid provoking God to jealousy?

2) Why do sins committed in one generation continue to influence a third or fourth generation within a family? How is a person's salvation likely to affect this type of situation?

3) Which is the most helpful way to counsel a fearful person who's convinced they're under a curse because their ancestors were practitioners of witchcraft?

---

[51] This prayer was first made on Monday, 24th January 2000. It expresses the need to pray about any heartfelt jealous feelings.

LS13: JOY

(Known also as *'Gladness'*)

LS13.1 Prelude

True spiritual joy should not be something 'worked up' but should be already present – welling up from within

LS13.2 Definition

This <u>largely shared</u> attribute of God's *'joy'* refers to His pleasure and happiness, portrayed in both His good-humoured wit and active desire to share that joy with those who follow Him.

Divine gladness is implied by the name **El Simchath Gili** – meaning *'God my exceeding joy.'* An example of this name being used in scripture occurs in Psalm 43:4 which states *"Then I will go to the altar of God, unto my God, my exceeding joy* (El Simchath Gili)*; yea upon the harp will I praise you, O God my God."* It demonstrates that God can fill His people with a sense of excitement during worship which may then be expressed through music.

LS13.3 Bible Exposition

Two further Bible passages demonstrating the existence of this attribute are Nehemiah 8:10 and John 17:13.

Nehemiah 8:10
"*Then he* [Nehemiah] *said to them, 'Go your way, eat the fat and drink the sweet and send portions to them for whom nothing is prepared. For this day is holy and the joy of the Lord is your strength."*

This exhortation follows a reading of scripture, just prior to the congregation being dismissed. It demonstrates the effortless link-up between holiness and joy with both attributes sitting comfortably together. Holiness should never lead to the kind of gloomy, introspective legalism which pervaded certain protestant circles toward the end of the nineteenth century. In contrast, holiness should always inspire active and joyful service. Joy should also characterise the day of rest – no matter whether it's on a Saturday or a Sunday. Over this issue, much could be learnt from the Jews who knew how to turn the Lord's Day into a celebration rather than a day of gloomy misery. Their Sabbath meals are an occasion of festivity in which all of the family participate. Not for them the dismal *'Sunday Sabbaths'* of Victorian times.[52] On a more balanced note, it's worth observing that God <u>does</u> give joy to His servants but it's never an uncontrolled frenzied hysteria, worked up through the employment of mass hypnosis techniques (often evidenced at large meetings). In reality, such a *'manufactured'* joy is false and cannot possibly last. However, true joy is present as a result of the Holy Spirit's work in a believer's life and is always a controlled joy that can even be present in very difficult circumstances. We already have a basis for joy through our relationship with Jesus, yet paradoxically we have a responsibility to nurture this joy and to express it through regular worship and the reading of scripture. When this is done the results can be very edifying – both to God and to His people. We should make way for a note of celebration in our Christian life and acknowledge that, in His goodness, there are times when the Lord likes to spoil His children. When such times happen, rejoice and be thankful!

John 17:13
"And now I come to you and these things I speak in the world that they may have joy fulfilled in themselves."

These words form part of the High Priestly prayer which Jesus made shortly before His arrest, torture and death. In them, He reveals that one of the key purposes of His ministry was to bring joy into the hearts of those who would believe in Him. Quite selflessly, He wanted His followers to share the boundless joy present between His Father, Himself and the Holy Spirit. Far from being a philosophical abstraction, there exists within the Trinity a continuously joyful interchange between each of its three members which began in eternity and will continue for forever. There is something boundless, unstoppable and wonderfully creative about divine joy. Its full manifestation will be seen in the afterlife when we shall experience it to its full extent – which is simply not possible here upon earth because of the presence of sin. However, this joy He promises is still available on this side of eternity and is more than able to survive amidst highly unfavourable circumstances. This is because it is a joy that celebrates and fully rejoices in what Christ did for us through His life, death and resurrection. In short, it is a joy that rejoices in the

---

[52] Children's swings in parks would be locked up – even on a Sunday afternoon. Young children, especially amongst the *'respectable'* middle classes were expected to sit through two long sermons – and the more hellfire and damnation in them the better.

bestowal of His gracious salvation. It rests, not in outward circumstances (which are fickle and changeable) but in the Person and work of Christ Himself. He is our focus for joy at the best and the worst of times.

When viewed alongside Psalm 43:4, these two passages show that:

1) True holiness is reflected in the amount of joy it produces

2) Joy is a source of strength in adversity

3) The Lord wants to share His joy with others

LS13.4 Application

In response to God's *'gladness'* believers would be wise to: -

1) Actively enjoy God's created gifts and His appointed day of rest

2) Accept that, whereas the devil came to spread misery, Christ came to give joy

3) Avoid equating holiness with a gloomy introspection and joy with a hysterical lack of self-control

At the close of this study it's reasonable to conclude that God is a giver of happiness, earnestly desiring that His people share the eternal joy existing in His Son, Jesus.

LS13.5 Conclusion

1) Divine *'joy'* shows that God may deal with the sin of apostasy by imparting an undergirding sense of joy to those believers called to challenge it

2) At His death, Jesus demonstrated this attribute by allowing this divinely ordained event to become a source of immeasurable happiness to those who would believe that He had died for their sins

For further study please refer to the words *'gladness' 'joy,'* or *'rejoice'* in any Bible Concordance or Dictionary

LS13.6 Epilogue

Ah, the joy that exists in you, oh Lord!
How great your gladness and Unfathomable pleasure
Welling up from the infinite depths of your being

Draw us deeper into your love
That we may rejoice in your joy and
Share it with others[53]

LS13.7 Questions

1) What are the results of knowing the joy of the Lord?

2) Why was Jesus able to manifest a true sense of joy shortly before His death?

3) How would you approach a Christian who has allowed their faith to degenerate into a system of rules and regulations? What influences may have robbed them of their sense of joy?

LS14: JUDGEMENT

(Known also as *'Condemnation'*)

LS14.1 Prelude

Learn to live with the 'Day of Judgement' constantly in view but do not become morbidly obsessed by it

LS14.2 Definition

This <u>largely shared</u> attribute of God's *'judgement'* refers to His ability to assess His Creation, to condemn the evil within it, to pass sentence upon it and to forcibly remove the evil so that it is no longer a menace.

Divine condemnation is implied by the name **Elohe mishpat** – meaning *'God of justice'* or *'of judgement.'* An example of this name being used in scripture occurs in Malachi 2:17 which states, *"You*

---

[53] This prayer was first made on Tuesday, 25th January 1999. It rejoices in God's joy and wishes to share it with others.

have wearied the Lord with your words. You say, 'Wherein have we wearied Him?' When you say, 'everyone that does evil is good in the sight of the Lord and he delights in them' or 'where is the God of judgement* (Elohe Mishpat)?'"* God appears to think well of those who would do evil and allows them to prosper in their wicked ways with no sense of impending judgement. This demonstrates that God can (from a distorted human point of view) appear to be grossly unfair in His judgements, even rewarding evildoers at the expense of the godly. However, the rest of scripture shows that this is not the case.

LS14.3 Bible Exposition

Two further Bible passages demonstrating the existence of this attribute are 1 Samuel 15:3 and Jude 14b-15.

1 Samuel 15:3

"Now go and smite Amalek and utterly destroy all that they have and spare them not; but slay men and women, infant and suckling, ox and sheep, camel and ass."

Given by Samuel as *"the words of the Lord"* to King Saul this instruction contains a terrible warning for Western Civilisation; but first it is necessary to ascertain exactly what it means. Firstly, it teaches that any given <u>culture can reach a point of no return when divine judgement becomes inevitable.</u>[54] Secondly, once judgement does strike it is often devastating in nature – sparing no one on grounds of gender, age, class or nationality. This applies whether the judgement is via natural means (*e.g.* plague) or man-made (*e.g.* foreign conquest). Thirdly, 1 Samuel 15:3 demonstrates that God will, if necessary, take ruthless measures against those who threaten the spiritual health of His people – if the Amalekites had been allowed to survive they would have enticed the people of Israel into idolatry – thus preventing them from exercising their redemptive purpose. What these words do <u>not</u> represent is a charter for genocide. What may have been necessary for the survival of the Israelites in a particular situation is <u>not</u> applicable to the Church whose mandate is to spread the good news of salvation. A failure to observe this distinction has led to many a tragedy. Nevertheless, we would be wise to heed the warning that societies may become so corrupt that the Lord has no choice but to remove them – if He is to

---

[54] Exodus 17:8f showed that the sin of Amalek's people had originally been to oppose the Israelites' entry into the land promised to Abraham. They had also continued in the worship of idols which often required the sacrifice of children.

uphold His divine holiness. The question remains, *'How near is Western Civilisation to this point?'*

Jude 14b-15
"Behold, the Lord comes with ten thousands of His Saints to execute judgement upon all and to convince all that are ungodly among them of all their ungodly deeds which the ungodly have committed and of all the hard speeches which ungodly speakers have spoken against Him."

This is a quotation from the Jewish apocalyptic Book of Enoch and occurs in the context of a warning against false teachers who have *"crept in unawares"* (Jude 4a). Acting as *"spots in your feasts of charity"* and being *"complainers, walking after their own lusts"* (Jude 12a & 16a). As a consequence, their doom is inevitable, their fate decided just as it had been for the people of Amalek. God is revealed as the Being who overthrows false teachers, His methods for doing so varying from one situation to the next. He may sometimes allow pretentious, puffed-up false teachers to say and do such ridiculous things in public that no right-minded person could possibly take them seriously. This is very much the case with those bearded eccentrics in Israel who claim to be Elijah or Jesus Christ. Possessed with a proud madness, such people think they are important but in reality their only importance lies in their unwitting contribution to the field of psychology.[55] Equally belligerent are those self-appointed Bible teachers who adopt an over-rigid stance concerning the exact order of events leading up to the return of Jesus. False teaching appears to possess an innate tendency to lead to negative attitudes, corrupt speech, sinful lifestyles and moral depravity. In the end, Christ will return to put an end to all of the nonsense spoken in His name and His saints will be with Him to see it. However, until that moment arrives, it would be wise to take great care in what we think and say about God. Let none of us be numbered amongst those false teachers who have been ordained to a bitter condemnation, (Jude 4a). They will have found out the hard way that God is not to be trifled with.

---

[55] One such person (written about in a popular magazine) actually had the name *'Elijah'* marked in broad lettering on his briefcase. The same could be said of those *'aspiring Elijah's'* to be found on the Internet. To gently yet firmly point out that their predictions of global revival do not quite tie in with the Biblical picture of the *'Last Days'* makes them livid, to say the least.

When viewed alongside Malachi 2:17, these two passages show that: -

1) The Lord is relentlessly thorough in His judgements against evildoers

2) The Lord may condemn whole societies as well as particular individuals

3) Our thoughts, words and actions will all be judged

LS14.4 Application

In response to God's *'condemnation'* believers would be wise to: -

1) Hold God in awe

2) Watch what they think and say about God

3) Avoid envying false teachers even when, in material terms they appear to be very successful

At the close of this study it's reasonable to conclude that God is a remorseless judge of evil nations and false teachers who actively oppose His purposes

LS14.5 Conclusion

1) Divine *'judgement'* reveals how God may deal with the sin of apostasy by destroying those nations which have turned against His laws

2) At His death, Jesus demonstrated this attribute by being abandoned by His Heavenly Father on the cross in order that He could receive the judgement we deserved. He became sin for us so that all of God's wrath would be directed to Him and not to us.

For further study please refer to the words *'Judge'* or *'Judgement'* in any Bible Concordance or Dictionary

LS14.6 Epilogue

Please God, don't ever allow me to become a false teacher, never let me speak lies in Your Name, Amen[56]

LS14.7 Questions

1) What are the characteristics of a Godless nation?

2) Why does the Lord take such a severe stance toward false teaching?

3) How can we avoid becoming false teachers?

4) How can we avoid succumbing to false teaching (even when plausibly presented by a respected figure of authority)?

LS15: MYSTERY

(Known also as 'Hidden Invisibility')

LS15.1 Prelude

Only God can understand everything about God

LS15.2 Definition

This largely shared attribute of God's *'mystery'* refers to His ability to hide Himself, to be invisible and to act in an inexplicable manner, beyond normal human comprehension. This means that He can make Himself unapproachable so that people neither see Him nor feel His presence.

Divine invisibility is implied by the name **Elohim Mistatter** – meaning *'hiding God or Gods.'* An example of this name being used in scripture occurs in Isaiah 45:15 which states, *"Truly you are a God who hides yourself* (Elohim Mistatter), *O God of Israel, the Saviour."* It demonstrates that God can hide Himself in order to test the faith of His people.

---

[56] This prayer was first made on Wednesday, 26th January 2000, having been used since 1977. It expresses the need to actively pray against becoming a teacher of falsehood.

LS15.3 Bible Exposition

Two further Bible passages demonstrating the existence of this attribute are Deuteronomy 29:29 and 1 Corinthians 13:12.

Deuteronomy 29:29
"*The secret things belong to the Lord our God but those things which are revealed belong to us and to our children, that we may do all the words of this Law.*"

These words follow an exhortation to obedience. They imply that truth can be divided into *'knowables'* i.e. those things which can be known about God and *'unknowables'* – those things which cannot be known about Him in this life. Included amongst the *'unknowables'* are such difficult issues as the precise reason why God allows suffering or why He saves some people whilst passing others by. It is extremely important to make a distinction between these two types of truth – the *'knowable'* and *'unknowable.'* Often theologians err because they try to work out the answer to questions that can never be answered in this life. Even worse, once critics have refuted the answers given by those same theologians they think they can dispose of Christianity altogether. This is not the case because all that's happened is that they have disposed of certain bad arguments made in defence of Christianity. Attempting to fathom the *'unknowable'* becomes most apparent when unwise believers try to work out the precise dates of Creation, the rapture of the Church or the Second Coming of Christ. Such deluded individuals are committing the sin of proud presumption by claiming to know more than God has revealed and running counter to His wishes. They foolishly ignore the warnings our Lord made against date fixing in Mark 13:32 and Acts 1:7. At the other extreme are those (mainly unbelievers) who claim that only a little can be known about God. Such people take refuge in a vague and comfortable scepticism which believes in nothing in particular. The result is that faith, if present at all, is often lacking in clarity and they flounder about in unnecessary confusion. In order to gain and adhere to a well-defined, knowable and trustworthy Christian faith each believer should avail himself/herself of those truths that have already been clearly defined in scripture (a summary of which can be found in the Apostles' and Nicene Creeds). The responsibility remains to avoid speculating upon what cannot be known whilst applying those truths which can be known. Knowledge implies responsibility and when it comes to *"those things which are revealed"* those believers with families are to live by *'those things'* and then to pass them on to their children.

1 Corinthians 13:12
"*For now we see through a glass darkly but then face to face; now I know in part but then shall I know as also I am known.*"

This emphasis upon divine mystery is repeated in these words which probably originated in a long-lost ancient hymn, celebrating divine love.[57] If the great apostle could admit to knowing *'only in part'* then how much more must we? Oddly enough, the more we seem to know about God the more we realise how much we do not know. Becoming a Christian is like paddling near the coast – in time we may get to know our own immediate shoreline but lying ahead is an endless expanse of water. Nevertheless, our comparative ignorance of godly matters does not absolve us from the responsibility to *'grow in love.'* Patience is required to do this because such a growth does not come all at once. However, our patience is strengthened when we realise that our destiny is to see Jesus *'face to face.'* We shall spend much of eternity gazing upon someone who is the ultimate personification of love. Far from being absorbed into some impersonal *'cosmic consciousness'* we shall enjoy an individual, unceasing relationship with Jesus. Far from being suppressed, our distinctive personal characteristics will be enhanced. It is only when that happens in the afterlife that our knowledge of God will become more complete. In the meantime, our responsibility is to grow in both love and knowledge. To help us do this it is necessary to refer constantly to scripture in order to define the boundary between the *'knowables'* and the *'unknowables.'* Doing this is not always easy because a distinction needs to be made between those things which we cannot know now and those which are not to be known this side of eternity. Unless this distinction is made, it is impossible to grow further in our understanding. We will also discover that it is not those things we do not understand that make us uncomfortable but rather those which we do understand clearly – the doctrine of hell being a case in point. Growing in the knowledge of God brings both joy and sorrow.

---

[57] Incidentally, it is worth noting that the reference to a glass refers to the polished brass mirrors employed in Roman times. These gave only a very dim reflection.

When viewed alongside Isaiah 45:15, these two passages show that:

1) God may choose to hide certain truths from His people because they are not yet ready to receive them at a particular point in human history

2) Even without sin, limited human minds could never grasp everything there is to know about God

3) A positive relationship can exist between knowledge and love

LS15.4 Application

In response to God's *'invisibility'* believers would be wise to: -

1) Allow the mystery of God to teach them humility

2) Accept that, in this life, we cannot know everything about God

3) Avoid trying to discover what we should not know (the *'unknowable'*) about God or at the other extreme, lazily ignoring what we <u>should know</u> (the *'knowable'*) about God

At the close of this study it's reasonable to conclude that God may choose to reveal or to keep secret certain, hidden mysteries

LS15.5 Conclusion

1) Divine *'mystery'* shows that God may deal with the sin of apostasy by behaving in a way that an apostate would not anticipate

2) At His death, Jesus demonstrated this attribute by indicating that the full benefits of His atonement might not be fully understood in this life – to many of His contemporaries it seemed inconceivable that God would put His Messiah through such an ordeal[58]

For further study please refer to the words *'hide,'* *'mystery'* or *'secret'* in any Bible Concordance or Dictionary

---

[58] In part, this was because they were expecting a glorious kingly Messiah who would evict the Romans from the land of Israel.

LS15.6 Epilogue

Lord, show me more truth from your Word but in a way and at a time you judge best[59]

LS15.7 Questions

1) What things may hinder people from truly understanding God?

2) Why does God choose to hide some truths from human understanding?

3) How can one grow in both knowledge and love at the same time?

LS16: SELF-REVEALING

(Known also as 'Communicativeness')

LS16.1 Prelude

The silence of God can be more chilling than His direst warnings

LS16.2 Definition

This <u>largely shared</u> attribute of God's *'self-revealing'* refers to His ability to speak, to engage in personal conversation with and to communicate in a variety of ways so that any believer may understand His purposes.

Divine communicativeness is implied by the term **Apokalupsis** – meaning *'sudden disclosure* or *'dramatic revelation.'* An example of this term being used in scripture occurs in Revelation 1:1 which states *"The Revelation* (Apokalupsis) *of Jesus Christ which God gave unto Him to show his servants things which must shortly come to pass; and He sent and signified it by His angel unto His servant John."* It demonstrates that God can speak in a way that grabs the attention of His intended audience.

---

[59] This prayer was first made on Wednesday, 2nd February 2000. It expresses the need to depend upon the Lord to show us His truth.

LS16.3 Bible Exposition

Two further Bible passages demonstrating the existence of this attribute are Daniel 2:28 and Luke 2:26.

Daniel 2:28

"And there is a God in Heaven who reveals secrets and makes known to King Nebuchadnezzar what shall be in the latter days. Your dream and the visions of your head upon your bed are these…"

Daniel's faith in God's communication skills was particularly helpful when the king's inability to interpret certain of his dreams (through his soothsayers) had put him into a dangerously ugly mood. Gathered around Daniel were envious courtiers who would not have hesitated to pounce should he have appeared to stumble or lose royal favour. However, bolstering Daniel's words was the certainty that God was present and willing to communicate. He could reveal truths that had hitherto been kept hidden from human eyes and could reveal them in ways that were sufficiently dramatic to win human attention. Sometimes, such ways (as in Daniel's case) could include speaking through visions and dreams. As believers, we should not usually seek for God to speak in overtly dramatic ways, but neither should we exclude the possibility. If God does choose to speak with us in such a dramatic way it would be unmistakeable. However, such dramatic means are <u>never</u> meant to puff up our own pride or to make us feel good. When God speaks with unusual clarity, it is always with a view to meeting a need or of showing some important Biblical truth which may have been challenged or neglected. Moreover, He will speak in a dramatic way only at a time of His own choosing. We cannot insist upon the Lord speaking to us dramatically. Should we do so, we will either get very frustrated or become open to a counterfeit communication. The healthier attitude is simply to be open to the Lord speaking dramatically should He wish to do so. Usually, God tends to speak quietly, either through His Word, through simple common sense, or through the circumstances in which we find ourselves. Should God choose to speak to us quietly, there is still the responsibility to listen and obey. He can communicate in both spectacular and in more unobtrusive ways.

Luke 2:26
"And it was revealed unto him [Simeon] *by the Holy Spirit, that he should not see death, before he had seen the Lord's Christ."*

Simeon was an old man who had waited a long time to see the Messiah. He was faithful and He was prayerful (indeed, the two qualities usually go together, for prayer is a manifestation of faith). Nevertheless, it had taken him years to receive a true revelation pointing directly to the Messiah. Exactly how *"it was revealed to him"* is not stated, but the words *"by the Holy Spirit"* denote some form of internal illumination. Here, it's worth pointing out that scripture is not against people receiving internal spiritual illumination – what it is against is the all too frequent habit of relying solely upon and also failing to test these *'illuminations'* once they've been received. When this happens far greater emphasis is given to this form of communication with Scripture being largely negated. In Simon's case, the effect of his illumination was the conviction that he would live to see the Messiah. This conviction was confirmed by the appearance of the *'holy family'* at the Temple. Simeon's case also demonstrates that much of the spiritual life may involve waiting patiently for God to speak or act. During such times it is necessary to carry on with life's practical activities – these may include prayer, work and constructive recreational pursuits. Such a godly waiting need not be a hard nor irksome thing. We are to wait upon the Lord and in due time He will act or speak in a way that is best.

When viewed alongside Revelation 1:1, these two passages show that: -

1) The Lord possesses one of the main attributes of personality, the ability to speak

2) The Lord may speak in either dramatic or quiet ways

3) The Holy Spirit may provide some internal form of personal enlightenment

L16.4 Application

In response to God's *'communicativeness'* believers would be wise to: -

1) Accept that God has the perfect right to choose when to speak to us in a dramatic way

2) Accept that there are times when we can do nothing but wait upon God

3) Avoid blindly accepting every *'interior illumination'* as being from God

At the close of this study it's reasonable to conclude that God is a communicative Being who reveals His will in a variety of ways

LS16.5 Conclusion

1) Divine *'self-revealing'* shows that God may deal with the sin of apostasy by dramatically warning those on the verge of committing it

2) At His death, Jesus demonstrated this attribute by revealing that God was His heavenly Father when, in agony He uttered *"Father forgive them for they know not what they do,"* (Luke 23:34a)

For further study please refer to the words *'mystery,' 'reveal,' 'spoke'* or *'spoken'* in any Bible Concordance or Dictionary

LS16.6 Epilogue

Heavenly Father, please reveal your will to me and show me a new and fruitful direction, one which will answer the question 'What am I to do with the rest of my life?'[60]

LS16.7 Questions

1) What factors may prevent God from revealing Himself to people?

2) Why is it best never to assume that every *'internal illumination'* is from God?

3) How would you deal with someone claiming to have received an inner revelation which urged them to behave in a dangerous and irresponsible way?

---

[60] This prayer was first made on Tuesday, 15th February 2000. It expresses the need to ask the Lord to show a new direction in life.

LS17: SUFFERING

(Known also as 'Endurance')

LS17.1 Prelude

If you doubt that God can suffer then think of the cross

LS17.2 Definition

This largely shared attribute of God's *'suffering'* refers to His ability to choose to suffer pain from His Creation and to feel grief or sadness at any degree of sin or human suffering.

Divine endurance is implied by the name **Yahweh Rapha** – meaning the *'Lord your healer'* (from sickness and suffering). An example of this name being used in scripture occurs in Exodus 15:26 which states *"'If you will diligently hearken to the voice of the Lord your God and will do that which is right in His sight and will give ear to His commandments and keep all His statutes; I will put none of these diseases upon you which I have brought upon the Egyptians; for I am the Lord who heals you* (Yahweh-Rapha).*"* It demonstrates that God can bring healing to fractured communities as well as to particular individuals living within those communities.

LS17.3 Bible Exposition

Two further Bible passages demonstrating the existence of this attribute are Genesis 6:6 and Mark 3:5.

Genesis 6:6

"And it repented the Lord that He had made man on the Earth and it grieved Him to His Heart."

These words describe the reaction of the Lord to the growing wickedness in the pre-flood world. Sin cuts deep into God, who is distressed when He sees His Creation completely marred by the effects of sin. He has a total hatred for any type of evil because He sees evil as destroying the beauty of His Creation. Incredible as it may seem the Almighty Creator has emotions that we need to respect. We cannot afford any type of insensitivity. Even more astonishing is the fact that God has always had the perfect freedom not to allow us to cause Him suffering. In this world, we have no choice but to suffer – it is an inescapable part of the human condition. (However, what we can do is to avoid eternal suffering in the afterlife – obtained when we place our trust in Jesus Christ as our Lord and Saviour.) In contrast, God did have a choice; He could have chosen not to be vexed by human sinfulness. The reason why He did not make such a choice was because He was a God of perfect love. The words *"it grieved Him to His heart"* is not a testimony of divine weakness, rather of divine love and a willingness to get involved in His world.

Mark 3:5
"And when He [Jesus] had looked roundabout on them in anger, being grieved for the hardness of their hearts. He said to the man 'stretch forth your hand,' and he stretched it out and his hand was restored, whole as the other."

Here, the Lord is standing before a critical audience who don't really believe He is the Messiah. They were so entrenched in their traditions that they'd utterly failed to see the fresh work God was doing through Christ. A creeping sense of unbelief had settled in their hearts. Such unbelief stirs a deep sense of anger in God, because it can be a symptom of an underlying contempt for His mercy. Through unbelief both individuals and also whole networks of Churches have cut themselves off from the sustaining power and mercy of God. They then wonder why they shrivel and die – apparently unaware that rank unbelief has taken the place of adherence to Biblical doctrine. This process happened to virtually all denominations within the United Kingdom during the second half of the twentieth century. Eventually, such unbelief leads to unresponsiveness toward God, where people react not so much with antagonism but with a nonchalant indifference. The Creator of the Universe has become casually ignored as if He were a failed consumer product. The end result of such a process is eternal death. Even truly regenerate believers in Christ face the continual challenge of guarding their hearts and ensuring they remain responsive to the will of God; and also of being long-suffering with others because God has been longsuffering with them.

When viewed alongside Exodus 15:26, these two passages show that: -

1) The Lord wishes to provide some degree of healing for the suffering already caused by sin

2) The Lord has freely chosen to allow human beings to vex Him with their sins

3) The Lord hates that hardness of heart which leads to unbelief

LS17.4 Application

In response to God's *'endurance'* believers would be wise to: -

1) Accept that, in this world, only a temporary and partial healing can be accomplished; complete healing comes only after this life has ended

2) Acknowledge the need to be sensitive to God's feelings

3) Avoid accepting that miracles can always act as a cure for unbelief

At the close of this study it's reasonable to conclude that God has an absolute hatred of evil. Through Christ's death upon the cross, (which He willingly suffered) He set in motion those events which will ultimately destroy suffering and evil.

LS17.5 Conclusion

1) Divine *'suffering'* shows that God may deal with the sin of apostasy by grieving over the sins committed in His name before taking action to deal with them

2) At His death, Jesus demonstrated this attribute by suffering acute physical, mental and emotional agony as well as the torment of thirst

For further study please refer to the words *'suffered'* or *'suffering'* in any Bible Concordance or Dictionary

LS17.6 Epilogue

Lord, be not absent in our sufferings
Be present to heal, to sustain and to deliver your people.
For the sake of your son Jesus Christ, please answer this prayer[61]

---

[61] This prayer was first made on Monday, 21st February 2000. It expresses the need to look to the Lord to help us in times of suffering.

LS17.7 Questions

1) Why do people reject the view that God can suffer?

2) Why does God allow Himself to suffer in His complete awareness of the sins of humanity?

3) How would you respond to the following statement; *'If God can suffer He must be weak and therefore does not merit our worship?'*

LS18: UNITY

(Known also as *'Indivisible Oneness'*)

LS18.1 Prelude

Believing in one God is easy; the devils also believe and they tremble?[62]

LS18.2 Definition

This largely shared attribute of God's *'unity'* refers to His complex but indivisible oneness. It constitutes a singleness of purpose, enveloped within the loving integration of the three Persons of the Trinity. This means that it is legitimate to believe in only one true God rather than in three separate Gods.

Divine oneness is implied by the name **El ohenu** – meaning *'our God.'* An example of this name being used in scripture occurs in 2 Kings 18:22 which states *"But if you say to me 'we trust in the Lord our God* (El ohenu); *is it not He whose altars and whose high places Hezekiah has taken away and said to Judah and Jerusalem 'you shall worship before this altar in Jerusalem?'"* Even a militant pagan committed to the destruction of the Jewish people could demonstrate that God can be trusted because He's not torn apart by conflicting aims and desires.

---

[62] James 2:19

LS18.3 Bible Exposition

Two further Bible passages demonstrating the existence of this attribute are Deuteronomy 6:4 and Mark 12:29.

Deuteronomy 6:4
"Hear oh Israel; the Lord our God is one Lord."

Present here is an example of an early Creed. It was known as *'the Shema'* (derived from the word *'hear'*). A Biblical precedent was therefore being given for the use of Creeds in both public and private worship. Interestingly enough, the Hebrew word for *'oneness'* is *'Echad'* – a meaning a complex, pluralistic oneness, a *'diversity within unity.'* This word allows for the possibility that there exists <u>one</u> God but <u>three</u> distinct Persons – Father, Son and Holy Spirit.[63] Significantly, the word for simple indivisible oneness (*'Yachid'*) is <u>not</u> employed here.[64] This is not to claim that this passage teaches the doctrine of the Trinity but that <u>it at least allows for the possibility</u> of Trinitarian teaching. Its main purpose was to stress the unique identity of God in an age all too prone to the worship of many different deities. It set the Israelites on a collision course with all of the surrounding religions existing at the time of Moses. The challenge was to put away idols and to worship the one true God. The words of *'the Shema'* nullify any notion that all religions are equally valid or that it doesn't matter which deity you worship as long as you sincerely wish to encounter the divine. Using *'the Shema'* assumes that the worshipper is serious about following the one true God. Also by regularly using *'the Shema'* the worshipper is inclined to listen carefully to what the Lord is saying through His Word – it is only by listening that we can obey God. A final connection is that found between Deity and Lordship. In His deity God is to be worshipped, but in His Lordship He is to be obeyed.

God is to be worshipped, but in His Lordship He is to be obeyed.

Mark 12:29
"Jesus answered, the first of all commandments is 'Hear oh Israel; the Lord our God is one Lord.'"

---

[63] Any comparison with the distinctions between the body, mind and spirit within human beings is of limited value. It's an analogy which shouldn't be pressed too far.

[64] The word *'Yachid'* would be more applicable to the unbreakable unity existing in single chemical elements like hydrogen, whilst *'Echad'* would be more applicable to chemicals compounds like water. Compounds occur where two or more elements are joined together (as is the case with hydrogen and oxygen to form water).

These words were uttered during a very heated religious controversy which saw our Lord's Messianic authority being severely challenged. In response He publicly re-affirmed the traditional Creed of Israel. Jesus, in effect, was saying *'I am orthodox because I too believe in the one true God.'* In light of this response, there is little doubt that, if pressed into a similar situation today, our Lord would unequivocally recite the Apostles' and Nicene Creeds. Unlike many in the modern Church He took Creeds seriously. To Him they were not just optional extras. If Jesus could confess the Bible-based Creeds of His day then how much more should we? It is time to restore Creeds to their rightful place of respectability within the Church – there are absolute truths which need to be publicly acknowledged and re-affirmed if we are to be true to our vocation as Christian believers.[65] Yet belief in absolute truth must <u>never</u> become an excuse for violence or the mass murder of those holding to different beliefs. If we really do hold to the absolute truths revealed in scripture then our treatment of those holding to other views should be fair and just. Truth does <u>not</u> need a crusader's sword to defend it.

When viewed alongside 2 Kings 18:22, these two passages show that: -

1) Corrupt men often oppose the unity of God

2) The worship of many gods is not an option for the Christian

3) Truth about God is to be preserved in Creeds, <u>not</u> through violence

LS18.4 Application

In response to God's *'indivisible oneness'* believers would be wise to:

1) Clarify their ideas concerning Gods identity

2) Appreciate the value of Creeds in public and private worship

3) Accept that there are absolute truths upon which wholesome lives can be built

---

[65] A detailed defence of these points will be found in the article *'Why Creeds?'* (see **Appendix 2** of *'The Leeds Liturgy'*)

At the close of this study it's reasonable to conclude that, although God strongly encourages the use of Creeds in both public and private worship they should <u>never</u> be used as an excuse for violence

LS18.5 Conclusion

1) Divine *'unity'* shows that God may deal with the sin of apostasy by reacting to it with a consistent hostility

2) At His death, Jesus demonstrated this attribute by humbly submitting His own will to His Father in order to fulfil a very costly act of obedience

For further study please refer to the words *'one'* or *'unity'* in any Bible Concordance or Dictionary

LS18.6 Epilogue

Hear, oh people
The Lord your God is one
He is of one nature
He is of one mind
He is of one will
His one desire is
That we be
One in fellowship with Him and
With each other[66]

LS18.7 Questions

1) How would you respond to the assertion that *'the Shema'* totally contradicts any idea of God being a Trinity?

2) How would you challenge the view that there is no Biblical foundation for the use of Creeds in either private or public worship?

3) Why did Jesus use a Biblical Creed during a time of fierce public controversy? What lessons can be learnt from this?

---

[66] This prayer was first made on Thursday, 24th February 2000. It expresses the need for divine unity to be reflected in the corporate life of God's people.

LS19: WILL

(Known also as *'Total Determination'*)

LS19.1 Prelude

The will of God is invincible
The will of God is all-conquering
The will of God demands our submission
For it is a will guided by an awesome love

LS19.2 Definition

This largely shared attribute of God's *'will'* refers to His ability to first make and then to implement firm choices. This means He has a fixed resolution to crush evil and to banish it from His Creation.

Divine determination is implied by the name **El neqamoth** – meaning *'God of vengeance.'* An example of this name being used in scripture occurs in Psalm 94:1 which states *"O Lord God to whom vengeance belongs* (El neqamoth); *O God to whom vengeance belongs show yourself."* It demonstrates that God can inspire people to cry out for justice when they have been wronged or subjected to oppression.

LS19.3 Bible Exposition

Two further Bible passages demonstrating the existence of this attribute are Ezra 7:18 and Acts 21:14.

Ezra 7:18
"And whatsoever shall seem good to you and to your brethren, to do with the rest of the silver and the gold do after the will of your God."

The Temple in Jerusalem is about to be restored and there is an air of religious excitement amongst Ezra's entourage who have already been provided with the resources to begin this work. The above words offer the bold assumption that it's possible both to know and to actively follow the will of God. His will is not something obscure or impossible to know. However, for the believer, knowing God's will on a specific matter is conditional upon him/her being in a right relationship with Him through Jesus Christ. This relationship can only ever come about when Jesus is believed upon as Lord and Saviour. Without faith there is no relationship with God and without this relationship there is no ability to ascertain His will. An unregenerate person has no interest at all in what God wants. At best they only have a vague sense of what to do. Very rarely is there spiritual light amongst the unregenerate. Where it does exist, it's often as a result of God's general grace which consists of His undeserved blessings, favours and mercies. These are bestowed upon all people, believers and unbelievers alike.[67] Thanks to divine mercy unbelievers may catch glimpses into the will of God but they are only glimpses. A reasonably full picture begins to emerge only after a relationship with God is in place and scripture begins to be read and understood. Ezra's example shows that, once God's will over a particular matter is clearly discerned, the next step involves taking appropriate action. This proactive approach fulfils Daniel 11:32 which states, *"the people who know their God shall be strong and do exploits."* The only exception to this is when we are specifically called to do nothing but await developments.

Acts 21:14
"And when he [Paul] would not be persuaded, we ceased, saying, 'the will of the Lord be done.'"

The apostle Paul was determined to return to Jerusalem even though he had many warnings of severe dangers lying ahead of him. The believers' weeping and sobbing had failed to dissuade him from his fixed intention. Inwardly, he seemed to realise that it was God's *'will'* for him to go to Jerusalem and to face much hardship, danger and rejection from his own people. Like Paul, the Lord may bring us into a dangerous situation in order to test our faith and to increase our spiritual fruitfulness.[68] Paul's example also demonstrates that sometimes the Lord warns us of perils ahead to better equip us to endure rather than to escape from them. At such times, it is God's will to strengthen our wills so that we can face difficult circumstances and bear good fruit. The Lord may bring us into situations of danger so that we can be effective witnesses to His Son Jesus Christ. However, to avoid any type of psychological collapse we must take care to ensure that it is the Lord and not our own foolish impetuosity

---

[67] Such blessings may include the provision of natural resources, good health and enjoyable human relationships.
[68] A debate has existed as to whether Paul was right or wrong to continue his journey to Jerusalem in the face of the warnings he'd received. Tentatively, my own view is that, as there was still quite miraculous evidence of divine blessing in the Jerusalem and post-Jerusalem phases of his ministry, he was right to have continued his journey. He showed no trace of the helplessness or the defeatism associated with those who stray from God's will.

taking us into what may prove to be a very risky situation. If it is the Lord, we should enjoy the peace which gives us great resilience amidst severe adversity.

When viewed alongside Psalm 94:1, these two passages show that:

1) The Lord will take vengeance upon evildoers only when He wishes to do so

2) The Lord's will is accomplished through the corporate activity of His people

3) The Lord may decide to lead His people into situations of danger in order to test their faith

LS19.4 Application

In response to God's *'total determination'* believers would be wise to:

1) Acknowledge that vengeance is best left in God's hands

2) Accept that God's will may guide believers into new avenues of service

3) Avoid rushing into dangerous situations out of mere impulse

At the close of this study it's reasonable to conclude that God's total determination (at times of His choosing) may challenge people to face very dangerous and difficult situations.

LS19.5 Conclusion

1) Divine *'will'* reveals that God may deal with the sin of apostasy by firmly resolving to punish hardened unfaithfulness

2) At His death, Jesus demonstrated this attribute by firmly resolving to die on behalf of sinners

For further study please refer to the words *'chose,' 'chosen,' 'will,' 'willing'* or *'wills'* in any Bible Concordance or Dictionary

LS19.6 Epilogue

Lord, please grant your servant the wisdom to know whether it is your will to face this dangerous situation or to actively avoid it[69]

LS19.7 Questions

1) What are the best ways to ascertain whether the Lord is calling us to face a dangerous situation or to avoid it?

2) Why may the Lord call His people to enter perilous life-threatening situations?

3) How would you challenge a young, immature believer, completely convinced that it's the Lord's will to smuggle Bibles into a country bitterly hostile to Christianity?

LS20: WONDER

(Known also as *'Total Beauty'*)

LS20.1 Prelude

A wise person marvels at the beauty of Creation
An even wiser person marvels at the beauty of the Creator

LS20.2 Definition

This largely shared attribute of God's *'wonder'* refers to His awesome, yet comely attractiveness to delight His Creation and to inspire much true worship.

Divine beauty is implied by the name **Elohe Thehilathi** – meaning *'God of my praise.'* An example of this name being used in scripture occurs in Psalm 109:1 which states *"Hold not your peace, O God of my praise* (Elohe Thehilathi)." It demonstrates that God can provoke spontaneous praise.

---

[69] This prayer was first made on Monday, 28th February 2000. It expresses the need to pray about potentially dangerous situations.

LS20.3 Bible Exposition

Two further Bible passages demonstrating the existence of this attribute are Psalm 27:4 and Revelation 15:3.

Psalm 27:4
"One thing have I desired of the Lord, that will I seek after; that I may dwell in the house of the Lord all the days of my life, to behold the beauty of the Lord and to enquire in His temple."

David's words were set in a context of exuberant worship with his heart hungering for the things of God. The Holy Spirit had created in him a desire to be with the Lord forever. He was a man who enjoyed a profoundly loving relationship with his Maker – a love that was deeply passionate yet free from the trite sentimentality often seen amongst those who claim to *'love the Lord.'* Moreover, his love expressed itself in an active and meticulous way. For David to *'behold'* the beauty of the Lord was something worth seeking after – his fervour is an example to challenge us all; indeed, if David could display such fervour when he had only a partial revelation then how much greater should our fervour be – not least because we have received the full revelation of Jesus Christ? When it comes to spiritual matters there can be no room for slothful indifference. Both wisdom and zeal are needed. Like David, we can also acknowledge that sometimes the only way to obtain the right answers from the Lord is to ask Him the right questions. In the Christian life, those who don't ask don't get, (James 2:4c).

Revelation 15:3
"And they sing the song of Moses, the servant of God and the song of the lamb, saying, 'Great and marvellous are your works, Lord God Almighty; just and true are your ways you King of Saints.'"

Coming into clearer view is a more meaningful portrayal of that reality which David could only dimly see. John was granted a tremendous vision of heaven whereby he heard fervent songs of praise inspired by the Lord's beauty. One can almost feel the waves of joy coming from the assembled heavenly throng. God was praised for being: -
1) Great
2) The author of many works
3) Lord
4) Almighty

5) Just

6) The royal and sovereign head of all of His people

In Heaven, the attributes of God provoke joyful worship. This suggests that <u>the divine attributes are not simply a matter of speculation but also a cause of celebration.</u> As a final point, it is worth noting how, in this passage, many diverse attributes are worshipped together as one unit. The saints in Heaven assume no contradiction between them and neither must we. Consequently, it is not only possible to celebrate the attributes themselves, but also to justly celebrate the harmony between them.

When viewed alongside Psalm 109:1, these two passages show that: -

1) The beauty of the Lord inspires praise

2) The beauty of the Lord inspires fervour

3) The beauty of the Lord is fully manifested in Heaven

LS20.4 Application

In response to God's *'total beauty'* believers would be wise to: -

1) Be joyfully fervent in their praise and worship

2) Actively seek the Lord by asking Him questions

3) Model their worship on that of the saints in Heaven

At the close of this study it's reasonable to conclude that God is a focal point of sung worship

LS20.5 Conclusion

1) Divine *'wonder'* shows that God may deal with the sin of apostasy by punishing corrupt religious people in such a way that a sense of awe is provoked in those remaining loyal to the truth

2) This attribute continues to be demonstrated by the priceless value Christ's death has in the heart of believers

For further study please refer to the words *'beauty'* or *'wonder'* in any Bible Concordance or Dictionary

LS20.6 Epilogue

Lord, your beauty is beyond compare
Your attractiveness so very fair
Your attributes bring much delight
For you are awesome in your might[70]

LS20.5 Questions

1) **What should our response be to the beauty of God?**

2) **Why is it legitimate to use songs and music in worship?**

3) **To what extent do you agree with the view that *'worship should be a matter of creativity rather than tradition?'* Give reasons for your answer.**

4) **How would you comfort a well-meaning but rather insecure believer who feels guilty because they do not possess any strong feelings about God?**

LS21: WORTHINESS

(Known also as *'Unlimited Value'*)

LS21.1 Prelude

We are only worth something because God is worth everything

LS21.2 Definition

This <u>largely shared</u> attribute of God's *'worthiness'* refers to His unbounded worth and precious value. This means that He should be the first priority in everyone's life.

Divine value is implied by the name **Elohim Chai** – meaning *'living God'* or *'Gods.'* An example of this name being used in scripture

---

[70] This prayer was first made on Monday, 28th February 2000. It expresses the need to allow the beauty of God to inspire a sense of excited devotion.

occurs in Isaiah 37:17 which states *"Incline your ear, O LORD and hear; open your eyes, O LORD and see: and hear all the words of Sennacherib which he has sent to reproach the living God (Elohim Chai)."* It demonstrates that God can appear very real to believers who are being threatened by those who represent the evil one.

LS21.3 Bible Exposition

Two further Bible passages demonstrating the existence of this attribute are Psalm 36:7 and Matthew 13:44.

Psalm 36:7

"How excellent is your loving kindness, O God! Therefore the children of men put their trust under the shadow of your wings."

This psalm is a hymn of praise to God's everlasting value. He is worshipped because He is worthy. Moreover, in times of danger we are able to flee to Him for protection for, in His unlimited worth, He has condescended to love us who have no worth. Our worthiness lies in Christ who is present in each believer by the Holy Spirit. An urgent priority today is for the Church to regain this sense of divine worth – indeed a low esteem of God rots the religion entertaining such views and can lead to great acts of cruelty.[71] In contrast, high views of God (based upon scripture) can be a source of much blessing – as demonstrated during the Great Evangelical Awakenings of the eighteenth and nineteenth centuries. These revivals led to fresh forms of worship, a new concern for mission and a strong encouragement of positive social reform. The campaign to abolish slavery and a succession of Factory Acts demonstrated that cruelty and the unjust exploitation of others were no longer casually accepted as being part of the natural order of things. The question all of us now face is *'How much do we value the Lord?'* This is a challenge that cannot be ignored for should we <u>not</u> value the Almighty then neither will we value our fellow human beings. Such a point has been amply demonstrated in the history of atheistic ideologies like Communism. Over the long term, it is only possible to value other people if we value the Lord. For many believers today, their first priority should be to regain a fresh understanding of divine worthiness. Only then is evangelism likely to have any positive effect.

---

[71] *E.g.* the cruel sacrifices practised by the Aztecs before the Spanish conquest in the sixteenth century. Behind these sacrifices lay the assumption that the gods were so weak that an endless supply of ritually offered human blood was needed to keep them functioning. They were sacrificing to demons, (1 Corinthians 10:20).

Matthew 13:44
"*Again the Kingdom of God is like a treasure hidden in a field which when a man has found he hides and for the joy of it goes and sells all that he has and buys the field.*"

In this parable, Jesus is evidently very determined to highlight the unlimited value of God's heavenly kingdom. This kingdom is worth all that we have. How we spend our money shows the worth we place upon that kingdom (the word *'kingdom'* referring to that realm where God exercises a direct rule, unchallenged by any form of rebellion). Appreciating the unlimited worthiness of the Lord produces a joyful self-sacrifice that, to outsiders, may seem foolish. One danger to be avoided is to over-identify the *'Kingdom of God'* with any visible humanistic movement, organisation or nation state. At their best, such corporate bodies may be blessed by God and used to fulfil some of His purposes but eventually *'the law of sin and death'* still comes into play – causing such bodies to rebel against God and to come under His judgement, (Romans 8:2). In this world, the real place to find God's Kingdom is in the minds and hearts of those committed to following Jesus and also in the good fruit they bear in their lives. Hence, we must look for the kingdom of God but we must look for it in the right places; these do not include any political or religious empires built by men.[72] God's kingdom is where He reigns and He can reign in our hearts, this possibility should be a major source of joy.

When viewed alongside Isaiah 37:17, these two passages show that:

1) Divine worthiness can provoke even godless people to acknowledge God's sovereignty

2) Divine worthiness inspires a sense of awe and joy

3) It's definitely worth submitting every area of one's life to God

---

[72] Confusing the Kingdom of God with a particular Empire was a mistake that Byzantines Christians made and it's one that right wing American Evangelical Christians risk repeating. If Christianity is to survive it must have the capacity to disengage from collapsing civilizations. Any failure to do so will lead to its extinction. Western Christians may have to learn this point the hard way.

LS21.4 Application

In response to God's *'unlimited value'* believers would be wise to: -

1) Appreciate that there are no limits to divine sovereignty

2) Be eager in their pursuit of God's will

3) Avoid equating God's Kingdom with even benevolent organisations, nation states, Empires or Civilizations

At the close of this study it's reasonable to conclude that God is of unlimited worth and should be valued for His own sake

LS21.5 Conclusion

1) Divine *'worthiness'* shows that God may deal with the sin of apostasy by highlighting the tragic way in which apostate individuals and groups devalue themselves in God's sight

2) At His death, Jesus demonstrated this attribute by making a sacrifice, the value of which is impossible to measure

For further study please refer to the words *'wonder'* or *'wonders'* in any Bible Concordance or Dictionary

LS21.6 Epilogue

Who can measure your worth, oh Lord?
Who can estimate your infinite value and
Set a scale upon your precious nature?
Not one of us can, for we are limited sinners
Prone to seeking your kingdom in all the wrong places
Without you, we are worthless
With you, we are worth everything
For Your Son, Jesus, died to make us worthy[73]

---

[73] This prayer was first made on Tuesday, 29th February 2000. It expresses the need to show joy at God's worthiness and the worth He has given us, through His Son, Jesus Christ.

LS21.7 Questions

1) What are the right and wrong ways to respond to the worthiness of God?

2) Why is it important to seek the extension of God's rule in our own hearts? How can such an extension happen?

3) How would you reply to the claim made by a particular religious group that they are the only true representatives of God's Kingdom on Earth?

4) How would you reply to the claim that *'The environmental movement represents a genuine expansion of God's Kingdom on Earth?'*

LS22: WRATH

(Known also as *'Furious Anger'*)

LS22.1 Prelude

Divine wrath is slow to kindle but fatal to underestimate

LS22.2 Definition

This <u>largely shared</u> attribute of God's *'wrath'* refers to His justified, passionate but self-controlled indignation and deeply felt hatred of evil. This means that He will crush evil entirely.
Divine anger is implied by the name **Elohim Zo'em** – meaning *'angry,' 'indignant God'* or *'Gods.'* An example of this name being used in scripture occurs in Psalm 7:11 which states *"God judges the righteous and God is angry* (Elohim Zo'em) *with the wicked every day."* It demonstrates that God can be unrelenting in His wrath.

LS22.3 Bible Exposition

Two further Bible passages demonstrating the existence of this attribute are Nahum 1:3 and Colossians 3:6.

Nahum 1:3
"The Lord is slow to anger and great in power and will not at all acquit the wicked. The Lord has His way in the whirlwind and in the storm and the clouds is the dust of His feet."

In order to convey the awesome nature of divine anger the Lord uses vivid natural imagery, creating a very clear picture in the minds of His hearers. Not much sympathy should be wasted on the Assyrians who are the target of Nahum's tirades. Theirs had been a brutally wicked empire, not above impaling unfortunate victims on long stakes or skinning them alive. In Assyria, violence was glorified and a *'might is right'* philosophy had been adopted in its dealings with other nations. Now it was Assyria's turn to receive exactly the same fate it had dealt out to others. God's anger is never hasty, but once kindled it can be devastating in its effects. His anger may be directed against whole cultures as well as individual evildoers within those cultures. Usually, divine anger is expressed by allowing people and nations to take the inevitable consequences of their own actions. They are given over to their own depraved minds and self-destructive behaviour patterns (Romans 1:18f). However, on occasion a dramatic divine intervention may take place to forcibly remove a particular evil. Those believers who are spiritually discerning often know when such a moment is occurring. Post war western civilisation has not yet been judged like Nineveh[74] but what does seem to be happening is a rapid filling up of *'the cup of wrath.'* One sin is being added to another and, all the while, people are gradually losing any sense of right or wrong. Even worse, many Churches have been given over to a retributive spiritual blindness so that leaders and members alike are no longer able to tell the difference between the Holy Spirit and an *'unclean spirit.'* This means that one of the chief restraints upon evil (the Holy Spirit) will have removed Himself from most of the Churches leaving them to their own devices. Sooner or later a point may well be reached when God's wrath is ready to overflow and judgement meted out via the hands of evildoers. Once this happens, it will signify the end of western society as we know it.

Colossians 3:6
"For which things the wrath of God comes upon the children of disobedience."

---

[74] Although the destruction of the New York Trade Centre on 11th September 2001 could well be an ominous portent – as could the London suicide attacks of 7th July 2005 and the banking crash of September 2008

In the previous verse, Paul had given a list of rather unpleasant human sins, including fornication, covetousness and idolatry, all of which are manifestations of the underlying sin of disobedience. Once people have set their hearts against God other sins tend to spring up as if they were poison toadstools on a decaying tree trunk. God's response can only ever be one of wrath. If this were not the case then He would simply become a passive accomplice to those evils which derive from sin. A God who was not angered by some of the great crimes in human history would not be a God worth following. Divine anger is the appropriate response to the presence of malicious wickedness, especially if such wickedness is done in the name of God! It might be helpful to think of it as a form of outraged love and, as such, used either to restrain or to remove evil. In addition, it is worth noting that God is angry at every specific sin we commit for His perfection cannot abide the slightest trace of imperfection. Not one sin will be overlooked on the Judgement Day. Indeed, our position would be utterly hopeless if it were not for Christ's work in pacifying God's wrath when He died upon the cross. For believers, Christ is like a shield, deflecting the hammer blows of God's awesome rage against our iniquity. Without this shield we would be eternally and deservedly lost. My urgent advice to anyone reading these words is to throw yourself upon the mercy of God and plead with Him to give you that faith in Jesus who is the only Person able to quell God's justified fury against our sin. Only through this faith can divine wrath be appeased. In the end, all of us will know either the full manifestation of divine love or the full manifestation of divine anger. If you want to enjoy the former then you must repent of your sins and believe in Jesus as your Lord and Saviour. Also, receive the Holy Spirit and be willing to be baptised through full water immersion that you may publically witness your identification with Christ's death, burial and resurrection. If you have acted upon this advice you will have received the Gospel which gives you eternal life.

When viewed alongside Psalm 7:11, these two passages show that:

1) The Lord never ceases to be angry toward the wicked

2) The Lord's wrath overthrows evil societies as well as individuals within them

3) Divine wrath is an appropriate response to human sinfulness

LS22.4 Application

In response to God's *'furious anger'* believers would be wise to: -

1) Accept that none of us can escape the Day of Judgement

2) Acknowledge that disobedience leads to many sins and the kindling of divine wrath

3) Avoid the full manifestation of divine anger by continuing to believe in Jesus as Lord and Saviour

At the close of this study it's reasonable to conclude that God's wrath is applicable at both the individual and wider social scale

LS22.5 Conclusion

1) Divine *'wrath'* shows that God may deal with the sin of apostasy by forcibly removing religious corruption

2) At His death, Jesus demonstrated this attribute by being subjected to a dreadful darkness (indicative of the presence of God's wrath at the crucifixion)
For further study please refer to the words *'anger,' 'fury,' 'rage'* or *'wrath'* in any Bible Concordance or Dictionary

LS22.6 Epilogue

Sovereign God, in this time of your anger remember that you sent Your Son Jesus to die on our behalf – thus taking the punishment we deserved for our sins[75]

LS22.7 Questions

1) What effect will divine anger have upon corrupt societies?

2) Why is it appropriate for God to be angry about our sins?

---

[75] This prayer was first made on Tuesday, 29th February 2000. It expresses the need to trust in the atoning work of Christ's death, especially during times when divine wrath is manifesting itself.

3) How would you challenge the view that, because of what Jesus did on the cross, God isn't angry with the world anymore?

LS23: ZEAL

(Known also as 'Enthusiastic Fervour')

LS23.1 Prelude

Foolish zeal is a curse but lazy indifference is a double curse; the first may be corrected, but the second is almost beyond cure

LS23.2 Definition

This <u>largely shared</u> attribute of God's *'zeal'* refers to His heartfelt, militant combativeness against evil and His fervent eagerness to carry out His plans to the tiniest detail.

Divine fervour is implied by the name **Yahweh Nakeh** – meaning *'the Lord who smites.'* An example of this name being used in scripture occurs in Ezekiel 7:9 which states *"And mine eye shall not spare, neither will I have pity. I will recompense you according to your ways and your abominations that are in the midst of you and you shall know that I am the Lord who smites* (Yahweh Nakeh).*"* It demonstrates that God can be zealous about overthrowing evil.

LS23.3 Bible Exposition

Two further Bible passages demonstrating the existence of this attribute are 2 Kings 19:31 and John 2:17.

2 Kings 19:31
"For out of Jerusalem shall go forth a remnant and they that escape out of mount Zion; the zeal of the Lord of hosts shall do this."

Represented here is a prophetic promise given to King Hezekiah during a time of great crisis when all seemed lost. God is shown to be a zealous guardian of a loyal remnant whom He miraculously preserves during times of great devastation. He comforts those who belong to that remnant with a vision of hope, inspiring them to remain faithful during difficult times when the small kingdom of Judah was threatened with annihilation by a cruel Assyrian foe. In our present day, an awful judgement <u>has</u> to come upon this increasingly godless world, but thankfully judgement will not be the end of the matter. Through it the Lord will preserve a remnant of both Jews and Gentiles who will play a major part in advancing God's kingdom. The reason for this preservation lies in God's own fervent determination to see His Kingdom established. Neither the strongest powers of Hell nor massive human rebellion will be able to prevent His purpose from being fulfilled. God's *'will,'* shall <u>inevitably</u> be done because He will zealously desire to make it so. A heartfelt appreciation of these facts would do much to improve the morale of those grievously disturbed at how things have turned out in the Church. Let those who still believe in Jesus cling to this vision of hope and be strengthened by it. Times may indeed be bad but with God on our side no justifiable reason exists to despair.

John 2:17
"And His disciples remembered that it was written, 'The zeal for your house does devour me.'"

This verse records the reaction of the disciples to Jesus having dramatically chased the money changers out of the Temple. A particular scriptural quotation came to their minds; its effect was to deepen their understanding of Christ's messianic ministry. They began to realise that God is zealously opposed to religious *'confidence tricksters'* who make use of His name solely as a means to defraud others. God forcibly drives such people away from His presence.[76] In His humility, the Lord <u>has freely chosen to subordinate Himself to His Word (Scripture)</u> because it's a perfect reflection of His own perfect mind. Usually, when there is talk of God being *'bigger than His Word'* an attempt is being made to foist some non-scriptural belief or practice upon God's people.[77] In reality, God and His Word are one and indivisible. Far from being *'above His Word,'* the Lord is <u>passionately</u> zealous to fulfil every detail of it. Christ demonstrated this zeal by cleansing the Temple where, at great risk to Himself, He went out of His way to fulfil just one Messianic prophecy. To be zealous for the *'Word'* is tantamount to being zealous for God. As a final point, it's worth adding that *'the Word'*

---

[76] He did this with the money changers in the Temple, with the late medieval indulgence sellers at the time of the Reformation and with those prosperity preachers of our present age whose ministry has ended in public disgrace.

[77] It is also interesting to note that when God acts in an astonishing way, (which may look to be slightly out of character) He justifies it by bringing to mind relevant scripture passages to those witnessing the action. Here, it is vital to emphasise that, whilst the Lord may act in a way contrary to our expectations, He will <u>never</u> act in a way contrary to Scripture. Any assertion that God is *'bigger than His Word'* is the talk of a fool.

helps keep our zeal (both individual and corporate) within reasonable bounds. Without it our enthusiasm for spiritual things would quickly degenerate into a foolish and dangerous fanaticism, wholly discrediting to God and His gospel of salvation. Yet it must be said that a certain amount of zeal is needed to prevent any study of Scripture from becoming a dry intellectual exercise. Zeal motivates us to apply scriptural teaching in our daily lives. Far from being fanatical, this zeal could be better described as an avid interest, a determination to obey scriptural teaching and a desire to share the Christian life with both believers and unbelievers.

When viewed alongside Ezekiel 7:9, these two passages show that through zeal, God is motivated to: -

1) Destroy those people and nations who militantly oppose His will

2) Preserve a remnant of believers during times of judgement

3) Directly confront religious corruption

LS23.4 Application

In response to God's *'enthusiastic fervour'* believers would be wise to: -

1) Ensure that we are part of God's remnant in this evil age

2) Acknowledge that we need to be zealous in our application of Biblical teaching

3) Avoid using the name and Word of God as a means of taking advantage of others

At the close of this study it's reasonable to conclude that God is a zealous guardian of His remnant people

LS23.5 Conclusion

1) Divine *'zeal'* shows that God may deal with the sin of apostasy by waging militant warfare against a harlot *'super Church,'* (which Revelation 17-18 suggests will have formed just before Christ's return)

2) At His death, Jesus demonstrated this attribute on the cross when confronting the forces of human and spiritual evil

For further study please refer to the words *'enthusiasm, fervour'* or *'zeal'* in any Bible Concordance or Dictionary

LS23.6 Epilogue

Loving God, please help me to combine both a fervent zeal and a calm wisdom so that I may effectively witness to yourself and to your Son, the Lord Jesus Christ, Amen[78]

LS23.7 Questions

1) What are the main characteristics of divine zeal?

2) Why is zeal such a necessary part of the Christian life? How can it be prevented from degenerating into a foolish fanaticism?

3) How would you respond to a fanatical person who uses the argument that *'God is bigger than His Word'* when attempting to justify some strange beliefs and practices?

---

[78] This prayer was first made on Tuesday, 29th February 2000. It expresses the need to balance zeal with wisdom in the Christian life.

Summary

Su1: Each of the above 23 <u>largely shared</u> attributes may be summarised as follows: -

1) Divine complexity: God's ability to possess many <u>apparently</u> diverse attributes, with no conflict or inner tension

2) Divine creativity: God's ability to plan, originate and construct things, either from nothing or by using existing raw materials

3) Divine emotion: God's ability to feel, be moved by, empathise with, sensitively relate to and freely identify with His Creation

4) Divine enlightenment: God's ability to give understanding, to guide, to mentally inspire, to show the truth and to teach, using a variety of methods

5) Divine eternity: God's ability to enjoy an unceasing, timeless, everlasting and perpetual existence

6) Divine faithfulness: God's ability to be consistently trustworthy, loyal and dependable in keeping all of His promises

7) Divine greatness: God's ability to display an awe-inspiring depth of character, immensity of being and dignified stateliness, embodied in His outstanding moral qualities

8) Divine heroism: God's ability to perform great deeds and to confront evil, whilst Himself accepting great suffering, pain and grief

9) Divine humanity: God's ability to become a limited human being – having all of the traits associated with humanity, but without sin

10) Divine humour: God's ability to amuse and to be amused by a lively combination of unexpected ideas or expressions

11) Divine intelligence: God's ability to think, reason, analyse and discern, as well as to perceive, so that He works in a logical and orderly way

12) Divine jealousy: God's ability to be protectively possessive of all of His people, leading Him to demand their total loyalty and abstention from all forms of evil

13) Divine joy: God's ability to feel a good humoured happiness, pleasure and delight

14) Divine judgement: God's ability to assess His Creation, to condemn the evil within it, to pass sentence upon it and to forcibly remove the evil so that it is no longer a menace

15) Divine mystery: God's ability to hide Himself, to be invisible and to act in an inexplicable manner, beyond normal human comprehension

16) Divine self-revealing: God's ability to speak, to engage in personal conversation with and to communicate in a whole variety of ways in order that any believer can understand His purposes

17) Divine suffering: God's ability to choose to suffer pain from His Creation and to feel grief or sadness at any degree of sin or human suffering

18) Divine unity: God's ability to display a complex but <u>indivisible oneness.</u> It constitutes a singleness of purpose, enveloped within the loving integration of the three Persons of the Trinity

19) Divine will: God's ability to make and implement firm choices, including the decision to crush evil and to banish it from His Creation

20) Divine wonder: God's ability to display an awesome, yet comely attractiveness to delight His Creation and to inspire much true worship

21) Divine worthiness: God's ability to possess unbounded worth and precious value

22) Divine wrath: God's ability to manifest justified, a passionate but self-controlled indignation and deeply felt hatred of evil

23) Divine zeal: God's ability to show a heartfelt, militant combativeness against evil and His fervent eagerness to carry out His plans to the tiniest detail

Su2: In relation to the sin of apostasy: -

1) Divine complexity shows that God may react to it in ways which may perplex those who have turned against Him

2) Divine creativity shows that God may deal with it by regarding it as a grievous violation of His created order – especially where sexual immorality is involved

3) Divine emotion shows that God may react to it with keenly felt repugnance, anger, sadness and grief

4) Divine enlightenment shows that God may deal with it by giving more than enough truth to those who have turned against Him so that they will be without excuse on the Day of Judgement

5) Divine eternity shows that God will react to it by inflicting eternal death upon those who stubbornly remain faithless toward His son Jesus

6) Divine faithfulness shows that God may deal with it by keeping His promise to inflict many curses upon those who cease to follow Him or to obey His teaching

7) Divine greatness shows that God may deal with it by publicly humbling those who've chosen to turn against Him (*e.g.* by allowing their names to be linked to scandalous behaviour)

8) Divine heroism shows that God may deal with it by empowering people to confront it in a bold and decisive manner

9) Divine humanity shows that God may deal with it by displaying human emotions like anger, grief and sorrow

10) Divine humour shows that God may deal with it by using irony to expose the pompous hypocrisy most often seen in those leaders who have hardened their hearts against the truth

11) Divine intelligence shows that God may deal with it by devising clever ways to thwart the proud schemes of apostates

12) Divine jealousy shows that God may deal with it by letting people reap the consequences of their own actions, *e.g.* allowing them to be cruelly oppressed by an idolatrous religion they had wished to follow

13) Divine joy shows that God may deal with it by imparting an undergirding sense of joy to those believers called to challenge it

14) Divine judgement shows that God may deal with it by destroying those nations which have turned against His laws

15) Divine mystery shows that God may deal with it by behaving in a way an apostate would not anticipate

16) Divine self-revealing shows that God may deal with it by dramatically warning those on the verge of committing it

17) Divine suffering shows that God may deal with it by grieving over the sins committed in His name before taking action to deal with them

18) Divine unity shows that God may react to it with a consistent hostility

19) Divine will shows that God may deal with it by firmly resolving to punish hardened unfaithfulness

20) Divine wonder shows that God may deal with it by punishing corrupt religious people in such a way that a sense of awe is provoked in those remaining loyal to the truth

21) Divine worthiness shows that God may deal with it by highlighting the tragic way in which apostate individuals and groups devalue themselves in God's sight

22) Divine wrath shows that God may deal with it by forcibly removing religious corruption

23) Divine zeal shows that God may deal with it by waging militant warfare against a harlot *'super Church,'* (which Revelation 17-18 suggests will have formed just before Christ's return)

Su3: During His death, Jesus demonstrated: -

1) Divine complexity by accomplishing an unlimited number of things – only a few of which can be known in this life

2) Divine creativity by confirming that God had devised a totally original solution to the problem of human sin

3) Divine emotion by being so moved by the plight of sinners that He chose to die an agonising death on their behalf

4) Divine enlightenment by showing the repentant thief where his destination would be in the afterlife

5) Divine eternity by giving eternal life to those remaining faithful to Him

6) Divine faithfulness by fulfilling every Biblical prophecy which had predicted this event

7) Divine greatness by suffering the worst forms of abuse without retaliation

8) Divine heroism by showing how He, as a mortal human being was willing to die an agonising death in order to save people from their sins

9) Divine humanity by suffering such human needs as thirst, whilst hanging upon the cross

10) Divine humour (irony) was present, in that the heathen Roman Centurion was able to show respect – even when his supposedly God-fearing compatriots could not

11) Divine intelligence by showing that God had an intelligent plan to thwart the wiles of Satan and to undo the harm caused by human sin

12) Divine jealousy by the rending of the Temple veil from top to bottom, clearly indicating that He would not allow <u>any</u> priestly hierarchy to obstruct this new relationship He'd established with His people

13) Divine joy by allowing this divinely ordained event to become a source of immeasurable happiness to those who would believe that He had died for their sins

14) Divine judgement by being abandoned by His Heavenly Father on the cross in order that He could receive the judgement we deserved

15) Divine mystery by indicating that the full benefits of His atonement might not be fully understood in this life – to many of His contemporaries it seemed inconceivable that God would put His Messiah through such an ordeal

16) Divine self-revealing by revealing that God was His heavenly Father when, in agony, He uttered *"Father forgive them for they know not what they do,"* (Luke 23:34a)

17) Divine suffering by suffering acute physical, mental and emotional agony as well as the torment of thirst

18) Divine unity by humbly submitting His own will to His Father in order to carry out a very costly act of obedience

19) Divine will by firmly resolving to die on behalf of sinners

20) Divine wonder by the priceless value Christ's death has in the heart of believers

21) Divine worthiness by making a sacrifice, the value of which is impossible to measure

22) Divine wrath by being subjected to a dreadful darkness (indicative of the presence of God's wrath at the crucifixion)

23) Divine zeal when confronting the forces of human and spiritual evil

C3:
THE FOURTEEN POTENTIALLY SHARED ATTRIBUTES

PS1: GENEROSITY

(Known also as *'Abundance'*)

PS1.1 Prelude

God is not a miser who gives only grudgingly to His people

PS1.2 Definition

This potentially shared attribute of *'generosity'* refers to God's bountiful open-handedness in giving abundantly to His people and withholding no good thing.

Divine abundance is implied by the name **Yahweh-Yireh** – meaning *'the Lord who provides'* or *'Lord Provider.'* An example of this name being used in scripture occurs in Genesis 22:14 which states *"And Abraham called the name of that place Yahweh-Yirah as it is said to this day, in the mount of the Lord it shall be seen."* It demonstrates that God can astonish people with His generosity.

PS1.3 Bible Exposition

Two further Bible passages demonstrating the existence of this attribute are Genesis 13:15 and Matthew 6:26.

Genesis 13:15
"For all the land which you see, to you will I give it and to your seed forever."

The words *"all the land"* highlight the generosity of the Lord, as does the promise that it will be given to Abraham's descendants *'forever.'* An unconditional promise is made with no suggestion that ownership of the land is applicable only to one particular historical time period. Also, the land shall never be permanently taken away (though periods of exile have since been necessary to deal with sin). If the Almighty could make such generous promises to Abraham's physical descendants then, He also makes similar promises to those who, through Jesus, have been adopted into Abraham's family. Not only does God make these promises – He also keeps them. This is because His promises reflect the abundant generosity of His nature. To deny that God will restore His Jewish people to a position of blessing is to deny His generosity. If the promise of Genesis 13:5

clearly means what it says then the only conclusion to draw is that <u>the Jewish people have a permanent right to the land promised to Abraham.</u> This is <u>not</u> to condone everything said or done in the name of the Jewish State of Israel, but it does involve recognizing that this State has a right to exist. Attempts to delegitimize it must be resisted so as not to become complicit in a further attempt to exterminate the Jewish people. If this happens another generation may have to learn the hard way that anti-Semitism is the most destructive of hatreds. Any attempt to get rid of the Jews can be a very messy business. It can ruin the perpetrators as well as the victims.

Matthew 6:26
"Behold the fowls of the air; for they sow not, neither do they reap, nor gather into barns, for your Heavenly Father feeds them. Are you not much better than they?"

The Lord comforts His disciples by showing how God's bountiful generosity operates in the world of nature. In this case, He is referring to those chains of food supply provided for every single creature. A pastoral image of birds, fields and barns must have filled the disciples' minds as they heard these words. Jesus was using imagery that would be meaningful to his audience. Like many other skilful Jewish Rabbis, He was teaching that what applied on a *'minor'* level also applied on a *'major'* level. Divine generosity works from the sub-atomic through to the cosmological scale. This can be readily seen in this galaxy alone where God has provided two hundred billion stars to edify the human mind. There are also an estimated one hundred billion galaxies also containing billions and trillions of stars. Large and small things alike tell of God's infinite abundance many of which are underlined still further by modern scientific discoveries. Our response to this can only be to remain respectfully silent and to marvel at how the God who created all of this should choose to become a tiny clump of cells in a virgin's womb.

When viewed alongside Genesis 22:14, these two passages show that: -

1) The generosity of the Lord is seen in the meeting of human needs

2) The making and keeping of generous promises serves to highlight God's bountiful character

3) The world of nature is one grand display of God's incredible abundance

PS1.4 Application

In response to God's *'abundance'* believers would be wise to: -

1) Know that God can meet needs in all sorts of generous ways

2) Accept the fact that the Jews will be restored to a position of divine blessing

3) Avoid worrying over whether He will provide for our needs

At the close of this study it's reasonable to conclude that God is both a maker and a keeper of wonderful promises which guarantee a generous provision for our needs

PS1.5 Conclusion

1) Divine *'generosity'* shows that God may deal with the sin of apostasy by delaying His judgements, so providing people with more time to repent, (2 Peter 3:9)

2) At His death, Jesus demonstrated this attribute by praying that God His Father would forgive those who had crucified Him, (Luke 23:34)

For further study please refer to the words *'generous'* or *'kindness'* in any Bible Concordance or Dictionary

PS1.6 Epilogue

Lord God of Israel
Please be generous and quickly
Get me out of the mess I'm in
In Jesus name, Amen[79]

---

[79] This prayer was first made on Friday, 26 November 1999. It expresses the need to ask God to show His generosity in times of great personal difficulty.

PS1.7 Questions

1) What prompted God to give the land of Israel to the descendants of Abraham for all generations?

2) Why may we be tempted to doubt God's generosity?

3) How would you challenge someone who is increasingly sceptical of God's generosity as a result of repeated personal disappointment?

PS2: GOODNESS

(Known also as 'Benevolence')

PS2.1 Prelude

One of the abilities the Lord has given to the believer is the capacity for him or her to thrill God's heart!

PS2.2 Definition

This <u>potentially shared</u> attribute of *'goodness'* refers to God's benevolent kindness, cordiality and caring friendship with His Creation. This means He wants only the best for it.

Divine benevolence is implied by the name **Yahweh-Rapha** – meaning *'the Lord your healer.'* An example of this name being used in scripture occurs in Exodus 15:26e which states *"For I am the Lord who heals you,"* (Yahweh-Rapha). It demonstrates that God can express his goodness through divine healing.

PS2.3 Bible Exposition

Two further Bible passages confirming the existence of this attribute are Zephaniah 3:17 and John 3:16.

Zephaniah 3:17
"The Lord your God in the midst of you is mighty. He will save, He will rejoice over you with joy, He will rest in His Love, He will rejoice over you with singing."

This prophecy refers to the final redemption of the saints that will take place at the end of time. Amazingly, the Lord is portrayed as singing joyfully over His people who must, by that stage, fill Him with a great deal of delight. One can almost imagine the Lord beaming with pleasure as He surveys a people who will have been purified of all their sins. It seems a little odd for humanity to actually have the capacity to fill God with pleasure but that does seem to be the case. Presumably, this is because He sees us through the prism of Christ's work on the cross. Sometimes, we need to lift our eyes above our current struggles in order to look up to God and to look forward to what we will be in Christ. Too many Christians make the mistake of being trapped in the *'here and now.'* They would be wise to adopt a long-term perspective of their affairs. It is helpful to recall that every day we are being prepared for eternal life with Jesus Christ.

John 3:16
"For God so loved the World, that He gave His only begotten Son, that whosoever believes in Him should not perish but have everlasting life."

This represents one of the most famous promises of scripture. Much more could be said concerning it, but in this present discussion it will be used only to show how it relates to divine goodness. It is found in the context of a conversation between Jesus and a senior Jewish religious figure, Nicodemus. When talking with Nicodemus the Lord showed a comprehensive awareness of His Father's plans to redeem the Earth from sin. These plans were an excellent reflection of the Father's goodness; showing His love for a sin-afflicted world. However, Jesus words presupposed a choice; Mankind could either accept the Lord's goodness (as supremely manifested in Jesus) or reject it by continuing in unbelief. Nicodemus faced that choice and so do we. The Lord's goodness is to be received but we must first believe that Jesus is God's only begotten Son. To deny God's ability to have a son is also to deny His goodness.

When viewed alongside Exodus 15:26, these two passages show that: -

1) The goodness of God is often shown in the work of divine healing

2) The Lord loves to rejoice over His people

3) God's goodness has been shown by sending His only begotten Son into the world and also by the presence of His Holy Spirit in the believer's heart

PS2.4 Application

In response to God's *'benevolence'* believers would be wise to: -

1) Acknowledge God's goodness when receiving a work of healing

2) Acknowledge the Lord's goodness with songs and praises

3) Avoid believing that God can have no sons

At the close of this study it's reasonable to conclude that God is a lover of humankind and thoroughly enjoys His handiwork when the element of sin has been removed

PS2.5 Conclusion

1) Divine *'goodness'* shows that God may deal with the sin of apostasy by ensuring that the schemes perpetuated by wicked apostates themselves become a means whereby the Gospel is further propagated, (Acts 8:1)

2) Jesus demonstrated this attribute by praying for sinners just before His death, (Luke 23:44)

For further study please refer to the words *'good'* or *'goodness'* in any Bible Concordance or Dictionary

PS2.6 Epilogue

Abba Father, let me sing out my praises to your goodness, for you're a wonderful Lord who does everything right. Cause me to testify to your benevolence in a bold but sensitive manner.[80]

---

[80] This prayer was first made on Monday, 29 November 1999. It expresses the need to let divine goodness inspire an enthusiastic praise.

PS2.7 Questions

1) How does God show His goodness to the believer?

2) Why is Nicodemus puzzled by Christ's statement in John 3:16? What is the most appropriate response to this passage?

3) How would you respond to an over-enthusiastic believer who keeps testifying to God's goodness in a congregation where there are a significant number of people suffering from bereavement, poverty or persistent ill health? In what ways would you try to curb his enthusiasm without destroying it?

PS3: GRACE

(Known also as *'unmerited favour'*)

PS3.1 Prelude

To know God's grace is the only way to know true freedom

PS3.2 Definition

This <u>potentially shared</u> attribute of *'grace'* refers to God's undeserved favour shown toward His Creation and to Humanity who, in their universal corruption, merit only the severest form of punishment.

Divine undeserved favour is implied by the name **Elohim rachun vechannun** – meaning *'merciful and gracious God.'* An example of this name being used in scripture occurs in Exodus 34:6 which states *"And the Lord passed by before him* [Moses] *and proclaimed The Lord, the Lord God, merciful and gracious* (Elohim rachun vechannun) *and longsuffering and abundant in goodness and truth."* It demonstrates that God can reveal attributes like goodness through direct revelation.

PS3.3 Bible Exposition

Two further Bible passages demonstrating the existence of this attribute are Genesis 6:8 and Ephesians 2:8.

Genesis 6:8
"But Noah found grace in the eyes of God."

The historical setting took place during a time of great wickedness when the Lord was abandoning people to their own evil ways. Five verses previous to this, the Lord had made the terrible statement *"My spirit shall not always strive with man."* In other words, He was abandoning a degenerate people to their own devices. Even worse, Genesis 6:7 revealed that the Lord had already resolved to destroy Mankind. Judgement by devastation was inevitable and yet at such an awful time it was still possible to find grace — how? Hebrews 11:4 provides the answer; *"By faith Noah, being warned by God of things not seen as yet, moved with fear, prepared an ark to the saving of his house."* Revealed here is the fact that grace is found through a reverent faith in God and His promises. No esoteric knowledge or magnificent spiritual experience is needed. The New Testament reinforces this point by revealing that the God of Israel sent His only begotten Son to die for our sins. His name is Jesus and today, through faith in Him, all of us may find grace in the eyes of God, no matter how much wickedness or apostasy may be going on around us. A simple yet true faith always results in practical obedience to the will of God as revealed in Scripture.

Ephesians 2:8
"For by grace you are saved, through faith, and that not of yourselves, it is the gift of God."

In these words, Paul pinpoints the relationship between grace and faith. If the paragraph above showed that faith was a means of receiving grace, then here faith is shown to be utterly dependent upon grace for its very existence. Grace gives the faith first of all to believe in the God of Israel and then it operates again so that people may receive the grace of salvation. Unlike Gnosticism, (whose teaching centres upon moving from one higher level of mystical knowledge to another) God's Word shows that spiritual knowledge is gained only as a result of faith. We are <u>not</u> placed into a right relationship with God through the acquisition of special knowledge but through simple faith that the Lord Jesus Christ died to save us from our sins before rising bodily from the dead three days later, (Romans 10:9). If this were not the case, any relationship with God would be confined to a small intellectual élite, convinced that they alone had exclusive access to *'special'* knowledge. Christianity would not appeal to ordinary people. What this passage also rules out is any idea that a relationship with God is something that can be engineered through human effort. Where grace is present there is no room for human boasting. No one but God can claim credit for such a relationship. This is a point Paul himself stressed in Ephesians 2:9. The Almighty is not like a corrupt border policeman, having to be bribed (by our good deeds or moralistic self-effort) before He will let us through. Sadly, this is the way many in the Church perceive Him.

When viewed alongside Exodus 34:6, these two passages show that: -

1) Divine grace prompts God to show mercy to sinful people

2) Divine grace can be found during evil times

3) Divine grace is both a cause and a result of faith

PS3.4 Application

In response to God's *'unmerited favour'* believers would be wise to: -

1) Actively seek God's grace during personal difficulties

2) Be aware that a final manifestation of grace may precede a severe and devastating judgement

3) Accept the futility of trying to please God through human effort alone

At the close of this study it's reasonable to conclude that God is a giver of faith (even when He is preparing to remove evildoers from the face of the earth)

PS3.5 Conclusion

1) Divine *'grace'* shows that God may deal with the sin of apostasy by miraculously providing for true believers, who are possibly being persecuted or trapped in bad Church situations

2) At His death, Jesus demonstrated this attribute by instructing His disciple (John) to take care of His mother, Mary (John 19:26-27)

For further study please refer to the words *'grace'* or *'gracious'* in any Bible Concordance or Dictionary

PS3.6 Epilogue

Lord, please provide grace to show grace to all who try my patience, Amen[81]

PS3.7 Questions

1) How can people receive divine grace?

2) Why did God destroy most of the human race in Noah's day?

3) How would you respond to a despairing Christian who argues that society has become so evil that there's no longer any point in witnessing to the Gospel?

PS4: HOLINESS

(Known also as *'Total Purity'*)

PS4.1 Prelude

Nothing discredits the notion of 'holiness' more than 'holier than thou' Christians. Pray that God would save us from such abject creatures.

PS4.2 Definition

This <u>potentially shared</u> attribute of *'holiness'* refers to God's moral purity and complete freedom from any trace of evil or sin. It also refers to His strongly felt repugnance toward all forms of corruption.

Divine purity is implied by the name **Elohim Qedhoshim** – meaning *'Holy God'* or *'God's.'* An example of this name being used in scripture occurs in Joshua 24:19 which states *"And Joshua said unto the people, you cannot serve the Lord for He is a Holy God* (Elohim Qedhoshim); *He is a jealous God; He will not forgive your transgressions nor your sins."* It demonstrates that God, should He so decide, can refuse to forgive human sin.

---

[81] This prayer was first made on Wednesday, 22nd December 1999. It expresses the need to ask for grace at a time when we are most tempted to lose our patience.

PS4.3 Bible Exposition

Two further Bible passages demonstrating the existence of this attribute are Leviticus 11:44 and 1 Peter 1:15.

Leviticus 11:44
"For I am the Lord your God; you shall therefore sanctify yourselves and you shall be holy for I am holy – neither shall you defile yourselves with any manner of creeping things that creep upon the earth."

One reason for the complex dietary laws in Books like Leviticus is to point out the irreconcilable opposition existing between the *'clean'* and the *'unclean.'* These represent the good and the evil which can exist in every area of life. However, it would be mistaken to view these qualities as two equally valid manifestations of the same God.[82] In turn, the words *"you shall therefore sanctify yourselves"* do not imply a state of personal holiness achieved through self-effort alone. Both Biblical teaching and the evidence of human history show that self-sanctification is impossible. (The example of the Pharisees confirms that self-sanctification often ends in self-satisfaction). Rather, this passage presupposes that the Lord has already brought us out of the *'Egypt'* of sin and has given us the freedom to co-operate in our own spiritual growth. It is also worth stating that God wants all of His people to be holy. Contrary to popular impression, holiness is not an attribute reserved for some *'super-spiritual'* religious caste. Rather, it is a characteristic to be displayed by all believers in the *'rough and tumble'* of everyday life. In practical terms, sanctification can involve anything from honesty in business dealings through to faithfulness to one's marriage partner.

1 Peter 1:15
"But He who has called you is holy, so be holy in all manner of conversation."

Here, the Apostle Peter is focusing upon the practical side of the Christian life. The level of holiness in a person is shown in the language he/she uses. Without being supercilious or false, Christians are expected to adopt a speaking posture free from profanity, harshness and backbiting gossip. This seems to be something of a *'tall order'* and yes, it happens all too often that we do speak harshly

---

[82] This is the error of Pantheism, a world view suggesting that God is equally present in everything. It forms the basis of Eastern religions like Hinduism.

or enjoy a piece of gossip that we should not be enjoying. Whilst we all fail to be <u>consistently</u> holy in our manner of conversation we can nevertheless state that if a professing Christian is <u>casually</u> profane or deceitful in their use of language something has gone badly wrong. In truth, such people perhaps have never really repented and believed in Christ. Christians should *'watch their lips,'* for by them and by their actions people will decide whether they are genuine followers of the Messiah. Also to be avoided is any slippery evasiveness of language which tends to deceive, not by what it says but by what it leaves unsaid. This sin is particularly common amongst religious ministers whose loyalty to Christ has begun to diminish. Their preaching tends to focus upon the *'nice'* things of Christianity like God's love and care. The less *'nice'* things like God's wrath and judgement of sin are conveniently ignored.

When viewed alongside Joshua 24:19, these two passages show that: -

1) The holiness of God challenges people to choose whether they are serious about following Him

2) The holiness of God draws a distinction between right and wrong

3) The holiness of God is displayed in the words of scripture

PS4.4 Application

In response to God's *'purity'* believers would be wise to: -

1) Think carefully before choosing to serve God in any capacity

2) Actively co-operate with God in the process of being made holy

3) Avoid company where there is likely to be suggestive or unpleasant conversation

At the close of this study it's reasonable to conclude that God is concerned that holiness extends into all aspects of life

PS4.5 Conclusion

1) Divine *'holiness'* shows that God may deal with the sin of apostasy by withdrawing His Holy Spirit from corrupt Churches, leaving them to be destroyed by human sin and the devil's wiles

2) Jesus demonstrated this attribute by experiencing the complete abandonment of His Father's caring presence as He took the punishment for human sin during His crucifixion

For further study please refer to the words *'holy,' 'holiness'* or *'sanctify'* in any Bible Concordance or Dictionary

PS4.6 Epilogue

Lord
Let your holiness
Fill my heart
Fill my lips and
Fill my actions
So that I may glorify your name
Through witnessing
Your truth to others
Amen[83]

PS4.7 Questions

1) Why can't people make themselves holy?

2) What are the likely effects of attempts at *'self-sanctification?'* Why is it something Christians should <u>never</u> attempt?

3) Why may it be difficult to maintain a holy manner of conversation with others? Suggest ways to maintain an unblemished conversation in a workplace full of profane language?

4) How can we help both ourselves and other believers to grow in personal holiness?

---

[83] This prayer was first made on Wednesday, 12th January 2000. It expresses the need to ask for divine holiness to influence all areas of one's life.

PS5: HUMILITY

(Known also as 'Modesty')

PS5.1 Prelude

When people boast of their humility reach for the sick bag!

PS5.2 Definition

This <u>potentially shared</u> attribute of *'humility'* refers to God's ability to willingly put aside His majesty in order to become weak and vulnerable; restraining and humbling Himself to better identify Himself with His Creation.

Divine modesty is implied by the name **Emmanuel** – meaning *'God with us.'* An example of this name being used in scripture occurs in Isaiah 7:14 which states *"Therefore the Lord will give you a sign; behold, a virgin shall conceive and bear a son and shall call His name Emmanuel."* It suggests that God can bear a son should He wish to do so.

PS5.3 Bible Exposition

Two further Bible passages demonstrating the existence of this attribute are Amos 7:3 and 1 Corinthians 1:25.

Amos 7:3
"The Lord repented of this [proposed punishment] *– It shall not be, says the Lord."*

In this dialogue with the prophet Amos, the Lord explicitly promises to spare His people from the disasters He was initially going to inflict upon them as a punishment for their sin. Amazingly, thanks to this attribute, it is possible for believers, in prayer, to cause the Lord to change His mind concerning a specific course of action. This can happen without there being any change in the essential nature of God. His change of mind has <u>not</u> lessened His divinity in any way. At this point, one can imagine the prophet's horror at a threatened judgement suddenly turning to relief as the Lord relents and changes His plans. Why then does an utterly perfect God condescend to change His mind in response to our feeble, often wayward prayers? The simple answer is that He wants our relationship with Him to be real. If it was not possible for us to change His mind on certain occasions then the Lord would be no better than an unscrupulous politician, going through the motions of consultation when a course of action had already been decided upon. Yet one note of caution needs to be sounded. We can never persuade Him to change His mind so that He would act in a way contrary to His Word or ask Him to do something obviously nonsensical. For example, God would never bring another Messiah in place of Jesus, wishing Him to be an alternative source of salvation. Neither would He change the present world into the shape of a square just for the fun of it. Instead, what He does do is to show enough flexibility to make prayer a worthwhile exercise. Prayer can change things in certain areas because, in His breath-taking humility, God has given His servants the privilege of being able to change His mind. It's up to us to use that privilege wisely.

1 Corinthians 1:25
"Because the foolishness of God is wiser than men and the weakness of God is stronger than men."

In this passage, Paul is dealing with the negative reaction to the Gospel which *"for the Jews is a stumbling block and for the Greeks foolishness,"* (1 Corinthians 1:23). This is because neither of these two groups understood the first thing about divine humility. In Jewish eyes God was viewed as a remote potentate, whereas in the eyes of sophisticated Greeks He was little more than a philosophical abstraction. Their theological perspective prevented them from seeing that, in the person of Jesus, God was humble enough to die a criminal's death in order to rescue people from their sins. When expiring upon the cross God, through Jesus, was challenging the world to face the fact that many of their most cherished religious and philosophical prejudices were hopelessly wrong. Nails driven through the limbs of Jesus were also nails driven into the heart of every single *'faith'* lying outside the boundaries of clear Biblical teaching. When Jesus died man-made religious-philosophical systems began to die too. Subsequent attempts to devise new systems have simply represented ways of trying to resuscitate a corpse. Sadly, human stubbornness throughout the ages has ensured that most people prefer to adhere to these *'dead systems'* rather than enjoy a personal relationship with the living God. By dying in the way that He did, Jesus demonstrated that both Rabbinic Judaism and Greek Philosophy adopted an equally naive approach to human nature and its many flaws. Neither of these two systems could grasp that, as a deliberate act of love, God <u>chose</u> to become a full human being in order to save people from their sins. He did not remain remote and distant.

When viewed alongside Isaiah 7:14, these two passages show that: -

1) The humility of God means that He need no longer to be viewed as an overbearing dictator, using arbitrary force to get His own way

2) The humility of God turns prayer into a meaningful exercise

3) The humility of God allowed Him to become part of the human race in the person of Jesus

PS5.4 Application

In response to God's *'modesty'* believers would be wise to: -

1) Attempt to discern those times when it may be possible to change God's mind

2) Abandon any undue confidence in man-made philosophical or religious systems

3) Avoid equating divine humility with a supercilious cowardice

At the close of this study it's reasonable to conclude that God is a self-effacing Being. His humility dashes human pride by showing that even the most cherished of philosophical beliefs has an erroneous view of God and His ways of working

PS5.5 Conclusion

1) Divine *'humility'* shows that God may deal with the sin of apostasy by restraining His judgements in response to heartfelt prayers made by his servants

2) At His death, Jesus demonstrated this attribute by meekly allowing brutal Roman soldiers to nail Him to a cross (without any show of defiance)

For further study please refer to the words *'humble,'* *'modesty'* or *'repent'* in any Bible Concordance or Dictionary

PS5.6 Epilogue

Lord, teach me to be humble but in a way that is not too embarrassing[84]

PS5.7 Questions

1) What are the best ways to grow in humility?

2) Why do people often find it hard to grasp the idea of humility?

3) How would you keep your patience with someone who boasts of their humility?

PS6: JUSTICE

(Known also as 'Impartial Fairness')

PS6.1 Prelude

People cry to God "Give us justice, give us justice," but if He did, they would soon be obliterated from the face of the Earth

PS6.2 Definition

This <u>potentially shared</u> attribute of God's *'justice'* refers to His impartial fairness and unprejudiced decision-making. This means that He always arrives at the right verdict – treating all people exactly as they deserve.

Divine fairness is implied by the name **Adon** – meaning *'my Almighty ruler and judge.'* An example of this name being used in scripture occurs in Genesis 18:32 which states *"And he* [Abraham] *said oh Lord* (Adon) *let not the Lord be angry and I will speak yet but this once; peradventure ten* [righteous men] *will be found there* [in Sodom] *and the Lord said I will not destroy it for ten's sake."* It demonstrates that God can display His justice toward whole communities as well as to particular individuals.

---

[84] This prayer was first made on Thursday, 13 January 2000. It expresses the inner unease which may be felt when praying for humility.

PS6.3 Bible Exposition

Two further Bible passages demonstrating the existence of this attribute are Isaiah 9:7 and Romans 3:5.

Isaiah 9:7
"*Of the increase of His government and peace there shall be no end, upon the throne of David and upon His Kingdom, to order it and to establish it with judgement and with justice from henceforth even forever. The zeal of the Lord of hosts will perform this.*"

The Lord is concerned with social justice in general and with those unfairly oppressed by corrupt structures within a given society. He wants fair treatment for all members of the human race, regardless of gender, age, race, or religious conviction. Even people who lead blatantly sinful lives are entitled to impartial treatment by the courts if they have been unfairly wronged. This point is borne out in this messianic prophecy which promises a kingdom wherein perfect justice will reign for all people. Obviously, the setting lies somewhere in the future and it would be foolish to attempt to usher in such a kingdom whose full manifestation can only be achieved by God Himself. This constituted one of the tragedies of Communism – where it tried to usher in a perfectly just society by human effort alone and the result was the Gulag – a network of prisons, extermination centres and slave labour camps which were the embodiment of injustice. Since the 1980s, the so-called '*Reconstructionist*' theologians in America risk repeating the same mistake of trying to build an imaginary perfect society by force. If they had their way the result would be the ultimate horror – Gulags in the name of Christ! One would have the gates of a future Auschwitz adorned with words from the Sermon on the Mount. Hopefully, such a scenario will remain a nightmare of the imagination – however, in days such as these one cannot be too sure. The current moves to create a New World Order based upon New Age Ideas should be watched with deep, prayerful concern. However, this is not to imply that God will do everything and that Christians should be unconcerned with matters of social justice. Far from it – Christians should be actively involved in implementing justice wherever they can. This is because they will be judged, at least in part, on the way they have treated others, (Matthew 7:12 & 25:31f) However, what they must grasp is that such an implementation can only ever give a preview of the kingdom that is to come. Yes, Christians may rightly campaign for justice, but they must realise that, at best, this can only ever bring about a partial and temporary manifestation of Christ's kingdom. The full realisation of the Kingdom of God will only ever come about at a time of God's choosing, (Acts 1:7).

Romans 3:5
"But if our unrighteousness commends the righteousness of God, what shall we say? Is God unrighteous who takes vengeance? (I speak as a man)."

The Apostle Paul has been showing that both Jews and Gentiles alike are under the wrath of God. He is being wholly realistic in his view of human nature. Paul also saw that God would be totally unjust if He took an indifferent *'never mind, it doesn't matter'* attitude to the sin which warps every human being. God is rightfully indignant about all of our shortcomings and His holiness constrains Him to take action against our wrongdoing. If that were the end of the story our plight would be an utterly hopeless one – resulting in death, judgement and hellfire for every human being. Mercifully, the story does not end there; Jesus was sent to satisfy divine justice and to open up the way for people to know God as their Father. Jesus did this through His sacrificial death upon the cross at Calvary. There, God's justice was displayed in all of its lofty majesty and there too it was satisfied. Nevertheless, it is unwise to set oneself up as a professional critic of divine justice. If we presume to ask Him to show justice by removing evil from the face of the earth He may well choose to make a beginning by removing us! All of us, to some degree, perpetuate evil in our lives. We would be far better asking God to show His mercy first before asking Him to display His justice over a particular matter. We must remember that God is just, but His notion of justice is far removed from our limited human understanding of it. This is because He sees things with a <u>perfect</u> clarity, something utterly unattainable for any human being.

When viewed alongside Genesis 18:32, these two passages show that: -

1) The kingdom of God will be characterised by a perfectly fair system of justice

2) The Lord is passionately zealous in an impartial yet fair justice for the disadvantaged members of society

3) The Lords standards of justice are far higher than any human being could ever imagine

PS6.4 Application

In response to God's *'fairness'* believers would be wise to: -

1) Accept that any man-made attempts to bring about a perfectly just society will have tragic consequences – even when attempted in the name of Christ

2) Accept that the responsibility still remains to campaign for justice as long as it is realised that such campaigns will only ever reflect a small foretaste of Christ's kingdom upon Earth

3) Avoid setting themselves up as professional critics of divine justice

At the close of this study it's reasonable to conclude that God is a scrupulously impartial observer of human affairs and justly angry with the many injustices in the world.

PS6.5 Conclusion

1) Divine *'justice'* shows that God may deal with the sin of apostasy by thwarting attempts made by apostates to usher in a better society

2) At His death, Jesus demonstrated this attribute by willingly taking the punishment we deserved for our sin

For further study please refer to the words *'just'* or *'justice'* in any Bible Concordance or Dictionary

PS6.6 Epilogue

Lord, bring justice to the world but in your way and in your time[85]

---

[85] This prayer was first made on Wednesday, 26th January 2000. It expresses the need to accept that God has His own timing over when to implement His justice.

PS6.7 Questions

1) What incorrect ideas do people entertain about divine justice?

2) Why do attempts to bring in a perfectly just society always end in tragedy?

3) How would you argue against the statement, *Matters of social justice are of no concern to the Christian?'* What would be the likely results of such a viewpoint be, were it ever adopted on a large scale?

PS7: LAW-GIVING

(Known also as *'Legitimate Authority'*)

PS7.1 Prelude

False teachers and false prophets may have power in the Church but that is not the same thing as exercising a <u>legitimate authority.</u> Keep this distinction in mind and you will be safe

PS7.2 Definition

This <u>potentially shared</u> attribute of God's *'law-giving'* refers to His ability to set perfectly authoritative standards which address both the realm of nature and human affairs. Any departure from these standards leads only to disastrous consequences to the orderly running of Creation.

Divine authority is implied by the name **Elohim** – meaning *'righteous God'* or *'Gods.'* An example of this name being used in scripture occurs in Psalm 7:9 which states *"Oh let the wickedness of the wicked come to an end; but establish the just – for the righteous God* (Elohim) *tries the hearts and emotions."* It demonstrates that God can use the law to express His righteousness.

PS7.3 Bible Exposition

Two further Bible passages demonstrating the existence of this attribute are Exodus 13:9 and Galatians 6:2.

Exodus 13:9
"And it shall be a sign to you upon your hand and for a memorial between your eyes that the Lord's law may be in your mouth; for with a strong hand has the Lord brought you out of Egypt."

To be effective, the laws of God must first be written by the Holy Spirit deep within our hearts and minds. This point is implied in the above command given by Moses just as the Israelites were about to leave Egypt (a nation at that time undergoing the severest of judgements). People appear to need a visible, physical reminder of who God actually is – there has to be something of immediate import to act as a preventive against drifting back into idolatry. Jesus instituted a similar reminder when He introduced the Lord's Supper as a physical reminder of His death. However, true spiritual growth can only ever take place <u>after</u> the Lord has done a special regenerative work in the human heart. Only the Holy Spirit can create any longing for the things of God. Should we yearn for Him, we can never take the credit for it. Such a trait <u>never</u> comes naturally to the human heart; but exists only because of a hidden, yet profound work, initiated and then continued by the Holy Spirit. His is always a positive influence, affecting our innermost being – influencing both heart and mind. This flatly contradicts certain mystical teachings associated with groups like the Quakers (which assumes the presence of an *'inner light'* or *'spark'* reaching out from humanity to the divine. In reality, it is always the Holy Spirit reaching out to us). The Jewish and Christian Faiths also contradict mysticism in their teaching that the Almighty did a very specific work in human history. The Deity is no impersonal *'it,'* (as mysticism often teaches) far removed from the affairs of His world – neither is He some vague *'cosmic consciousness.'* God is personal and He acts in human affairs. In the case of the Israelites, He rescued them from the slavery of Egypt and in the case of true believers He delivers them from slavery to sin. God has acted in human history by revealing His laws and, from behind the scenes He is continuing to work His purposes out. This applies to even the most tragic of events.

Galatians 6:2
"Bear one another's burdens and so fulfil the law of Christ."

Written by Paul to a congregation in bondage to legalism, these words confirm that the Church is not to consist of disparate individuals, having little to do with one another, except when attending Sunday worship. Whether we like it or not we are responsible to our fellow believers – even if they do belong to the *'awkward squad.'* Paul's words presuppose a sense of community and this is precisely the quality lacking in most churches today. Exactly how we *'bear one another's burdens'* will vary from one situation to another. At times it may be *'tea and sympathy,'* the provision of financial relief or the meeting of a physical need. Absent in this passage is any notion that pastoral care should be left to a *'ministerial elite'* or to a team of *'super counsellors'* – although this is not to deny that people may need to be referred to professional care should their problems be more complex in nature. Particularly in relation to the severely mentally disturbed this would prove a very sensible thing to do. Nevertheless, the fact remains that we cannot continue in our indifference to the state of our fellow brothers and sisters in Christ. The law of Christ is the law of love and this love must be expressed in the life of the Church if it is to maintain an effective witness in an increasingly hostile world.

When viewed alongside Psalm 7:9, these two passages show that: -

1) The law of God reflects His righteousness

2) There is no inner light in Man; only God can ever give us a longing for Him

3) The law of God is not opposed to the love of God

PS7.4 Application

In response to God's *'Law-making'* believers would be wise to: -

1) Appreciate the value of such external rites as Water Baptism[86] and Holy Communion

2) Acknowledge that God actively breaks into human affairs

3) Feel a responsibility and actively work toward a real sense of community with other believers

At the close of this study it's reasonable to conclude that God is able to intervene in human history to reveal His will and to declare His laws

---

[86] This refers to full immersion adult baptism and not to infant baptism, which the writer believes is unscriptural

PS7.5 Conclusion

1) Divine *'rule-making'* shows that God may deal with the sin of apostasy by inflicting specific penalties for the breaking of specific commands

2) At His death, Jesus demonstrated this attribute by being cursed for being hung on a cross, (Deuteronomy 21:21f)

For further study please refer to the words *'commandments,' 'law'* or *'statutes'* in any Bible Concordance or Dictionary

PS7.6 Epilogue

Lord, let your Law inspire love rather than fear in the hearts of those who long to obey you. Please do this for the sake of your son Jesus Christ, Amen[87]

PS7.7 Questions

1) What are the similarities and differences between *'the law'* of Moses and *'the law'* of Christ?

2) Why are visible aids (like the Sacraments) so necessary in the life of the Church? How can we prevent them from becoming an idol?

3) How can visible aids (like the sacraments) inspire people to care for one another in a practical way?

4) How would you respond to the complaint that God is unfair to expect impossibly high standards of behaviour and then condemn people for not meeting those standards?

---

[87] This prayer was first made on Thursday, 27th January 2000. It expresses the need to depend upon the grace of Jesus in order to receive a favourable answer to prayer.

PS8: LOVE

(Known also as *'Benevolent Compassion'*)

PS8.1 Prelude

Two options are available to people – to know God's love or to know His wrath

PS8.2 Definition

This <u>potentially shared</u> attribute of God's *'love'* refers to His undeserved self-giving, boundless, patient, kind and compassionate pity for His Creation. He would be willing to suffer to an unlimited degree (should this be necessary) in order to procure the best possible blessing for humanity.

Divine compassion is implied by the term **Agape** – meaning *'compassionate and self-giving God of love.'* An example of this name being used in scripture occurs in 1 John 4:8 which states *"He that does not love does not know God; for God is love* (Agape).*"* It demonstrates that God's love can be known and enjoyed by His people.

PS8.3 Bible Exposition

Two further Bible passages demonstrating the existence of this attribute are 2 Chronicles 2:11 and Romans 5:5.

2 Chronicles 2:11
"Then Hiram the king of Tyre answered in writing which He sent to Solomon, because the Lord has loved his people, he has made you king over them."

For once, what seems to be a rather flattering diplomatic note contains some truth. At the human level Hiram, a wealthy king of Tyre, wished to establish diplomatic relations with Solomon, the then newly appointed King of Israel. However, on the spiritual level the Holy Spirit was wishing to convey the message that divine love can increase our influence amongst open-minded people who may notice that we have something special. Here, one is reminded of the old saying that *'faith is not taught, it's caught'* and to some degree this is true. We *'catch'* our faith through it being manifested in the example of others. God also manifests His love by putting in place able governments. It is the Lord who establishes and overthrows worldly rulers. The Lord may also use the most unexpected of people to give help in times of need. Newly established upon the throne and wishing to build God's Temple, Solomon knew he needed trustworthy allies. Fortunately for him, the Lord caused Hiram, King of Tyre, to provide the needed support. When believers are seen to be truly loved by God then their witness becomes effective – outsiders want to have that same spiritual reality readily seen in those who know God. Believers always face the challenge of demonstrating that they live under the love rather than the wrath of God. Tragically, as a corporate body the Church in the Western World is visibly under God's wrath, yet many of those who call themselves believers are so blinded by various delusions that they still babble on about how much Jesus loves them. They are oblivious to their true state in the sight of God because they take the stance which says, *'No harm can befall us, we're the King's kids.'* Only a miracle will cause them to see reality.

Romans 5:5
"And hope does not make us ashamed because the love of God is shed abroad in our hearts by the Holy Spirit who is given to us."

Paul was exploring the nature of Christian salvation. He saw that divine love was conveyed to believers through the person of the Holy Spirit. Hence, divine love is not something attainable through human striving, but rather received in an attitude of humble faith. It's then possible for this love to bubble spontaneously from the believer's heart. Obviously, on a daily basis, this is not always the case – but even when we feel spiritually dry God's love is always there in the background, ready to restore our souls. Incidentally, the words *"the love of God"* refute the common mystical view that God is an impersonal *'it.'* When Paul wrote those words he was showing that God had the highest attribute of personality – which is love. Indeed, love does seem to play a significant role in uniting and directing all other personal attributes, including the ability to decide, think, feel and communicate. This implies that, where love is absent from our hearts, we are somehow incomplete in our personality. In the end, it's possible to realise that, not only is God the supreme embodiment of *'love'* but also of *'personality'* too.

When viewed alongside 1 John 4:8, these two passages show that God's love: -

1) Is conveyed to every believer by the Holy Spirit

2) Should be visibly shown in the lives of believers

3) Can be shown in the appointment of good rulers

PS8.4 Application

In response to God's benevolent compassion believers would be wise to: -

1) Accept that loving others is <u>not</u> an *'optional extra'* in the Christian life

2) Accept the responsibility and challenge of demonstrating that one is loved by God

3) Avoid behaving appallingly in the name of Jesus

At the close of this study it's reasonable to conclude that God is able to establish His love in the hearts of every believer

PS8.5 Conclusion

1) Divine *'love'* shows that God may deal with the sin of apostasy by displaying His love to those excluded by corrupt religious systems

2) At His death, Jesus demonstrated this attribute by showing a deep compassion for sinners

For further study please refer to the words *'compassion,' 'love'* or *'pity'* in any Bible Concordance or Dictionary

PS8.6 Epilogue

Lord
Show me your love
So that I can love others
In a way that redounds to
The glory of your son
The Lord Jesus Christ[88]

---

[88] This prayer was first made on Monday, 31st January 2000. It expresses the need to have an encounter with divine love in order to love others.

PS8.7 Questions

1) What obstacles may hinder us from loving others and how can such obstacles be overcome?

2) Why does God pour out His love in the heart of every believer? Describe the effect this love should have.

3) How can we remain receptive to divine love amidst the pressures and strains of daily living?

PS9: MERCY

(Known also as *'Forgiveness'*)

PS9.1 Prelude

The fact that we all need divine mercy is irrefutable – the problem lies in persuading others to accept it

PS9.2 Definition

This <u>potentially shared</u> attribute of God's *'mercy'* refers to His ability to forgive sins and to withhold punishment so that people are not given the penalty they deserve.

Divine forgiveness is implied by the name **Eloah Selichoth** – meaning *'God of forgiveness or kindness.'* An example of this name being used in scripture occurs in Nehemiah 9:17c which states *"but you are a God ready to pardon, gracious and merciful, slow to anger and of great kindness* (Eloah Selichoth) *and forsook them not."* It demonstrates that God can show many kindnesses to His people.

PS9.3 Bible Exposition

Two further Bible passages demonstrating the existence of this attribute are Daniel 2:18 and Ephesians 2:4.

Daniel 2:18
"That they would desire mercies of the God of Heaven concerning this secret that Daniel and his fellows should not perish with the rest of the wise men of Babylon."

The context of this verse is a time of great danger for Daniel and his friends. A despotic king is about to purge his court and this has ignited an atmosphere of fear. They are in very real danger for their lives – indeed their plight shows that there is nothing like a good dose of danger to arouse a fervent desire for the mercy of God. This in part explains the old saying; *'There are no atheists during in a storm at sea.'* Yet calling upon divine mercy and help in a time of peril is one thing, desiring it to change our lives and to bring us into a closer relationship with God is quite another. Usually, people only plead for divine mercy at a particular point in their lives (often with a view to being saved them from an imminent danger). However, for the rest of the time they are content to live their lives much as they wish. In the long term, the effect of such an attitude is eventual exclusion from God's mercy. People need to go beyond the point of praying *'God save us from danger'* and reach the stage where, with reasonable sincerity, they pray *'God save us from our sins.'* The only way to know divine mercy on a permanent basis is to surrender ourselves completely to God. (This is done by trusting that He sent His Son the Lord Jesus Christ die for our sins and to bring us into a relationship with Himself.) In the meantime, we need to pray for the grace to avoid a frivolous attitude toward divine forgiveness. It's there if we want it, but do we want it wholeheartedly or just at times when we feel afraid or in danger?

Ephesians 2:4
"But God, who is rich in mercy for His great love wherewith He loved us,"

With great enthusiasm, Paul is highlighting the blessing that results from believing in Jesus as Lord and Saviour. We can know the riches' of divine mercy but only on condition that we place our faith in Jesus as our redeemer from sin. In short, we receive divine mercy on God's terms – not our own. No one should expect this mercy if they are unwilling to submit to the Lordship of Jesus. The problem with many religious people is that they want divine mercy on their own terms; they see it as a reward for their *'good deeds.'* Yet mercy earned is not mercy at all. By nature, mercy is something freely given when we do not deserve it, (Luke 18:9-14). Hence, even in the lives of the Godless some degree of mercy may be apparent; they may be endowed with good health or a happy family life and or with some measure of career success. Christians should not be too surprised when the ungodly receive such blessings for the Lord is indeed rich in mercy. Neither should believers forget that divine mercy often operates at those times when they are most unaware of it. God's mercy is also shown through those things which do not happen to us as well as those that do. Failure can be a *'severe'* mercy in the sense that it may prevent us from going down a wrong avenue – it may even represent a forcible re-direction from a wrong to a right course of action.[89]

When viewed alongside Nehemiah 9:17c, these two passages show that: -

1) The mercy of God can restrain the anger of God

2) The mercy of God can be shown in unexpected ways

3) Divine mercy represents an application of divine love

PS9.4 Application

In response to God's *'forgiveness'* believers would be wise to: -

1) Appreciate the greatness of God's mercy already shown to them

2) Accept that God's mercy saves them from sins as well as from immediate physical danger

3) Avoid restricting divine mercy to a select group of people or to a narrow religious area of life *e.g.* church going and bible study

At the close of this study it's reasonable to conclude that God shows us mercy only because Jesus died to save us from our sins

PS9.5 Conclusion

1) Divine *'mercy'* shows that God may deal with the sin of apostasy by sparing apostates the full consequences of their faithlessness in order to give them a chance to repent

2) At His death, Jesus demonstrated this attribute by asking His Father to forgive those who were crucifying Him, (Luke 23:34)

---

[89] This observation was made during August 2006 when the writer was undergoing a painful yet emphatic re-direction which, by April 2007, had taken him into the area of self-publication. Circumstances had left him with no other alternative.

For further study please refer to the words *'forgiveness,' 'merciful'* and *'mercy'* in any Bible Concordance or Dictionary

PS9.6 Epilogue

Ah Lord, be merciful to your stricken people and teach them to value your forgiveness[90]

PS9.7 Questions

1) What is the difference between divine mercy and human permissiveness, (which allows for a lax, *'it doesn't matter'* attitude toward sin)?

2) Why may people want God only in times of danger and not at any other time? How can this attitude be changed?

3) How would you respond to the following attitude; which says *'God is merciful so I can do what I like?'*

PS10: PATIENCE

(Known also as *'Persevering Self-restraint'*)

PS10.1 Prelude

Be thankful for divine patience but do not presume upon it.

PS10.2 Definition

This <u>potentially shared</u> attribute of God's *'patience'* refers to His long-suffering slowness to anger and His patient persistence with people – even in the face of the most outrageous provocation.

Divine self-restraint is implied by the name **Elohim Nose** – meaning *'Forgiving God'* or *'Gods.'* An example of this name being used in scripture occurs in Psalm 99:8 which states *"You answered them* [the prayers of the Israelites] *O Lord, you were a God who forgave them* (Elohim Nose), *even though you took vengeance on their*

---

[90] This prayer was first made on Tuesday, 1st February 2000. It expresses the need for many in the Church to adopt a respectful attitude to divine forgiveness.

inventions [man-made idols]." It demonstrates that God can answer our prayers because He has forgiven our sins.

PS10.3 Bible Exposition

Two further Bible passages demonstrating the existence of this attribute are Nehemiah 9:17 and 1 Peter 3:20b.

Nehemiah 9:17
"*And* [our fathers] *refused to obey, neither were they mindful of your wonders that you did among them, but hardened their necks and in their rebellion appointed a Captain to return to their bondage. But you are a God ready to pardon, gracious and merciful, slow to anger and of great kindness and you did not forsake them.*"

These words form part of a prayer of repentance, recalling God's wonderful deeds in Israel's history and highlighting the corruption present in the human will. A sharp contrast is made between human stubbornness and divine patience. God's persevering self-restraint is shown in His: -
1) Desire to pardon
2) Abundance of grace and mercy
3) Slowness to anger
4) Extreme kindness
5) Loyalty
6) Self-restraint.

Evidently, signs and wonders were not a cure for unbelief. Indeed, true godly miracles sometimes serve only to further entrench people in their godless state. When left alone human volition will always choose things that displease God, simply because it's in deep bondage to sin. Freewill, (in the sense of being able to choose God-honouring courses of action) simply does not exist for the godless. Adams fall has left us all with an in-built programme to sin. However, this doesn't mean that we're unable to make sensible choices, but even here, the taint of sin prevents them from being pleasing to God. Real freewill can only exist after a prior work of the Holy Spirit. It is He who smashes the chains of sin and allows us to make choices that please God. Yet even where there is no overt wilfulness we may still provoke the Lord through crass insensitivity. It's a good thing that God is patient otherwise the human race would have been destroyed long ago.

1 Peter 3:20b
"The longsuffering of God waited in the days of Noah, whilst the ark was preparing, wherein a few, that is eight souls, were saved by water."

A reference is made here to Christ's descent into the abode of the dead during the period of time between His death and resurrection. The full reasons as to why He made such a descent need not be explored here, but what can be pointed out is that Noah's ark was meant to call people to repentance. Yet, in the final result, only eight were saved. There was a mass refusal to respond to the grace of God whilst it was available. This passage warns us not to presume upon divine patience which, if manifested, is an attribute demanding our response. God is patient, not in order for us to do what we like, but because He wants us to receive His salvation offered through His only begotten Son, the Lord Jesus Christ. In the end, divine patience has to run out otherwise it would lead to an unhealthy toleration of evil. The door of salvation does not always stay open. On a more practical note, God's patience should inspire us to deal patiently with those whom we would normally find difficult. When our patience runs out with a certain trying individual then we need to make a conscious decision to ask for more patience. Such a request does not preclude the need to confront such individuals, should the need arise – but it does ensure that any confrontation would be undertaken in the right attitude.

When viewed alongside Psalm 99:8, these two passages show that:

1) The patience of God restrains His anger

2) The Lords patience prevents Him from destroying the human race

3) The patience of God allows time for people to repent of their sins

PS10.4 Application

In response to God's *'persevering self-restraint'* believers would be wise to: -

1) Receive God's free offer of salvation whilst it remains available

2) Show sensitivity to how God feels about things

3) Request more patience when relating to particular individuals

At the close of this study it's reasonable to conclude that God is capable of restraining His anger in order to give people more time to repent

PS10.5 Conclusion

1) Divine *'patience'* shows that God deals with the sin of apostasy by taking a very long time to judge those who have turned against His will, (2 Peter 3:8-13)

2) At His death, Jesus demonstrated this attribute by not responding to the mockery He suffered when nailed to the cross, (Matthew 27:39-44)

For further study please refer to the words *'long-suffering'* or *'patience'* in any Bible Concordance or Dictionary

PS10.6 Epilogue

God of patience, please enable me to show more tolerance toward even the most foolish of your people[91]

PS10.7 Questions

1) In what ways do we presume upon the patience of God?

2) Why, in relation to humanity, does God's patience run out in the end?

3) How would you respond to those using divine patience as a justification for continuing in a life of sin?

---

[91] This prayer was first made on Wednesday, 9th February 2000. It expresses the need to pray for patience in human affairs.

PS11: PEACEFULNESS

(Known also as 'Total Harmony')

PS11.1 Prelude

Beware of those who promise peace on condition that you submit to their authority

PS11.2 Definition

This <u>potentially shared</u> attribute of God's *'peacefulness'* refers to His perfect lack of inner conflict, His settled stillness and calm, even in the face of outrageous antagonism and militant rebellion from sections of His Creation.

Divine harmony is implied by the name **Yahweh-Shalom** – meaning *'the Lord is peace or complete wholeness.'* An example of this name being used in scripture occurs in Judges 6:24 which states *"Then Gideon built an altar there unto the Lord and called it Yahweh-Shalom. Unto this day it is yet in* [the territory of] *Ophrah of the Abi-ezrites."* It demonstrates that God can create a sense of peace during times of worship.

PS11.3 Bible Exposition

Two further Bible passages demonstrating the existence of this attribute are Genesis 1:26a and John 14:27.

Genesis 1:26a
"And God said let us make Man in our image, after our likeness."

These words represent part of the Creation narrative in which the members of the Godhead are portrayed in mutual consultation. Absent is any form of conflict or disagreement. Indeed, how could there be conflict in a divine Being, characterised by the highest levels of perfection? In addition, this excerpt shows how humanity really is able to share in some of the attributes of God; peacefulness representing just one such attribute. Thanks to the agency of the Holy Spirit all Christians can (over a lifetime) grow in this steadfast quality. Thus in this life, we can to a very limited degree, possess some of God's attributes, because originally we were made to be like Him. Divine harmony also means that God is completely at ease within Himself, unsettled neither by inner conflict nor unfulfilled desire. It is this, peacefulness which characterises the relationship between God the Father, God the Son and God the Holy Spirit. The Trinity is *'one,'* partly because the three Persons who make up that body are at utter peace with one another. This enables them to share a common purpose in redeeming those who would place their faith in Jesus. It also allows each member of the Trinity to fill the other members. This means that where one Person of the Trinity is present the others are also. The Godhead cannot be divided.

John 14:27
"Peace I leave with you, my peace I give to you, not as the world gives, give I to you. Let not your hearts be troubled, neither let them be afraid."

The Lord Jesus Christ is making His farewell speech to His disciples. A horrible ending to His earthly ministry is drawing near, but incredibly the Lord is still at peace within Himself. Christ's peace differs from that of the world in that it is independent of circumstances, actually enduring in spite of them. Also, it is a spiritual peace bringing personal wholeness; it is not a peace imposed by force of arms or diplomatic manoeuvring. Above all, it is an eternal peace given directly by God Himself. With such peace, it is possible for believers in Christ to endure the most terrible of persecutions. Also, it is far more than having a *settled conscience* – hugely important though that is – it is a supernatural peace, one <u>not</u> *'worked up'* on human strength or as a result of some form of mass manipulation. It is a peace able to endure through great suffering. Of utmost importance is the responsibility to zealously guard this peace by refusing to give in to any serious form of sin. Nevertheless, it is possible for this peace to break into our lives when we are at the end of our natural human resources. Should this happen, just be thankful, for it is a sure sign that God is with us. Inner peace is one of the most precious gifts God can give to His children. Sometimes, in order to test and strengthen our faith He may withdraw it for a while, just as He did with Christ in the garden of Gethsemane. However, if we are faithful, He will always restore it.
When viewed alongside Judges 6:24, these two passages show that:

1) The peace of God gives a powerful unity of purpose

2) There is complete and utter peacefulness between each member of the indivisible Trinity

3) The peace of God leads to personal wholeness

PS11.4 Application

In response to God's *'total harmony'* believers would be wise to: -

1) Make a careful distinction between worldly peace and godly peace

2) Accept that there are no inner conflicts within God

3) Avoid fear and accept the responsibility of safeguarding God's inner peace by placing all cares into His hands

At the close of this study it's reasonable to conclude that God is a giver of that peace which still remains during times of adversity

PS11.5 Conclusion

1) Divine *'peacefulness'* shows that God may deal with the sin of apostasy by not allowing global rebellion to disturb His own sense of inner peace

2) At the point of His death Jesus demonstrated this attribute by peacefully commending His Spirit to His heavenly Father, (Luke 23:46)

For further study please refer to the words *'Peace'* or *'Quiet'* in any Bible Concordance or Dictionary

PS11.6 Epilogue

Praise you
Father, Son and Holy Spirit

Praise you
For the eternal peace existing between each of you

Praise you
For sending that peace to well up within my own heart[92]

---

[92] This prayer was first made on Wednesday, 9th February 2000. It expresses the joy which comes when God's peace is present in a believer's heart.

PS11.7 Questions

1) What are the main differences between a worldly peace and the true spiritual peace of God?

2) Why can the peace of God be such a blessing to believers during times of difficulty?

3) How would you respond to a distressed believer complaining of a lack of inner peace?

PS12: RIGHTEOUSNESS

(Known also as *'Correctness'*)

PS12.1 Prelude

The time to get right with God is now
The means to get right with Him
Is to believe in His Son
The Lord Jesus Christ

PS12.2 Definition

This <u>potentially shared</u> attribute of God's *'righteousness'* refers to His inherently perfect moral standards, where everything He thinks, says and does is utterly right and free from fault.[93]

Divine correctness is implied by the name **Yahweh-Tsidkenu** – meaning *'the Lord our righteousness.'* An example of this name being used in scripture occurs in Jeremiah 23:6 which states *"In his days Judah shall be saved and Israel shall dwell safely: and this is his name whereby he shall be called, THE LORD OUR RIGHTEOUSNESS* (Yahweh-Tsidkenu).*"* It demonstrates that God can freely give people <u>His</u> righteousness.

---

[93] According to Grudem (1994) p.203, the terms *'righteousness'* and *'justice'* belong to the same Hebrew and Greek word groups and can therefore be used interchangeably. However, in the English language a more precise differentiation has taken place and is the one used here.

PS12.3 Bible Exposition

Two further Bible passages demonstrating the existence of this attribute are Ezra 9:15 and Romans 1:17.

Ezra 9:15
"O Lord God of Israel you are righteous; for we remain yet escaped as it is this day. Behold, we are before you in our trespasses; for we cannot stand before you because of this."

After a prayer of sorrowful confession, Ezra acknowledges the righteousness of God, shown in both His mercy and His judgements. This passage demonstrates that none of us can stand before God on our own merits. From God's perspective, we have nothing to offer. We are simply rebellious sinners, deserving only eternal punishment. As Christians, we only enjoy a positive relationship with our Maker because of the righteousness His Son provided through His atoning death upon the cross. This was a sacrifice which satisfied the requirements of divine holiness and enabled God to give His Holy Spirit to motivate us to turn away from sin. It must be stated quite categorically that there is a right and a wrong way to acquire righteousness. The wrong way is to try and earn it through all sorts of man-made works, *e.g.* scourging one's own body with whips, saying a set number of prayers or giving a fixed amount of money to charity. Based upon human pride or fear, such striving achieves only the illusion rather than the substance of righteousness. As Jesus pointed out in Luke 18:10-14, people are no nearer to God as a result of it. The right way begins by realistically acknowledging that every attempt to earn righteousness through man-made efforts is as ineffective as launching a firework to get to the Moon. It just will not work. What needs to be done is to sorrowfully confess sin and ask God to give His righteousness through Jesus. We are to believe in Jesus as our only Lord and Saviour who died on our behalf so that our false, man-made righteousness could be exchanged for His righteousness, freely given to us. If such a belief proves difficult all we can do is to cry *"Lord, help me in my unbelief!"* (Mark 9:24c). Once a relationship with God as Father has been established then those good works that are genuinely pleasing to Him can begin to be done. In short, divine righteousness is there for us to receive as a loving, free gift, not as something to be earned. A failure to observe this vital distinction can lead to cruel bondage. It is the ultimate of follies to attempt to please God through our own efforts. They can never be good enough for Him.

Romans 1:17
"For therein is the righteousness of God revealed from faith to faith; as it is written, 'the just shall live by faith.'"

With great skill Paul is introducing one of the main themes of this whole epistle, carefully showing how the statement made in Habakkuk 2:4b still applies in his own day. However, when placed in a contemporary context, what was then meant by *'faith'* now differs markedly from its original meaning. In many Evangelical Churches (who often claim to follow Paul's teachings) faith is often confused with a nominal consent in which a person *'does God a favour'* by choosing to accept Jesus Christ as Saviour. Faith then becomes a sort of *'insurance policy,'* guaranteeing a place in Heaven! Such a superficial notion of faith is far removed from that which Paul prized most dearly. As a first century Jewish Rabbi, Paul saw faith as being a humble, cleaving to God and His promises made in scripture. The word *'faith'* could just as easily be transformed into *'faithfulness'* and still be in accord with the original Biblical meaning. If there is no ongoing faithfulness, then there is no faith and where there is no faith there is no relationship with God. This is because a healthy relationship depends upon an element of trust (faith) and if this element is lacking no such relationship exists. In its outreach, the Church must clarify its definition of faith – otherwise it's in danger of offering a false Gospel. Perhaps the failure to offer the true Gospel explains, in part, why the Western Church is in its present dire condition. God Himself is a creator of both faith and righteousness. Through the agency of the Holy Spirit, He created the faith that exists within our hearts and through His Son He created a way in which sinners may receive His righteousness. Over the course of our lives, He helps our faith to grow and to mature so that it can withstand times of adversity. Admittedly, we have our own part to play in the development of our faith, but this may only become effective following a definite commitment to Christ as Saviour and Lord. True faith in Christ is a free gift from God – not something which can be *'worked-up'* through psychological manipulation or group pressure. Instead, it results from a hidden work of the Holy Spirit within our hearts.

When viewed alongside Jeremiah 23:6 these two passages show that: -

1) The Lord alone gives us righteousness

2) The effect of divine righteousness is to humble human pride

3) Divine righteousness can be received only through a God-given faith

PS12.4 Application

In response to God's *'correctness'* believers would be wise to: -

1) Accept the fact that it is impossible to earn the righteousness of God

2) Praise God for freely giving His righteousness

3) Avoid any confusion concerning the meaning of words like *'faith'* or *'righteousness'* (the former is equated with trust and the latter with adherence to perfect moral standards)

At the close of this study it's reasonable to conclude that God exposes and utterly condemns our deep-rooted sinfulness. He does this in order to pinpoint our desperate need for His righteousness

PS12.5 Conclusion

1) Divine *'righteousness'* shows that God may deal with the sin of apostasy by determinedly punishing those who militantly oppose Him.

2) At His death, Jesus demonstrated this attribute by fulfilling every requirement of the Mosaic Law

For further study please refer to the words *'righteousness'* or *'righteous'* in any Bible Concordance or Dictionary

PS12.6 Epilogue

Lord, save me from my sins
For the sake of your son, Jesus
Bestow the righteousness that
Only you can give[94]

---

[94] This prayer was first made on Tuesday, 15th February 2000. It expresses the need to actively pray to receive God's righteousness.

PS12.7 Questions

1) Why do we try and gain righteousness by our own futile efforts?

2) Why is a correct understanding of words like *'faith'* and *'righteousness'* so necessary to healthy Christian growth?

3) How may we receive the righteousness of God and what may be its likely effect in our lives?

PS13: SIMPLICITY

(Known also as *'Straightforwardness'*)

PS13.1 Prelude

Divine truth is simple to understand but impossible to accept without divine grace

PS13.2 Definition

This <u>potentially shared</u> attribute of God's *'simplicity'* refers to His straightforward, perfectly balanced personality, free from conflicting desires so that He can be implicitly trusted and readily understood; even during the most difficult of times.

Divine Straightforwardness is implied by the name **Eli** – meaning *'my God.'* An example of this name being used in scripture occurs in Psalm 22:1 which states *"My God* (Eli), *my God, why have you forsaken me?"* It demonstrates that God can still be called upon even when we feel totally abandoned by Him.

PS13.3 Bible Exposition

Two further Bible passages demonstrating the existence of this attribute are Numbers 6:26 and Hebrews 13:20.

Numbers 6:26
"May...The Lord lift up His countenance upon you and give you His peace."

These words form part of a prayer of blessing and show that there is often a strong sense of peace whenever and wherever God chooses to reveal Himself. Present is that invigorating stillness which can sometimes be experienced in country Churches during sunny, summer afternoons. We are to pray that the Lord will lift up His countenance upon people and give them His peace. This means His *'Shalom'* peace which produces personal wholeness and integration. God uses such a peace to settle our minds and bring us to a better understanding of His will. Through His peace God reveals His simplicity. However this peace is something is a blessing reserved for the righteous; for the wicked there should be no peace, because if there was they would have no incentive to repent of their evil ways. Christians are never to ask God to give peace to those who have set themselves against His will, for as scripture warns *"there is no peace for the wicked,"* (Isaiah 48:22 & 57:21). Also, believers should take care to maintain a basic simplicity of heart and a straightforward goodness in their character as the presence of sin causes people to make things needlessly complicated, especially in the area of human relations. The challenge for the Christian is to be simple but also mature. The simplicity lying at the very heart of God means that any attempt by Satan to *'play one attribute off against another'* in order to rob God of His perfection is always doomed to failure. The attributes of divine Holiness and divine Love can never be opposed to one another although many in Western Christianity casually assume just such an opposition. United in simplicity each divine attribute can <u>never</u> be forced into some form of artificial conflict.[95] God's attributes have <u>always</u> co-existed as <u>complementary</u> aspects of His Divine nature. They can never be altered nor improved upon. Thus the simplicity of God is an important basis for the unity of God.

Hebrews 13:20
"Now the God of peace, that brought again from the dead our Lord Jesus Christ, that great shepherd of the sheep, through the blood of the everlasting covenant."

---

[95] The relationship between divine holiness and divine love is more fully explored in *'The Phantom Conflict.'*

These words represent the closing blessing of a wonderful epistle and reveal the simplicity, peace and power co-existing within the heart of God. These attributes worked flawlessly together in raising Jesus from the dead. They also meant that Christ Himself is the only true source of permanent peace, because he assumes the shepherd's role of protecting and looking after his flock. The presence of this role suggests that He can also communicate His will in a simple and straightforward manner that establishes a good rapport with His intended audience. This explains why scripture contains so many different literary forms. These forms are meant to communicate God's will to different audiences with a wide range of intellectual sophistication. In addition, it is important to accept that peace is conditional upon obedience to God's will as revealed in scripture. Happily, such obedience does not have to be perfect but it does mean that we must be serious about obeying those truths that we do understand and putting them into practice. As implied earlier, knowledge of divine simplicity is, to some extent, conditional upon obedience. Sin complicates matters but faithfulness to God gives scope for the Holy Spirit to remove any serious confusion afflicting our sinful minds. Sadly, whilst many are aware of the need for peace of mind and simplicity of character, this is often sought after in all the wrong places *e.g.* alcohol, drugs and Eastern Meditation – all of which tend to blank out the human mind and hinder rational thinking. People end up being *'simple'* in the wrong sense of the word. Where divine peace enhances our humanity, the false peace of Satan diminishes it by turning us into unthinking zombies. A similar point applies at the international level of peace between nations states. The example of King Solomon and Hiram of Tyre shows that treaties and trade agreements are all very well (and they can be a means of facilitating a true and Godly work) but they are not a substitute for the straightforward peacefulness and simplicity in relationships that only the Lord can bring, (1 Kings 5). At best they provide a glimpse into the nature of those qualities.[96] By all means look for peace and simplicity in living – but take care to look for it from *'the Prince of peace'* rather than *'the Prince of darkness'* who will offer many attractive, quack remedies. One has only to view the window display of a New Age shop to recognise that this is the case.

---

[96] Ultimately, Bible prophecy suggests that many nations will look for a World Dictator to provide peace. Should this happen, the human race will stand on the brink of a truly awful carnage.

When viewed alongside Psalm 22:1, these two passages show that:

1) The Lord's peace is a manifestation of His simplicity

2) There is no way in which one attribute can be in conflict with another

3) The Lord is full of peace and strength

PS13.4 Application

In response to God's '*straightforwardness*' believers would be wise to: -

1) Actively want others to know the peace of God

2) Accept the need for personal simplicity

3) Avoid looking for peace from the wrong sources

At the close of this study it's reasonable to conclude that God is a giver of stillness to those troubled in heart

PS13.5 Conclusion

1) Divine '*simplicity*' shows that God may deal with the sin of apostasy by allowing apostates to twist Biblical teaching in such ways as to thoroughly confuse themselves

2) At His death, Jesus demonstrated this attribute by displaying a simple faith in God after His cry of dereliction

For further study please refer to the words '*quietness*' or '*simple*' in any Bible Concordance or Dictionary

PS13.6 Epilogue

Thank you Lord for your simplicity, may it be a source of blessing for all whom you call me to pray for, Amen [97]

---

[97] This prayer was first made on Wednesday, 16th February 2000. It expresses thankfulness to God for His divine simplicity.

PS13.7 Questions

1) What is the relationship between the simplicity of God and the peace of God?

2) What is the difference between a Godly simplicity and an unhealthy, childish simple-mindedness? Why do believers often find it very hard to acquire a Godly simplicity?

3) What is the difference between a true Godly peace and the false peace offered by Satan through various forms of eastern meditation?

PS14: UPRIGHTNESS

(Known also as *'Infallible Truthfulness'*)

PS14.1 Prelude

Only those who have passed beyond death have an infallible perception of truth

PS14.2 Definition

This <u>potentially shared</u> attribute of God's *'uprightness'* refers to His absolute reliability, His trustworthy freedom from error and His realistic sense of perception, so that He is the one source of all correct moral standards. In scripture, *'truth'* is assumed to have a positive moral quality. It refers to far more than factual accuracy.

Divine truthfulness is implied by the name **Elohe Amen** – meaning *'God of truth.'* An example of this name being used in scripture occurs in Isaiah 65:16 which states *"That he who blesses himself in the earth shall bless himself in the God of truth* (Elohe Amen) *and He that swears in the earth shall swear by the God of truth; because the former troubles are forgotten and because they are hidden from my eyes."* It demonstrates that God can keep His promises to bless those who trust in Him.

PS14.3 Bible Exposition

Two further Bible passages demonstrating the existence of this attribute are Isaiah 45:19 and 2 John 1.

Isaiah 45:19
"*I have not spoken in secret in a dark place of the earth. I said not unto the seed of Jacob seek me in vain. I the Lord speak righteousness; I declare things that are right.*"

The Lord is drawing attention to the difference between His revelation and other so-called revelations delivered by pagan deities. In contrast to these pagan revelations (which were often delivered in caves for greater effect but really amounted to little more than crude fortune telling) the Lord's revelation comes true. Not one unconditional prediction He makes ever fails. Consequently, waiting and seeking to know God's will is not a waste of time. His Word can be trusted as a source of correct guidance. Evidence for this can be seen in the preservation of the Jewish people against all conceivable odds. Another witness is the way in which the Gospel has been propagated amongst all nations in spite of the many follies committed by the Gentile Church. God speaks correctly because He is truth. For Him to lie or to be mistaken is to go against the grain of His nature. He delivers truths in which we can trust. At this juncture it is worth emphasising that Isaiah 45:19 is not an untypical passage. Scripture, throughout both Testaments, makes such astounding claims about its own infallible authority that all of it must be accepted as true or it is the most carefully crafted lie in human history. What is not left open is the option of believing that, although some of it may represent God's Word, the rest of it is untrue. This stance begs the question over how the *'truthful'* sections can be clearly distinguished from the *'less truthful'* sections. The different teachings of scripture are all inter-connected through logic[98] and by frequent backward and forward *'mutual'* referencing between texts.[99] The Bible is an entire package in which either all of it is God's Word or none of it is. We cannot arbitrarily select favoured portions of it and discard the rest. If we do, the result is a loss of spiritual power, (Revelation 22:19).

---

[98] One example of a logical connection occurs between the attributes of holiness and wrath. Logically, the presence of unlimited holiness suggests that God would react to sin with unlimited wrath. Similarly, God's total presence (Omnipresence) suggests He knows everything that is going on (Omniscience). The existence of one attribute therefore suggests the existence of others. Implicit in divine holiness is divine wrath; whilst implicit in divine omnipresence is divine omniscience.

[99] For example, Psalm 22:1 references forward to Christ's words in Matthew 27:46, whilst these same words refer backward to Psalm 22:1.What is taking place between both passages is a system of mutual referencing.

2 John 1
"*The elder unto the well beloved Gaius, whom I love in the truth,*"

Truth and love go together. Where a truth is present an opportunity to love exists! Indeed, if truth without love degenerates into a bigoted fanaticism, then love without truth becomes a misguided sentiment, resulting in more harm than good. Both qualities (truth and love) need to be present if spiritual growth is to take place. Indeed, if truth is lost in the Church, love is often the next to follow. The apostle John perceived this very thing when he wrote this warm-hearted introduction to Gaius – who seems to have held a responsible position in the Church. John also realised that adherence to error undermines the capacity to love. To value good doctrine is not to go against love – rather, it is a key element in making love possible. The relationship between these two attributes is positive. Truth and love are partners, not foes and both are needed to build real unity amongst regenerate Christians. A knowledgeable belief in biblical truth is a necessary precondition for love. It also deters any inclination to woolly thinking for *'love of the truth'* encourages that clarity of mind which forms the basis of effective Christian living.

When viewed alongside Isaiah 65:16, these two passages show that:

1) Truthfulness is part of God's nature

2) The unconditional predictions of God are always fulfilled

3) Truth and love co-exist

PS14.4 Application

In response to God's *'infallible truthfulness'* believers would be wise to: -

1) Adopt a confident attitude toward scripture

2) Appreciate the difference between the divine revelation of scripture and oracles emanating from false religions

3) Avoid an indifferent attitude to truth

At the close of this study it's reasonable to conclude that God is a giver of reliable teachings, all of which help His people to grow in truth and love

PS14.5 Conclusion

1) Divine *'uprightness'* shows that God may deal with the sin of apostasy by treating individual apostates in exactly the way they deserve

2) At His death, Jesus demonstrated this attribute by speaking words characterised by both truth and love

For further study please refer to the words *'truth'* or *'uprightness'* in any Bible Concordance or Dictionary

PS14.6 Epilogue

Lord, show me more of your truth
Please provide a better understanding of your Word
So that I can grow in my love for you and
For even the most difficult of people[100]

PS14.7 Questions

1) Why should a revelation from a non-biblical source be rejected even when it is factually correct?

2) Why does conflict appear to persist between true doctrine and the need to grow in love? What effect is this misunderstanding likely to have upon the life of the Church?

3) How would you answer the argument that states *"It isn't doctrine but love that matters?"*

---

[100] This prayer was first made on Friday, 25th February 2000. It expresses the need to prayerfully employ truth as a means of growing in love.

Summary

Su1: Each of the above 14 potentially shared attributes may be summarised as follows: -

1) Divine generosity: God's bountiful open-handedness in giving abundantly to His people and withholding no good thing

2) Divine goodness: God's benevolent kindness, cordiality and caring friendship with His Creation

3) Divine grace: God's undeserved favour toward His Creation and to Humanity who, in their universal corruption, merit only the severest form of punishment

4) Divine holiness: God's moral purity and complete freedom from any trace of evil or sin; also His strongly felt repugnance toward all forms of corruption

5) Divine humility: God's willingness to put aside His majesty in order to become weak and vulnerable, restraining and humbling Himself to better identify Himself with his Creation

6) Divine justice: God's impartial fairness and unprejudiced decision-making in order to arrive at the right verdict whilst treating all people exactly as they deserve

7) Divine Law-Giving: God's perfectly authoritative standards in which address both the realm of nature and human affairs

8) Divine love: God's undeserved self-giving, boundless, patient, kind and compassionate pity for His Creation

9) Divine mercy: God's willingness to forgive sins and to withhold punishment so that people are not given the penalty they deserve

10) Divine patience: God's long-suffering slowness to anger and His patient persistence with people – even in the face of the most outrageous provocation

11) Divine peacefulness: God's lack of inner conflict, His settled stillness and calm even in the face of outrageous antagonism and militant rebellion from sections of His Creation

12) Divine righteousness: God's ability to display inherently perfect moral standards, where everything He thinks, says and does is utterly right and free from fault

13) Divine simplicity: God's ability to enjoy a straightforward, perfectly balanced personality, free from conflicting desires so that He can be implicitly trusted and readily understood; even during the most difficult of times

14) Divine uprightness: God's ability to show absolute reliability, trustworthy freedom from error and realistic sense of perception, so that He is the one source of all correct moral standards

<u>**Su2:**</u> In relation to the sin of apostasy: -

1) Divine generosity: shows that God may deal with it by delaying His judgements, so providing people with more time to repent,

2) Divine goodness: shows that God may deal with it by ensuring that the schemes perpetuated by wicked apostates, themselves become a means whereby the Gospel is further propagated

3) Divine grace: shows that God may deal with it by miraculously providing for true believers who are possibly being persecuted or are trapped in bad Church situations

4) Divine holiness: shows that God may deal with it by withdrawing His Holy Spirit from corrupt Churches, leaving them to be destroyed by human sin and the devils wiles

5) Divine humility: shows that God may deal with it by restraining His judgements in response to heartfelt prayers made by His servants

6) Divine justice: shows that God may deal with it by thwarting attempts made by apostates to usher in a better society

7) Divine Law-Giving: shows that God may deal with it by inflicting specific penalties for the breaking of specific commands

8) Divine love: shows that God may deal with it by displaying His love to those excluded by corrupt religious systems

9) Divine mercy: shows that God may deal with it by sparing apostates the full consequences of their faithlessness in order to give them a chance to repent

10) Divine patience: shows that God deals with it by taking a very long time to judge those who have turned against His will

11) Divine peacefulness: shows that God may deal with it by not allowing global rebellion to disturb His own sense of inner peace

12) Divine righteousness: shows that God may deal with it by determinedly punishing those who militantly oppose Him.

13) Divine simplicity: shows that God may deal with it by allowing apostates to twist Biblical teaching in such ways as to thoroughly confuse themselves

14) Divine uprightness: shows that God may deal with it by treating individual apostates in exactly the way they deserve

<u>Su3:</u> During His death, Jesus demonstrated: -

1) Divine generosity: by praying that God His Father would forgive those who had crucified Him

2) Divine goodness: by praying for sinners just before His death

3) Divine grace: by instructing His disciple John to take care of His mother, Mary

4) Divine holiness: by experiencing the complete abandonment of His Father's caring presence as He took the punishment for human sin during His crucifixion

5) Divine humility: by meekly allowing brutal Roman soldiers to nail Him to a cross (without any show of defiance)

6) Divine justice: by willingly taking the punishment we deserved for our sin

7) Divine Law-Giving: by being cursed for being hung on a cross

8) Divine love: by showing a deep compassion for sinners

9) Divine mercy: by asking His Father to forgive those who were crucifying Him

10) Divine patience: by not responding to the mockery He suffered when nailed to the cross

11) Divine peacefulness: by peacefully commending His Spirit to His heavenly Father

12) Divine righteousness: by fulfilling every requirement of the Mosaic Law

13) Divine simplicity: by displaying a simple faith in God after His cry of dereliction

14) Divine uprightness: by speaking words characterised by both truth and love

C4:
THE FIFTEEN BARELY SHARED ATTRIBUTES

BS1: ABSOLUTE BEING

(Known also as 'Independent self-existence')

BS1.1 Prelude

To deny the existence of God is like denying the existence of a large rock hurtling toward you at break-neck speed. The result of both denials is the same – death.

BS1.2 Definition

The barely shared attribute of *'absolute being'* refers to God's objective, free existence. It also means that He is the first cause of everything and could exist quite independently of His Creation.

Divine self-existence is implied by the name **YHWH** (pronounced *Yahweh*) – meaning *'absolute, self-existent Lord God'* and/or *'Sovereign Master.'* An example of this name being used in scripture occurs in Exodus 15:2 which states; *"The Lord* (Yahweh) *is my strength and song and He is become my salvation. He is my God and I will prepare Him a habitation; my father's God and I will exalt Him."* It demonstrates that God can be exalted through prayer and worship.

BS1.3 Bible Exposition

Two Bible passages witnessing to this attribute are Exodus 3:14 and John 8:58.

Exodus 3:14
"And God said to Moses [at the beginning of his ministry] *I AM that I AM (Ehyeh Aser Ehyeh) and He said you shall say to the children of Israel I AM has sent me to you."*

In this revelation, given personally to Moses, the Lord reveals Himself as a *'being'* of supreme authority. He clearly displays two fundamental divine attributes which constitute personality. These are the ability to be completely self-aware and to communicate that self-awareness. These words confirm that Moses was not dealing with some impersonal *'cosmic force'* but rather a very real, speaking and acting personality. Moreover, as a divine person the Lord has the right to send people to discharge a task which may lie beyond their natural human strength that they may learn to humbly depend upon His power. For Moses, the task was to deliver the Israelites from Egypt. For others the task may be to live with a difficult relative; whatever this task care must be taken to discharge it faithfully. However, in everything we do need to ensure that we are under divine authority otherwise it will useless. The impossible task will remain impossible. Faith in God is inextricably connected to a sense of total dependence. Yet, in that dependence, is the freedom to become the people we could have been if no sin had intruded into our lives. True freedom doesn't lie *'in doing our own thing,'* but is a result of doing God's thing, in God's way and at God's time. This was a lesson which Moses learnt only after much hardship and failure. His life was to demonstrate that knowing God's will is one thing, knowing when and how to apply it is quite another.

John 8:58
"Jesus said to them [His religious enemies] *I say to you, before Abraham was I AM."*

These words represent the climax of a highly provocative sermon that drove the enemies of Jesus into an absolute rage. His words resound even today and still have the power to cause great offence. Here, he went far beyond the claim to being the perfect image of God, but actually claimed to be God. The use of *I AM* meant that Jesus was the same supreme, eternal Lord who spoke to Moses through the burning bush. All of the attributes of Deity belonged to Him in fullest measure. He left no room for manoeuvre; people either had to worship the Messiah as being absolute God or to reject Him as a wild blasphemer, worthy of death under Jewish Law. Jesus went out of His way to leave His audience with no other choice. Accepting Him as a good teacher or great prophet wasn't good enough. Unlike other faiths, Christianity does not require its adherents to submit to a body of law or custom – instead it demands complete submission to an active and living divine being that once walked the streets of Nazareth as a humble Jewish carpenter. In the end the audience whom spoke to made their decision – we in our present time and place need to make ours.

When viewed alongside Exodus 15:2, these two passages show that: -

1) The name YHWH confirms that God enjoys an absolute and unchanging existence as a divine being. Lending weight to this is the fact that *Ehyeh Aser Ehyeh* could also be translated to mean, *"I will be what I will be."* God is the only ultimate reality.

2) The Lord did not come into being due to any external agency. He has always enjoyed a totally independent, ceaseless existence. Consequently, He will always remain above human understanding, even after He has revealed His will to us through scripture.

3) God is not a projection of the human mind. Man cannot *create* God through his own thoughts, hopes and fears. Rather, it is more a matter of Man being viewed as a special Creation brought into existence by the one true God.[101]

BS1.4 Application

In response to God's *'self-existence'* believers would be wise to: -

1) Accept that God exists independently. Faith in Him should lead to the same reverence that Moses displayed when He approached the burning bush. Christians need to be wholly confident that the Lord of Heaven and Earth will communicate His will to those able to listen.

2) Realise that belief in such an *'Absolute Being'* differentiates them from most other people.

3) See the Lord as a person deserving of the greatest respect. There must be a radical turnaround where God *'Almighty'* replaces God *'almatey.'* Any superficial over-familiarity should be abandoned in favour of a greater degree of genuine respect.

At the close of this study it's reasonable to conclude that God is a communicating personality who makes astonishing claims both to challenge people and to reveal something of His nature.

BS1.5 Conclusion

1) *'Absolute Being'* shows that God may deal with the sin of apostasy by beginning a new work outside of those Churches that refuse to obey His will

---

[101] Admittedly, humanity has shown an incessant capacity to create an almost infinite multitude of false god's. However, their supposed existence should never be taken as proof that a one true God does not exist.

2) At His death, Jesus demonstrated this attribute by showing that God was free to solve the problem of sin in His own way, without any external constraint

For further study please refer to the words *'I am,' 'Lord'* or *'Yahweh'* in any Bible Concordance or Dictionary

BS1.6 Epilogue

Oh Lord, let us forever realise that you do exist – particularly at those times when we are most tempted to forget you, Amen[102]

BS1.7 Questions

1) What does the title *'I am'* reveal about God?

2) Why did Jesus use the title *'I am,'* knowing it would cause outrage amongst an audience who'd be left in no doubt that He was claiming to be God?

3) How would you answer the statements, *'Surely conflicting views about the Almighty prove that the whole concept of God is really only a product of the human imagination?'*

BS2: ADEQUACY

(Known also as *'Competence'*)

BS2.1 Prelude

God is not a beggar, depending upon human schemes in order to accomplish His purposes. Those who treat Him as such end up as beggars themselves.

BS2.2 Definition

The barely shared attribute of *'adequacy'* refers to God's sovereign control and provision of circumstances to meet every type of human need and to bring happiness to all of His Creation.

---

[102] This prayer was first made on Thursday, 11 November 1999. It expresses the need to depend upon God to show us that He still exists.

Divine competence is implied by the name **Yahweh El Gemolah** – meaning *the Lord our recompense* or *reward*. An example of this name being used in scripture occurs in Jeremiah 51:56 which states, *"Because the spoiler is come upon her, even to Babylon and her mighty men are taken, every one of their bows is broken; for the Lord God of recompense* (Yhwh El Gemolah) *shall surely requite."* The ability to give rewards is one manifestation of divine adequacy. It demonstrates that God can reward people on the basis of their deeds.

BS2.3 Bible Exposition

Two Bible passages demonstrating the existence of this attribute are Exodus 3:12 and Mark 10:30.

Exodus 3:12

"And He [the Lord] *said* [to a fearful Moses], *Certainly I will be with you and this shall be a token to you when you have brought forth the people out of Egypt. You shall serve God upon this mountain."*

The Lord is reassuring a troubled Moses at Mount Sinai by informing him that his call to perform humanly impossible tasks will be vindicated by circumstances. For us too, God's presence is a sufficient aid in our tasks (even when they produce little result). However, whilst calling us to such tasks the Lord will challenge our faith by presenting us with a choice – either to believe or not to believe in His ability to provide for our needs. This is a choice which every disciple of Christ is called upon to make. A relationship with God has the potential to liberate us from unrighteous fearfulness and to give comforting or guiding scriptural words a certain sense of sharp reality. Divine adequacy may be experienced in hard times as well as good. The Lord we follow is not a *'fair weather'* God – with us only during the easier parts of our lives.[103] On the contrary! He remains with us throughout our lives; this fact alone should serve as a source of great comfort. We may safely assume that when God promises to be with us, He means what He says. Should we be engaged in any genuine ministry, we can trust the Lord to provide the resources needed to sustain it.

---

[103] Saying such comforting words may seem easy but they were originally drafted only two days after receiving a demand for nearly £400 from a certain government department on Saturday, 13th November 1999. Thankfully, the writer later discovered that this had been due to an administrative error.

Mark 10:30
"But he [the faithful disciple] *shall receive a hundredfold now in this time, houses* [and] *brethren, lands with persecutions and in the world to come eternal life."*

Jesus is making a comforting promise to his disciples who appear to have been troubled by some teaching he had just given on marriage and divorce. As a true prophet, He was looking ahead to the corporate life that would be enjoyed by the Church. In contrast, disciples like Peter had certain personal insecurities to overcome before they could fully enter into a new sphere of ministry. They were still at an early stage of spiritual development. Behind these words is the assumption that the Church should be a mutually supportive community. Where this sense of community is absent the Church is dead and only a charade of Christianity is being played out. Nevertheless, even amidst today's apostasy, faithful believers can still hope for something tangible in this world as well as the next. They may not be endowed with an abundance of material prosperity but they will receive enough to meet their needs and to be a blessing to others. Belief in divine adequacy can therefore inspire a firm sense of hope. It's a belief that can save us from a thousand worries.

When viewed alongside Jeremiah 51:56, these two passages show that: -

1) God will often comfort His servants during moments of perplexity

2) Divine adequacy is sufficient to secure eternal life and to provide a variety of blessings in this world

3) God can fully satisfy every type of need in those who know Him through Jesus Christ

BS2.4 Application

In response to God's *'competence'* believers would be wise to: -

1) Allow the clear-cut promises of scripture to be a source of comfort

2) Accept that the faithful Christian life will involve persecution as well as blessing

3) Be aware that the Lord can sustain His people throughout difficult circumstances

At the close of this study it's reasonable to conclude that God is a liberator who frees His people from fear whilst simultaneously providing for their various needs

BS2.5 Conclusion

1) Divine *'adequacy'* shows that God may deal with the sin of apostasy by only blessing those who remain faithful to His scriptures

2) At His death, Jesus demonstrated this attribute by showing that He had adequately provided a perfect sacrifice to fully appease divine wrath against human sin

For further study please refer to the words, *'provide'* or *'provision'* in any Bible Concordance or Dictionary

BS2.6 Epilogue

Heavenly Father, teach us always to trust in your adequacy – especially during times of great affliction.[104]

BS2.7 Questions

1) In what ways may God provide for our needs?

2) How may we meet the needs of others so that they can be helped to grow in their relationship with God?

3) Why is it often hard to believe in the adequacy of God? Suggest ways in which such a belief may be made easier?

4) How might scripture and (common sense) be used to refute the false view that Mark 10:30 represents an automatic guarantee of *'health and wealth'* for every Christian? List the damaging consequences which may arise from adopting such a false view.

---

[104] This prayer was first made on Monday, 15 November 1999. It expresses the need to go on trusting that God will provide for our needs, even in difficult times

BS3: GLORY

(Known also as 'Renown')

BS3.1 Prelude

Where true doctrine is ignored, worship fails.

BS3.2 Definition

This <u>barely shared</u> attribute of *'glory'* refers to God's radiant splendour and justifiable fame which causes Him to be a fit object of human adoration.

Divine renown is implied by the name **El Hakkabhodh** – meaning *'God of glory or God the glorious.'* An example of this name being used in scripture occurs in Psalm 29:3 which states; *"The voice of the Lord is upon the waters; the God of glory* (El Hakkabhodh) *thunders, the Lord is upon many waters."* It demonstrates that God can reveal His glory through the forces of nature.

BS3.3 Bible Exposition

Two further Bible passages demonstrating the existence of this attribute are Habakkuk 2:14 and Romans 11:36.

Habakkuk 2:14
"For the Earth shall be filled with the knowledge of the glory of the Lord as the waters cover the sea."

Filled with a buoyant spiritual joy, the prophet Habakkuk foresees a time when knowing God in a very deep and profound way will become commonplace. The word *'glory'* in this verse is *'Kabod,'* meaning weight or heaviness; thus implying that God has an infinite *'weight'* of honour. His existence will be evident to all. In this present age of global spiritual rebellion this promise has yet to be fulfilled (possibly during a future age after Christ's return). Despite two thousand years of Gospel preaching, those who genuinely know the Lord God of Israel constitute only a tiny proportion of the human race. The Gospel has been heard but the nations as a whole have not favourably responded. On a more optimistic note, disaster and doom is not the end of the story – the teachings of God <u>will</u> prevail across the whole of the world. However, realism about human nature confirms that only Christ Himself can bring about such a triumph. For now Christians are to witness to the light they have. Also, to avoid disillusionment, they should forget such silly notions as *'winning the world for Jesus'* or *'taking the nations for Christ.'* These imply the ludicrous possibility that the Church can seize the levers of power in order to establish a New World Order which will glorify God and prepare the way for Christ's return. Overlooked is the teaching of Acts 1:7-8 which shows that the Churches role is to be a faithful witness to Christ in the nations and not a political power over them. The Church always betrays its mission when it's more interested in establishing a new social order rather than in declaring the gospel of Jesus Christ. Such an interest shows that it has departed from its original purpose.[105]

Romans 11:36
"For in Him and through Him and to Him are all things, to whom be [the] *glory forever, Amen."*

These words are a spontaneous outburst of praise, coming at the end of a long theological analysis concerning the doctrine of God's purposes for Israel. For the Apostle Paul, doctrine was not in the least bit boring but was, for him, an occasion to worship. He saw God as the beginning and end of all things. Paul's words testify exuberantly to the fact that God's glory will neither fade nor diminish in its strength but will last forever. This is in marked contrast to the glory of men whose pomp and show lasts only *'for a season.'* Let wholesome Bible doctrine act as fuel to our worship. Allow theology to turn into doxology, (an enthusiastic praise of the Creator God). Remember, if we do not take our doctrine seriously then something will be amiss with our worship. A major role that doctrine performs is to show us the One whom we should adore; a good theology should act as a springboard to worship. Without a basis in sound theology, worship often becomes nothing more than a trite demonstration of human emotionalism. It really is necessary to grasp just what a great privilege it is to be involved in worship. God could, of course, glorify Himself without any help from us. From eternity, endless expressions of devotion have mutually taken place between the three members of the Trinity. However, God has allowed us to worship Him, not only because He's entitled to it but because it does us good. At the very least, true worship can have a therapeutic value in calming our

---

[105] In Sociology, this problem of an organisation's departure from its original mission is known as *'goal displacement.'* It's absolutely rife throughout every branch of Christianity.

anxieties and focussing our attention upon an infinitely positive Being. We can acquire the spiritual intelligence that enables us to discern God's will and see our place in the wider scheme of things. At its very best, worship can replace an unhealthy self-absorption with a healthy God-absorption that can invigorate us and help us to live out our daily lives in a way that benefits others. True worship produces much good, both spiritually and psychologically and we should never neglect it.

When viewed alongside Psalm 29:3, these two passages show that:

1) The work of God in Creation should inspire true worship

2) The glory of the Lord will be known in all of the nations in a very deep and striking way

3) The study of difficult theological issues can excite an emotional praise and worship of God

BS3.4 Application

In response to God's *'renown'* believers would be wise to: -

1) Admire His handiwork in Creation

2) Admit that good theology is the basis of all good worship

3) Accept that it's right and personally beneficial to glorify God, even though He is perfectly capable of glorifying Himself

At the close of this study it's reasonable to conclude that God glorifies Himself by enlightening the world through gospel preaching and through the maintenance of spectacular natural processes

BS3.5 Conclusion

1) Divine *'glory'* shows that God may deal with the sin of apostasy by using the schemes perpetuated by wicked apostates to rebound to His, (rather than their own) glory, (Acts 2:22-24)

2) At His death, Jesus demonstrated this attribute by showing that even the worst form of suffering could gain long-term renown

For further study please refer to the words *'glory,'* *'glorify'* or *'glorification'* in any Bible Concordance or Dictionary

BS3.6 Epilogue

All glory be to you, O Lord
For your many awesome attributes show that
You are worthy of endless praise
Both in the Heavens and upon the Earth[106]

BS3.7 Questions

1) How can we glorify God in our praise and worship? To what extent should worship be a corporate as well as an individual activity?

2) Why, if God is so capable of glorifying Himself does He still require the praises of human beings?

3) How would you answer the charge that God must be *'power mad'* to require so much praise?

BS4: IMMANENCE

(Known also as *'Total Involvement'*)

BS4.1 Prelude

God is involved in the world, but the problem is that most people do not see it

BS4.2 Definition

This <u>barely shared</u> attribute of *'immanence'* refers to God's active and caring presence, His committed involvement and total participation in everything He has made.

Divine involvement is implied by the name **Elohe Mesrachoq** – meaning *'God who is not distant or afar off.'* An example of this name being used in scripture occurs in Jeremiah 23:23 which states *"Am I*

---

[106] This prayer was first made on Friday, 25 November 1999. It expresses how God's wonderful nature causes Him to merit unlimited praise from both angels and human beings alike.

a God at hand says the Lord and not a God afar off (Elohe Meshrachoq)?" It demonstrates that God can be close to his faithful servants even during periods of national disaster.

BS4.3 Bible Exposition

Two further Bible passages demonstrating the existence of this attribute are Psalm 3:5 and Acts 17:25.

Psalm 3:5
"I lay down and slept; I awoke for the Lord sustained me."

This passage shows that God is present even when the believer is completely oblivious to the fact. Most commonly He sustains us through natural processes but on occasion He will be with us in a miraculous way. His total involvement with His own Creation offers both hope and challenge. Hope in the sense that God identifies with our problems by becoming involved and helping us through them and challenge because God is also alongside us even when we sin. This never means that He's there to condone the sin but to record it and hold us accountable for it unless we accept His means of forgiveness by believing on the Lord Jesus Christ. For many, this means that God is *'too close for comfort.'* There is no escaping His acute observation of our lives. Men may run from the Lord but they may as well be running from the air they breathe. To escape His presence is impossible. However, others complain that God is absent, little realising that His absence is only apparent and not real. Even in times when He seems most absent, God is there to sustain us in our afflictions. Our trust in God is developed in the midst of our trials, for through them we begin to learn what faith really means. Should God feel absent all that has happened is that either adversity has dimmed one's sense of the divine presence or that the Lord Himself has temporarily withdrawn some of His comforts in order to increase our faith and to make us less dependent upon spiritual experiences.[107]

Acts 17:25
"Neither is God worshipped with men's hands as though He needed anything; He gives to all, life and breath and all things."

---

[107] Such a withdrawal is <u>not</u> to be confused with the retributive desertion reserved for those having hardened their hearts against the truth. God will <u>never</u> permanently forsake those who are faithful to Him.

The folly of idolatry lies in its assumption that God depends upon man-made artefacts to enable Him to contact the human race. In reality scripture clearly teaches that He simply has no need for such things because His Spirit pervades the whole of His Creation. Thus, it is we who depend upon Him for absolutely everything. Without the breath of His Holy Spirit all that now exists would instantaneously cease to be. In these words, Paul is robustly challenging the polytheistic idolatry he has just seen on Mars Hill in Athens. The problem with many forms of idolatry is that they do not expect God to do anything particularly constructive. He is either viewed as a bloodthirsty demon (as in the old Aztec religions) or as some abstract nonentity (portrayed in much of Liberal Theology.) Once such views are entertained the worship of God becomes impossible. To worship God aright we must view him a right. More technically; <u>a correct doxology</u> (worship) must be preceded by <u>a correct theology</u>. Minds must be cleared of error before the heart can even begin to worship properly.[108] This was the approach followed by the Apostle Paul in this verse.

When viewed alongside Jeremiah 23:23, these two passages show that: -

1) The Lord expressly denies that He is remote or far removed from the afflictions of His people

2) The Lord uses natural processes, *i.e.* sleep, to refresh His saints

3) The presence of God means that He does not have to be worshipped through the use of man-made objects, (idols)

BS4.4 Application

In response to God's *'total involvement'* believers would be wise to: -

1) Take comfort from the Lords presence during difficult times

2) Know when to rest and to enjoy the blessings of sleep

3) Avoid viewing God as a dependent Being, needing the input of man-made strategies and techniques as the means whereby He can exert even a modicum of influence

---

[108] This approach is followed in *'The Leeds Liturgy'* (see p.306 for further details).

At the close of this study it's reasonable to conclude that God is a Being whose Holy Spirit pervades even the smallest parts of His Creation

BS4.5 Conclusion

1) Divine *'immanence'* shows that God may deal with the sin of apostasy by recording all of the sins committed by apostates so that they can be condemned on the Day of Judgement

2) At His death, Jesus demonstrated this attribute by caring for others whilst He Himself suffered terribly

For further study please refer to the words *'near'* or *'sustain'* in any Bible Concordance or Dictionary

BS4.6 Epilogue

Praise you for your total involvement in my life Lord, but help me realise that you are present in the bad times as well as the good, in Jesus Christ's name, Amen[109]

BS4.7 Questions

1) What natural and supernatural agencies may God use to sustain His people? Why does He seem to prefer the use of natural agencies?

2) Why might people find it difficult to believe that God is near them?

3) How might a recently bereaved person best be comforted (especially when feeling that God has deserted them)?

---

[109] This prayer was first made on Tuesday, 18th January 2000. It expresses the need to thank God for His active participation in our lives.

BS5: IMMUTABILITY

(Known also as *'Stability'*)

BS5.1 Prelude

God may not change, but that does not mean He is boring

BS5.2 Definition

This <u>barely shared</u> attribute of God's *'immutability'* refers to His perpetual sameness, unalterable consistency and lack of any change in any of His attributes or His aims.

Divine stability is implied by the name **El Abikha** – meaning *'the God of your father or fathers.'* An example of this name being used in scripture occurs in Genesis 49:25 which states *"Even by the God of your father* (El Abikha) *who shall help you and by the Almighty who shall bless you with blessings of the deep that lie under, blessings of the breasts and of the womb."* It demonstrates that God always wants to give His people an unlimited number of blessings.

BS5.3 Bible Exposition

Two further Bible passages demonstrating the existence of this attribute are Jeremiah 10:10 and Hebrews 13:8.

Jeremiah 10:10
"*But the Lord is the true God. He is the living God and an everlasting King. At His wrath the Earth shall tremble and the nations shall not be able to abide His indignation.*"

Here, an unfavourable comparison is being made between divine stability and the fickleness of the people of Judah. In this one statement, many divine attributes are crammed together as an interlacing network of interconnected characteristics. God is at once alive, everlasting, sovereign and wrathful whether we like it or not. He is well able to deal with nations as well as individuals. The essential immutability of His nature is shown by His possession of an everlasting and totally complete set of attributes. Hence, every divine characteristic outlined in this study will last forever and will never change in its essential nature. It is also worth adding that, as God never changes, His divinely revealed truths never change either. The

Almighty does not remould the truth in order to please the whims of human beings. He is unchanging in all of His innate character. This means that today He reacts to hardened sin in exactly the same way He did in the time of Jeremiah – with wrath, judgement and forcible removal.

Hebrews 13:8
"Jesus Christ, the same yesterday and today and forever."

In terms of personality, Jesus is wholly consistent – despite His glorified status He is exactly the same Jesus as revealed in the Gospels. A contrast can be drawn between the eternal stability of Christ and the dangerous instability of many false teachers who tailor their doctrines to the prevailing climate of opinion. The real Jesus is no *'mystical'* or *'Cosmic Christ,'* differing from the One revealed in scripture. If, in John 14:6, Jesus claimed to be the only way to God it is then absurd to expect Him to later assert, through some mystical vision, that all religions represent a possible way to God. Should this happen some form of deception is in the making. One is either being deceived by a figment of one's own imagination or by a demon masquerading as Jesus. Divine immutability ensures that the real Jesus would never contradict Himself. One final point is that Christians can possess the strength to withstand opposition because they are linked to a divine Being who is completely stable in all of His ways. He will never let us down. God is present during the darkest times of our lives.

When viewed alongside Genesis 49:25, these two passages show that: -

1) God displays the same characteristics in His dealings with the human race

2) The Lord is unalterably consistent in how He deals with humanity

3) Jesus is not going to change His ways, even when people change their ideas about Him

BS5.4 Application

In response to God's *'stability,'* believers would be wise to: -

1) Recall God's consistency in His dealings with past believers

2) Accept that anger against sin is an innate part of His character

3) Avoid constructing false ideas concerning the identity of Jesus

At the close of this study it's reasonable to conclude that God is totally consistent in the ways in which He deals with people

BS5.5 Conclusion

1) Divine *'immutability'* shows that God may deal with the sin of apostasy by completely refusing to compromise any of His moral standards

2) At His death, Jesus demonstrated this attribute by being punished *'once and for all'* for sin – thus fulfilling God's plan of salvation and abolishing (making obsolete) the temporary sacrificial rules laid down by God in the Mosaic Law

For further study please refer to the words *change* or *changes not* in any Bible Concordance or Dictionary

BS5.6 Epilogue

Father, you are unchanging in all of your ways; yet what a marvel it is that sometimes you give us the ability to change your mind through our feeble prayers, Amen[110]

BS5.7 Questions

1) What comfort may the truth of divine stability bring to our lives?

2) Why, if God is perfectly consistent, does He sometimes allow the prayers of His people to change His mind over a particular issue?

3) How would you comfort someone who feels that the Lord has failed to keep a particular promise of scripture?

---

[110] This prayer was first made on Wednesday, 19th January 2000. It expresses the amazing fact that, within certain limitations, God is consistent about permitting us to change His mind, through prayer.

BS6: INFINITY

(Known also as *'Unlimited Extent'*)

BS6.1 Prelude

From God's perspective the Universe is like a tiny grain of sand trapped beneath His little toe nail

BS6.2 Definition

This <u>barely shared</u> attribute of God's *'infinity'* refers to His unlimited extent and boundless freedom from any external constraint – so there is never any end to Him.

Divine unlimited extent is implied by the name **Adonai** – meaning *'Almighty ruler and judge.'* An example of this name being used in scripture occurs in Exodus 4:1 which states *"And Moses answered and said, but behold they will not believe me, nor hearken to my voice; for they will say that the Lord* (Adonai) *has not appeared to you."* It demonstrates that God's power can be difficult to believe in.

BS6.3 Bible Exposition

Two further Bible passages demonstrating the existence of this attribute are Psalm 147:5 and Luke 1:35.

Psalm 147:5
"Great is our Lord and of great power. His understanding is infinite."

Represented here is a psalm in praise of God's power and creativity. There is no limit to His understanding; He can grasp every cause and every effect for His Spirit is present everywhere in Creation and even beyond it. He understands our every thought and mood change and monitors our deepest instincts. He understands us better than we do ourselves. Yet even though God's Spirit reaches to the deepest core of our being, we cannot fully grasp God. Indeed, without the revelation of scripture we would know next to nothing about Him. At best, we would dimly apprehend that He is a distant *'creator'* or *'mysterious power'* who pervades the universe in order to hold it together. Such a deity would resemble the *'impersonal first cause'* of Greek Philosophy or the vague *'cosmic consciousness'* of Eastern Thought. However, He would not resemble a loving, heavenly Father graciously sending His only Son to die in order to redeem people from their sins. Such things can only be known through divine revelation. Nevertheless, contemplating the endless infinity of God can only make our heads bow in humble adoration. By making us feel so little, it restrains any inclination to commit the sin of pride. Strongly reinforced is the impression that we totally depend upon Him for everything – even life itself.

Luke 1:35
"And the Angel answered and said to her [Mary] *The Holy Ghost shall come upon you and the power of the Highest shall overshadow you. Therefore also the Holy Thing which shall be born of you shall be called the Son of God."*

An Angel of the Lord is comforting Mary by stressing that God can do everything as long as it remains in accord with His Holy Love. No external constraints hinder His power and no *'being'* in Creation can thwart His will. Nevertheless, it is necessary to observe a distinction between a <u>forced</u> limitation and a <u>moral</u> limitation to God's power. God has the total power to do everything, but morally He won't because He is faithful and true to His Word. He will <u>never</u> act in a way that is either evil, absurd or against scriptural teaching. Internal constraints do exist. Moreover, the Lord has the humility to restrain His power in order to accommodate the limitations of humanity. To deny this possibility is to go against scripture. He became a limited human being in Jesus Christ – totally in accordance with His love. God the Father truly did begat a Son to display the extent of His love and care for us. Should He have been too remote and uncaring to have done such a thing how could we have ever loved such a God? We would only ever be able to relate to Him (or it) as a grovelling slave. Such a subservient relationship would be dominated by fear, lacking in any real love and mercy. By definition, an infinite being has an unlimited ability to partake of the finite. The presence of this attribute confirmed that <u>God could become a man and did so in the person of Jesus Christ.</u> He did this in order to save us from our sins and to grant eternal life to all who would believe in Him. Through Jesus we are adopted children who can relate to God as *'Father.'* There is no need for a slave mentality in the Christian faith for *'the truth has set us free'* from the tyranny of sin, society and Satan, (John 8:32). We need to praise God for the infinite mercy He has shown us. May we never take it for granted!

When viewed alongside Exodus 4:1, these two passages show that:

1) The human race is often loath to acknowledge the unlimited sovereignty of God

2) The Lords limitless understanding makes it possible for Him to know everything concerning limited human beings

3) Divine infinity made it possible for God to become a human being in the form of Jesus

BS6.4 Application

In response to God's *'unlimited'* extent believers would be wise to: -

1) Accept that, even at its best, the human mind can only ever possess a very limited insight into the nature of God

2) Accept that God is an infinite Person with personal attributes

3) Avoid the error which denies that God can ever become a human being[111]

At the close of this study it's reasonable to conclude that God is a Being who is simultaneously unlimited and personal; out of sheer love He became the man Jesus Christ in order to redeem sinners

BS6.5 Conclusion

1) Divine *'infinity'* shows that God may deal with the sin of apostasy by ensuring that it produces everlasting loss for those who knowingly and persistently commit it

2) At His death, Jesus demonstrated this attribute by producing an unlimited number of everlasting blessings – only a few of which can be enjoyed in this life

For further study please refer to the words *'impossible'* or *'possible'* in any Bible Concordance or Dictionary

---

[111] To accept it is to adopt a very restricted view of both His love and power

BS6.6 Epilogue

God of infinite love and perfect creativity
Help me to follow a course of life that is
Both fruitful and faithful to Your Holy Will[112]
Please answer this prayer
For the glory of your great name, Amen

BS6.7 Questions

1) What may hinder people from believing that God became a human being to rescue people from their sin?

2) Why did God take on human limitations when His awesome power alone would have been enough to destroy evil? How would you respond to the objection that *God has no sons?*

3) How would you answer an eastern mystic who believes God to be an infinite *'it,'* a *'Being beyond personality?'*

BS7: OMNIPOTENCE

(Known also as *'Total Power'*)

BS7.1 Prelude

When God displays His total power, the effect is to enhance and not to diminish our humanity.

BS7.2 Definition

This <u>barely shared</u> attribute of God's *'omnipotence'* refers to His ability to control every single part of Creation, even when it is in militant rebellion against His will. When manifested to a great degree the effect of this total power is to enable people to be more and not less human in character and outlook.

Divine total power is implied by the name **El Shaddai** – meaning *God Almighty* or *God all-powerful*. An example of this name being used in scripture occurs in Genesis 17:1 which states *"And when*

---

[112] This prayer was first made on Thursday, 20th January 2000. It expresses the need to draw upon God's unlimited resources in order to live out the Christian life.

Abram was ninety years old and nine, the Lord appeared to Abram and said unto him, I am the Almighty God (El Shaddai); *walk before me and be perfect."* It demonstrates that God can both control the universe and speak to individual people at the same time.

BS7.3 Bible Exposition

Two further Bible passages demonstrating the existence of this attribute are Jeremiah 32:17 and Matthew 26:53.

Jeremiah 32:17

"Ah! Lord God; behold, you have made the Heaven and the Earth by your great power and stretched out arm and there is nothing too hard for you."

Here, a terrific statement of faith was being made during a time of tremendous suffering. Creation itself was being viewed as an expression of His divine power and nothing was impossible to God, so long as it did not militate against His Holy Love. For us today, an acknowledgement of this same divine power enables us to face life's difficulties and irritations. However, there is a distinction between God giving the power to escape from suffering or granting the power to endure it. It is a strange paradox that in the Christian life, times of wonderful divine deliverance are interspersed with long periods of personal trial where prayers for relief seem to go unanswered. Hence, when faced with a difficult situation it is always best to discern whether God's intention is to bestow the power to get us out of it or to get us through it. Divine power is available for the believer to use, but only ever in accordance with the will of God. We cannot *'call down'* this power (or invoke it through *'wordy'* prayer) to fulfil our own vain ambitions. Sadly, many individual Christians and Churches suffer a crisis of powerlessness because they want divine power to bless what is essentially a selfish agenda *i.e.* to gain a high social status. They never grasp that God's power is only given to those who are actively following His will and not their own. Nor do they accept that in His sovereignty, the Lord gives His power to who He wishes and in what measure He sees fit. It is never, never to be viewed like a tap we can turn on and off at will. That is human presumption and pride and at its worst. What can be relied upon is that enough divine power will be given to complete any task that God has set for us. If God has called us to a work that, humanly speaking, is impossible then He will provide the strength to accomplish it. This was something the great heroes of faith found to be true and it's also something we can calmly place our confidence in too, (Hebrews 11:4f).

Matthew 26:53
"*You think that I cannot pray to my Father and He shall presently give me more than twelve legions of angels?*"

On the eve of His death, Christ was at the crisis point of His ministry. He realised that His Heavenly Father's power was available to Him but also that it was not His will to deliver Him from the cross. His call was to endure (and not to escape from) the unimaginable suffering. Unlike sinful human beings – who have been alienated from God by their iniquities – Jesus had, by virtue of His holy life, a perfect right to ask for angelic assistance. In the face of severe temptation, Jesus chose not to exercise that right in order to accomplish His mission of redeeming humanity from sin. He restrained His power when the occasion called for it and by so doing, Christ identified with the powerlessness of the human condition. His actions also demonstrated that God might call us down a certain direction that we would not naturally have chosen. Taking such a direction can be very hard, especially where suffering is involved. At such points, it's perhaps essential to remember that divine power is only available for God's work and for those who have submitted to His will. When a step of obedience has been taken the believer begins to be quietly aware of God's unlimited power in aiding and sustaining them amidst difficult circumstances. He finds that dependence upon God brings true freedom. Only He can end the crisis of powerlessness besetting many Churches today. The acceptance of this point is a vital precondition for revival.

When viewed alongside Genesis 17:1, these two passages show that: -

1) The power of God made Creation possible

2) The power of God means He can do anything so long as it remains in accordance with His Holy Love

3) God may restrain His power in order to identify with human powerlessness

BS7.4 Application

In response to God's '*total power*' believers would be wise to: -

1) Acknowledge the difference between the power to deliver and the power to endure

2) Accept that the power of God should be used only in accordance with the will of God

3) Be willing to go down the direction God has for them, even though it may be against their original preferences

At the close of this study it's reasonable to conclude that God uses His power to help people to accomplish His purposes

BS7.5 Conclusion

1) Divine '*omnipotence*' shows that God may deal with the sin of apostasy by suddenly removing apostates from positions of prominence

2) At His death, Jesus demonstrated this attribute in His endurance when God's wrath being poured out upon Him

For further study please refer to the words '*Almighty*' or '*Power*' in any Bible Concordance or Dictionary

BS7.6 Epilogue

Dear Lord, please teach me to use your power wisely and in such a way that accomplishes your ends rather than my own, Amen[113]

BS7.7 Questions

1) What reasons underlie the powerlessness of many local Churches? How can we avoid a similar powerlessness in our own lives?

2) Why did Jesus choose not to exercise His right to *call down* angels to save Him from the cross?

---

[113] This prayer was first made on Thursday, 3rd February 2000. It expresses the need to know how to use divine power wisely and in a way that follows God's own agenda and not our own.

3) How would you respond to the argument that, because God can do what He likes, His power can make people fall over, laugh hysterically or make animal noises?

BS8: OMNIPRESENCE

(Known also as *'Total Presence'*)

BS8.1 Prelude

Do not grumble if the Almighty presents himself in a way that you do not expect, but remember that He will always present Himself in ways that accord with scripture

BS8.2 Definition

This barely shared attribute of God's *'omnipresence'* refers to His ability to be everywhere at once, both inside and outside of the known Universe. His presence can be manifested in a wide variety of ways.

Divine total presence is implied by the name **El Roi** – meaning *'God all-seeing'* or *'the 'God who sees.'* An example of this name being used in scripture occurs in Genesis 16:13 which states *"And she [Sarah] called the name of the Lord that spoke to her, 'You God see me.' for she said, 'Have I also looked after Him who sees me* (El Roi).'" It demonstrates that God can watch over His people even in the most stressful of situations,

BS8.3 Bible Exposition

Two further Bible passages demonstrating the existence of this attribute are Psalm 139:8 and Matthew 6:32b.

Psalm 139:8
"If I ascend to Heaven you are there and if I make my place in Hell you are there."

This Psalm implies that any reflection upon God's presence is meant to provoke worship. Indeed, the more we know God, the more we can praise Him in an effective manner. Nowhere is excluded from His divine presence. In Hell He is present in His wrath and in Heaven He is present in His love. There is no escaping from the Lord; to run away from Him is fruitless; to hide from His Spirit is futile. People who try to flee from the Lord are like deep-sea fish trying to escape the ocean. For evildoers, the reality of God's presence is a source of nagging condemnation – no wonder they try to block it from their minds. However, for faithful followers of Jesus Christ, God's presence is a source of great joy, as indeed it was for the Psalmist. No matter how frightful the circumstances, the Lord is present in some capacity or other. Also, inner holiness is kindled by the realisation that there is no such thing as a *'secret '*sin. Secret from other people possibly – but not from God; should someone decide to sin in a furtive and secretive manner God would still be present in His capacity as judge. When atheist philosophers proclaim *'the death of God'* all they are really proclaiming is their own inability to discern God's presence. It is not so much *'the death of God'* but rather the spiritual deadness of the philosopher in question which is on show. In reality, the loudly trumpeted claim that *'God is dead'* is nothing more than a proclamation of spiritual deadness on the part of those making that claim. Far from proving God's non-existence all they have done is to prove that they have no wish for Him to exist. However, God most certainly does exist and is very much alive and present but most profess no wish to be aware of the fact. Yet, for the believer the presence of God can be a source of tremendous joy. It really is something to get excited about. We may truly thank the Lord for His presence and as believers in Christ, we can enjoy it forever.

Matthew 6:32b
"For your heavenly Father knows that you have need of these [material] *things."*

Christ has been instructing His disciples on prayer, being especially keen to draw their attention to the sharp contrast between the prayers believers should make and those common only to pagans. Those that are pagan in origin may well be motivated by faith but this faith is not in the God of Israel. Rather, it is a faith reliant upon an idol or other god-like figure – no credence being given to God the Father, who delights in making generous provision for His people. Jesus is also making it clear that His Father already knows a believer's needs in advance because He is deeply present in every area of life. Not one of our needs fails to be noticed. This fact should give a steady sense of confidence in prayer, based upon a wise faith and not fear. It is possible to join with the writer's wife in praying, *"May fear always be far from me."* When answered, this prayer produces a wonderful sense of liberation. In addition, our petitions to

God must be based upon real needs and not selfish wants. The former He has promised <u>always</u> to meet; the latter He has not. In prayer we should be free to rejoice in the goodness of God's presence but when making our requests we should not confuse our needs with our wants. The Lord knows our needs far better than we do.

When viewed alongside Genesis 16:13, these two passages show that: -

1) The Lord is present everywhere

2) The Lord manifests His presence in different ways

3) The total presence of the Lord means that He can meet our every need

BS8.4 Application

In response to God's *'total presence'* believers would be wise to: -

1) Realise the futility of trying to run away from God

2) Actively rejoice in, and draw comfort from God's complete presence

3) When praying, avoid confusing needs with wants

At the close of this study it's reasonable to conclude that when His children pray to Him, God is present to meet every legitimate need.

BS8.5 Conclusion

1) Divine *'omnipresence'* shows that God may deal with the sin of apostasy by exposing to public view the greed and secret schemes of apostates

2) At His death, Jesus demonstrated this attribute by showing that God can play many different roles whilst manifesting His presence

For further study please refer to the words *'present'* or *'presence'* in any Bible Concordance or Dictionary

BS8.6 Epilogue

Abba Father, may your Holy Spirit preserve an awareness of your wonderful presence in my own heart and in the hearts of all those who believe in you and in your Son, Jesus, Amen[114]

BS8.7 Questions

1) Why may God's total presence be either a source of joy or a source of fear?

2) How would you answer the charge that due to the presence of evil and suffering God simply can't be present in the world?

3) How would you comfort a disheartened believer who feels that God is utterly absent?

BS9: OMNISCIENCE

(Known also as *'Total Knowledge'*)

BS9.1 Prelude

God knows each one of our sins long before they have been committed

BS9.2 Definition

This barely shared attribute of God's *'omniscience'* refers to His ability to be aware of, to recall and to retain detailed information about everything, in and beyond all of His Creation.

Divine total knowledge is implied by the name **El Deoth** – meaning *'God of knowledge.'* An example of this name being used in scripture occurs in 1 Samuel 2:3 which states *"Talk no more so exceeding proudly; let not arrogance come out of your mouth – for the Lord is a God of knowledge* (El Deoth) *and by Him actions are weighed."* It demonstrates that God can weigh our actions on the basis of what He knows about us.

---

[114] This prayer was first made on Thursday, 3rd February 2000. It expresses the Holy Spirit's role in causing people to be aware of the presence of God.

BS9.3 Bible Exposition

Two further Bible passages demonstrating the existence of this attribute are Isaiah 40:14 and Acts 15:18.

Isaiah 40:14
"With whom has He taken counsel and who instructed Him and taught Him the path of judgement and taught Him knowledge and showed Him the way of understanding?"

The prophet Isaiah had been drawing attention to the grandeur of God by emphasising that God cannot be taught by any man because He has no need to learn anything. God's knowledge is utterly complete and thoroughly detailed; this means that nothing can be hidden from Him. Superficially, these statements of fact imply that prayer is a waste of time – why pray to the Lord if He already knows our needs in advance? The answer to this objection is quite simple; the purpose of prayer is <u>not</u> to tell the Lord things that He knows already – but is a wonderfully effective means of deepening a loving relationship with Him. The fact that God is already familiar with our needs <u>should act as an incentive to pray.</u> His ability to know all of our needs implies that He already knows the best manner in which to meet them. In His perfect knowledge, the Lord may meet our needs in ways we could not possibly have anticipated. His total knowledge can give us the faith to pray. However, His glad-hearted willingness to meet our needs does not mean He will answer prayers geared to meeting our selfish wants – even when we mistake these wants for legitimate needs. Sometimes when He does grant us the selfish want we had prayed for, it is only with a view to teaching us that the object or person we longed for wasn't good for us. Unless care is taken to retain a submissive attitude toward the Lord we may find, to our cost, that human selfishness can pollute the inner-sanctum of the prayer life. Returning to a more positive note, it is possible to find that prayer can act as a form of therapy in which we pour out our troubles to the Lord whilst giving space to the Holy Spirit to do a work of healing in our hearts. Prayer has value precisely because God <u>is</u> omniscient. Through it we both listen and talk to our Maker – giving Him scope to minister His love.

Acts 15:18
"Known to God are all of His works from the beginning of the world."

These words were penned in response to a controversy over whether new Gentile believers in the Messiah should submit to circumcision. James is arguing from the scriptures that they should not. On public display is the supreme confidence that God knows what He is doing in all of His works – be they Creation, Redemption or Judgement. He is the heavenly overseer, carefully supervising each particular area. Moreover, the Lord knows what specific or general *'works'* He wants to perform through us; nothing is a mystery to Him. In His knowledge He may call us to do mighty works in full public view; or alternatively, to accomplish tasks which remain hidden from human gaze. Nevertheless, both are of equal value in the Lord's sight. No good work is to be despised just because it's unspectacular or fails to gain widespread recognition. One temptation into which we easily fall is that of believing we know better than God. We may think that we have a better way to promote *'revival,'* to preach the Gospel or to increase the influence of Christianity in society. However, to adopt this stance always results in long-term failure and many Churches throughout England have *'self-destructed'* through this proud way of thinking. The presence of futile gimmicks like *'The Decade of Evangelism'* (during the early 1990s) served only to confirm that most remaining Churches have learnt nothing. They've failed to appreciate that God is the author of all *'good works.'* Consequently, Christians need to discern the will of God and then to actively follow His leading. As I Corinthians 3:11-15 warns, our works on judgement day will be *'tested with fire'* in order to see whether they were God-inspired and durable in their benefits. If not, we may have to endure the anguish of realizing that they were a complete waste of time and that we have forfeited certain heavenly awards.

When viewed alongside 1 Samuel 2:3 these two passages show that: -

1) God's total knowledge means that He is familiar with our every need

2) The Lord knows us better than we know ourselves

3) The Lord exercises detailed supervision over all of His works

BS9.4 Application

In response to God's *'total knowledge'* believers would be wise to: -

1) Adopt an attitude of humility in prayer

2) Accept that no one has the right to tell God what to do

3) Avoid trying to deceive God

At the close of this study it's reasonable to conclude that God is a skilful teacher who imparts true knowledge to the hearts and minds of believers

BS9.5 Conclusion

1) Divine *'omniscience'* shows that God may deal with the sin of apostasy by recording every sin an apostate commits so theirs will be an utterly fair verdict on the Day of Judgement

2) At His death, Jesus demonstrated this attribute by fulfilling the many detailed Bible prophecies foretelling this event

For further study please refer to the words *'known,'* *'knowing'* or *'knowledge'* in any Bible Concordance or Dictionary

BS9.6 Epilogue

All knowing God, teach me to humility concerning the knowledge I possess and cause me to accept that you know far better than I do how best to run my affairs[115]

BS9.7 Questions

1) What effect should divine omniscience have in our lives?

2) Why is it easy to think that we know better than God? What are the most likely results of this attitude?

3) How can we grow in both spiritual knowledge and humility?

---

[115] This prayer was first made on Monday, 7th February 2000. It expresses the need to acquire humility alongside knowledge.

4) In what way would you respond to someone who has allowed his/her doctrinal knowledge to become a source of overbearing arrogance?

BS10: OMNIWISDOM

(Known also as *'Total Shrewdness'*)

BS10.1 Prelude

Few people are more tiresome than those who use faith as an excuse for stupidity rather than as a basis to acquire wisdom

BS10.2 Definition

This <u>barely shared</u> attribute of God's *'wisdom'* refers to His ability to devise perfect plans and to fulfil them in the best possible way.

Divine shrewdness is implied by the name **Theodidkatos** – meaning *'God taught'* or *'God teaching.'* An example of this name being used in scripture occurs in 1 Thessalonians 4:9 which states *"But as touching brotherly love you need not that I write to you; for you yourselves are taught of God* (Theodidkatos) *to love one another."* It demonstrates that God can teach us to love.

BS10.3 Bible Exposition

Two further Bible passages demonstrating the existence of this attribute are Job 9:4 and James 3:17.

Job 9:4
"He [God] *is wise in heart and mighty in strength. Who has hardened himself against Him and prospered?"*

Here, Job was testifying to divine wisdom amidst terrible personal suffering. He went out of his way to show that to deliberately harden one's heart against God is to commit a sin of total folly. Job clung to the belief that a person's relationship with God (or lack of it) can influence their circumstances. He was realistically aware that the Lord was the fount of all true wisdom. Any hardening of the human heart against God may happen suddenly (often after traumatic circumstances) or in slow, incremental stages because of habitual sin. The latter may begin with a progressive indifference toward the things of God, (often expressed in feeble excuse-making rather than outright antagonism). A sense of spiritual perception may then be lost and replaced by a *'couldn't care less'* attitude toward the truth. An undiscerning zeal for a particular error may begin to take centre stage. Finally, as the human heart becomes ever more hardened a cold deadness toward important Biblical teaching develops. This often heralds *'the point of no return'* – where resistance to God has become so entrenched that any ability to comprehend Him has long since dissipated. When challenged, people in this state will often wonder what all the fuss is about or may well adopt an attitude of glib flippancy or sulky petulance. What they will <u>not</u> do is to exhibit any genuine willingness to repent. Perhaps more people will have found themselves in Hell through apathy than through any other single sin. An attitude of slothful indifference to the things of God is something in which no Christian can afford to indulge.

James 3:17
"But the wisdom that is from above is first pure, then peaceable, gentle and easy to be entreated – full of mercy and good fruits, without partiality and without hypocrisy."

James, the writer of these words was expounding the practical side of Christianity, characterised by: -
1) Purity
2) Peacefulness
3) Gentleness
4) A willingness to be available to help those in need
5) Mercy
6) The bearing of a wide range of good spiritual fruits
7) Impartiality
8) Honesty
9) Compassion
10) A non-hypocritical stance

Wisdom acts as the basis for the above ten qualities. Especially encouraging is the fact that it is available on request. When facing a perplexing decision one can ask for wisdom and it is granted without reservation or qualification. Through an infusion of wisdom we are enabled to make those right choices which honour God. It is amazing how a clear way ahead can be seen in an area previously characterised by total confusion. God is there to help us with our choices but we must have the faith to ask Him for His wisdom, (James 1:5-8). All this is in opposition to man-made *'worldly wisdom,'* which seeks to gain truth by relying solely upon human reasoning or intuition alone, with little or no regard for God's Word. Too often the results of such wisdom are <u>the very opposite of those listed above.</u> Human wisdom cut loose from the teaching of scripture becomes foolishness (Romans 1:22). Moreover, this type of wisdom can be open to satanic influence, the devil using it to construct elaborate systems of thought (*i.e.* Liberal Theology) which serve only to further obscure or denigrate the Gospel.

When viewed alongside 1 Thessalonians 4:9, these two passages show that: -

1) True wisdom helps the believer to grow in love

2) Divine wisdom may still be acknowledged during times of suffering

3) The wisdom of God has many positive characteristics and these distinguish it from *'the wisdom of the world'*

BS10.4 Application

In response to God's *'shrewdness'* believers would be wise to: -

1) Allow God to teach us wisdom through His Word

2) Avoid any incremental hardening against God

3) Ask for divine wisdom when faced with complex choices or difficult decisions

At the close of this study it's reasonable to conclude that God is a giver of wisdom to perplexed believers

BS10.5 Conclusion

1) Divine *'wisdom'* shows that God may deal with the sin of apostasy by giving loyal followers the wisdom needed to deal with particular apostate situations

2) At His death, Jesus showed this attribute by demonstrating that God had devised the wisest way to deal with human sin – one that neither destroyed humankind nor compromised His divine attributes

For further study please refer to the words *'wise'* or *'wisdom'* in any Bible Concordance or Dictionary

BS10.6 Epilogue

"May the Lord grant me the wisdom that this world cannot give; in particular I ask for the wisdom to know the best way ahead in a certain course of action."[116]

BS10.7 Questions

1) How can a *'hardening of heart'* against God be avoided?

2) Why is God willing to give wisdom to those who ask for it?

3) How would you pray for wisdom when faced with a difficult decision?

BS11: PERFECTION

(Known also as *'Faultlessness'*)
BS11.1 Prelude

Finding fault with God is one of the biggest time-wasting activities known to the human race – yet we all do it!

BS11.2 Definition

This barely shared attribute of God's *'perfection'* refers to His wholeness, completeness and total freedom from every fault. No positive quality is absent from Him and no negative quality is present in Him.

Divine faultlessness is implied by the name **Theos** – meaning *'God to be worshipped.'* An example of this name being used in scripture occurs in Romans 12:2 which states *"And be not conformed to this world: but be transformed by the renewing of your mind, that you may prove what is that good and acceptable and perfect will of God (Theos)."* It demonstrates that God can give us those personal qualities needed to resist negative cultural influences.

---

[116] This prayer was first made on Tuesday, 8th February 2000. It expresses the need to keep any prayers for wisdom both short and simple.

BS11.3 Bible Exposition

Two further Bible passages demonstrating the existence of this attribute are 2 Samuel 22:31 and Matthew 5:48.

2 Samuel 22:31
"As for God, His way is perfect; the word of the Lord is tried. He is a shield to all those that trust in Him."

In this sung Psalm of thanksgiving, David joyfully acknowledges the perfection of God's work and His Word. David's acceptance of divine perfection had enabled him to display a courageous faith, shown through many gallant deeds. It is easy to imagine his exultation as he recalls the Lord's provision and protection over the course of a turbulent life. The imagery used here may have formed the basis of Paul's words in Ephesians 6:16. Of particular interest is the assumption that God's Word can be tried and tested during difficult times. There are means to verify its truthfulness – it does not have to be blindly accepted. Near the end of his life, David acknowledged that the path in which God had led him was the best way even though it had not always been easy – nor necessarily David's first desire. When looking for a fresh direction in life, we can (as long as we consult humbly with God) be confidant that it is the way that is best for us. Moreover, it shall be a way wherein the Lord will be glorified for it will bear much fruit.

Matthew 5:48
"Be perfect, even as your Father who is in Heaven is perfect."

Jesus is throwing out an apparently impossible challenge to His still immature disciples. So what was He trying to do? The answer becomes clearer when one realises that the Greek word for perfect is *'Telos'* which actually means *'maturity'* or *'completeness.'* Aspiration and growth towards maturity should be our objective in this life. Full perfection will come only in the afterlife – there will never come a time in this life where we can say *'full perfection has been gained, we have arrived.'* Those who adopt such a stance quickly demonstrate their imperfection by displaying a certain shortness of temper when it is challenged. Yet there is a definite wisdom in the challenge Jesus made. He was urging His followers to aim for the very best; only then would they realise their full potential in God. He was thus lessening the risk of them settling for that indifferent mediocrity which is such a disfiguring feature of modern Church life today. Aiming for perfection (maturity, completeness) does not mean we shall attain it, but it does mean that we will have gained a whole lot more than would otherwise have been the case. In one sense, the Christian life can be compared to sitting for an exam; aim for 100% and you will obtain 80%, but aim for only 80% and you may achieve only 50%. Always in Christ, there is a responsibility to aspire toward the very best. Let us accept this challenge and then we will grow in faith. Our constant goal must be to attain complete personal and spiritual maturity. On this matter, we must be very persistent.

When viewed alongside Romans12:2, these two passages show that: -

1) The perfection of God lends legitimacy to worship

2) The perfection of God is reflected in both in His work and Word

3) The perfection of God stimulates personal holiness

BS11.4 Application

In response to God's *'faultlessness'* believers would be wise to: -

1) Remain confident in any given struggle

2) Have confidence in the Word of God

3) Aim for complete maturity in the Faith

At the close of this study it's reasonable to conclude that God is a Being who is completely without fault.

BS11.5 Conclusion

1) Divine *'perfection'* shows that God may deal with the sin of apostasy by devising the perfect means to expose apostates for who they really are

2) At His death, Jesus demonstrated this attribute by offering a totally perfect sacrifice for sin which permanently abolished the need for any other sacrifices to appease God's wrath

For further study please refer to the words *'fault'* or *'perfect'* in any Bible Concordance or Dictionary

BS11.6 Epilogue

Faultless God, please grant me the strength to appreciate your perfection even though at present I've been laid low by illness[117]

BS11.7 Questions

1) What is the evidence for divine perfection in either the works or Word of God?

2) Why is it necessary to aim for perfection even though it will not be attained in this life?

3) How would you use scripture to refute someone who (on the basis of Matthew 5:48) believes they actually have attained a state of *'sinless perfection?'*

BS12: SELF-SUFFICIENCY

(Known also as *'Total independence'*)

BS12.1 Prelude

The first step to apostasy often takes place when people think God is in need of their services

BS12.2 Definition

This <u>barely shared</u> attribute of God's *'self-sufficiency'* refers to His ability to freely exist without the aid of His Creation. It also refers to His ability to implement His plans even in the face of severe opposition from both angelic and human beings.

Divine total independence is implied by the name **El elyon** – meaning *'God most high.'* An example of this name being used in scripture occurs in Psalm 78:56 which states *"Yet they* [the Israelites] *tempted the Highest God* (El elyon) *and kept not to His testimonies."*

---

[117] This prayer was first made on Thursday, 11th February 2000, whilst the writer was suffering from a flu virus. It expresses the need to remain appreciative of God, even during times of illness.

It demonstrates that God can retain His dignity in the face of the fiercest human provocation.

BS12.3 Bible Exposition

Two further Bible passages demonstrating the existence of this attribute are Psalm 2:4 and Philippians 1:6.

Psalm 2:4
"He that sits in the heavens shall laugh; the Lord shall hold them in derision."

Here, the Lord's reaction to a major rebellion by the Earth's rulers is being recorded. It is one of derisory scorn because the Lord sees there is something rather pathetic about the strutting pretences of men. In the end, evildoers tend to destroy themselves. Admittedly, in this world they may seem to *'get away with it'* but after death there comes a most terrible judgement. God sees the end result of human rebellion even if we don't. What this passage does achieve is the ruling out of any idea that God is somehow beholden to the human race – He isn't! Rather, we are beholden to Him for everything! God would still be God even if, in a global referendum, 100% of people decided that He didn't exist or that Lucifer should be made God in His place. The Lord God of Israel does not depend upon human approval to carry out His plans. There is nothing we can do to strip Him of His Deity. In particular, the modern Church must stop patronising God by inferring that He is some sort of cosmic *'wimp,'* desperately needing our assistance to evangelise the world. Much of the Church today seems convinced that the Almighty needs the help of a *'Marketing Consultant'* or *'Public Relations Expert'* to ensure that His name receives the right publicity. Psalm 2:4 gives God's reaction to this kind of nonsense. To patronise Him is to insult Him.

Philippians 1:6
"Being confident of this very thing; that He, who has begun a good work in you, will perform it until the day of Christ."

These words form part of a eulogy for the Philippians who have stood loyally by Paul and the Gospel. In a note of resounding confidence, Paul states that it is God who begins, continues and finishes the work He has planned to carry out in the lives of His servants. The apostle grasped that the call to be a co-worker with God is a tremendous privilege which derives solely from divine grace. His own sufferings had taught him that we are not left to discharge this role on our own paltry strength. The fact that a large number of Christians are floundering in lives and ministries which produce nothing constructive probably indicates that they are *'doing their own thing'* rather than God's. Permanent ineffectuality is a sign that something is wrong. Unless there are mitigating medical circumstances, those who are continually ineffective have neither known nor been obedient to God's calling upon their lives. Following the Lord can pose frustrating difficulties, but in the midst of these, divine grace is sufficient to endure them and to finish the task at hand. Consequently, it is possible to enjoy the confidence that God is at work in us and will encourage us through any crisis or prolonged trial. The good Lord tirelessly works to mould our lives in a way that is pleasing to Him. Hence, in Christianity, it is possible to enjoy a legitimate sense of destiny and be *'purpose-driven'* in the proper biblical sense. Sometimes, the Lord may allow others to complete a work we were unable to do through no fault of our own. A case in point was the way the Lord used King Solomon to build the Temple – a work that his father King David had started. Wisdom would suggest that we should worry less about whether we can complete the task God has for us. We may not complete it, but God will do so in His own way and time, using whomever He wills to do so.

When viewed alongside Psalm 78:56, these two passages show that: -

1) The Lord reacts strongly to human disobedience

2) The Lord does not need human help to accomplish His plans

3) The Lord Himself ensures that the purpose of each believer's life is accomplished

BS12.4 Application

In response to God's *'total independence'* believers would be wise to: -

1) Accept the wisdom of not tempting God with our disobedience

2) Acknowledge that fretting over evildoers is a waste of time

3) Avoid worrying about whether the task God has for us will be completed

At the close of this study it's reasonable to conclude that God is able to mould each believer's character through the influence of His Holy Spirit and the providential ordering of external circumstances

BS12.5 Conclusion

1) Divine *'self-sufficiency'* shows that God may deal with the sin of apostasy by creating *'new church movements'* to replace those that have gone apostate

2) At His death, Jesus demonstrated this attribute by being able to accomplish God's will in the face of human cruelty and opposition

For further study please refer to the words *'I Am'* or *'sufficient'* in any Bible Concordance or Dictionary

BS12.6 Epilogue

Lord, vindicate the promise of your Word and enable me to accomplish the work to which you have called me[118]

BS12.7 Questions

1) What is the best way to appreciate divine self-sufficiency?

2) Why does the Lord hold those who militantly rebel against Him *'in utter derision?'* What should our own reaction be to them?

3) How can a diffident believer, suffering a serious setback, be encouraged to believe that God will actually bring to completion the task He has for them?

---

[118] This prayer was first made on Wednesday, 16th February 2000. It expresses the need for God to actively fulfil the promises made in His Word.

BS13: SOVEREIGNTY

(Known also as *'Lordship'*)

BS13.1 Prelude

It's a good job God is in control of human affairs because we most certainly are not!

BS13.2 Definition

This barely shared attribute of God's *'sovereignty'* refers to His ability to master and reign over the Creation He rightfully owns. He has the capacity to work through human free will, to fully master evil and to successfully implement all of His aims. Through this attribute God displays His kingly authority.

Divine Lordship is implied by the name **Kurios** – meaning *'Lord, Sir'* or *'reverend Master.'* An example of this name being used in scripture occurs in Revelation 22:5 which states *"And there shall be no night there and they need no candle, neither light of the sun for the Lord God* (Kurios) *gives them light and they* [the saints] *shall reign forever."* It demonstrates that God can and does control all of the events of our lives.

BS13.3 Bible Exposition

Two further Bible passages demonstrating the existence of this attribute are Psalm 93:1 and Revelation 11:15.

Psalm 93:1
"The Lord reigns, He is clothed with majesty. The Lord is clothed with strength, wherewith He has girded Himself. The world is also established that it cannot be moved."

This exuberant psalm is designed to cause a stir and to gain attention. It points out that divine sovereignty can bring a sense of power and stability, enabling people to deal effectively with any personal crisis. The realization dawns that God can be relied upon precisely because He is God. In addition, because of His all-powerful sovereignty, the Lord has established the physical world in its present precise location. (This applies to the other objects in the Cosmos too, the Universe itself bearing testimony to God's sovereignty.) Obviously the words *"the world is also established, that it cannot be moved,"* are poetry and need not to be accepted as a precise scientific description, but they do teach that God is in perfect control of His Creation. To maintain this control, the Lord often employs natural means, *i.e.* using the planet Jupiter to sweep away much of the cosmological debris that would otherwise come crashing into the Earth. The world is *established* because the Lord designed other worlds to provide protection for this one. Moreover, the sheer grandeur of these other worlds shows something of the grandeur of the Lord. Further discoveries in Cosmology all lend weight to this point.[119]

Revelation 11:15
"And the seventh angel sounded and there were great voices in Heaven saying, 'the kingdoms of this world are become the kingdoms of God and of His Christ and He shall reign forever and ever.'"

This pronouncement depicts God's sovereignty over the very darkest chapters of human history where the Gospel has been rejected by every nation. Unlike the power of earthly kingdoms, God's power is constant and eternal. His rule over the most rebellious of nations means that His judgements apply at a collective as well as an individual level. No wonder the angels get excited and praise Him with a noisy exuberance. The God we follow is the Lord of history as well as the Lord of Creation. Humanity may rebel but inevitably it is the Lord who triumphs. God shares His kingly authority with Christ, so that, in our prayers, we not only have access to a tender High Priest, familiar with our infirmities, (Hebrews 4:14f), but we also enjoy the friendship of a mighty King who can do great things on our behalf. He is a King worthy of our deepest respect. Such points are important because many believers do not have a clear idea about the God to whom they are praying. Moreover, as the days become

---

[119] In passing, it's worth mentioning that one of the blessings of being a regenerate Christian believer is the ability to appreciate the wonderful *'design'* present in God's Creation. Sadly, this is a point that those who don't believe in God are unable to comprehend. Any attempt to persuade unbelievers to accept Christianity on the basis of *'design'* tends usually to be a complete waste of time. It's the equivalent of trying to explain the colours of a rainbow to a person blind from birth. Represented here is a flawed method of evangelism which can be used by any religion – there's simply nothing distinctly Christian about it. Admittedly, such *'Natural Theology'* does have value in reinforcing a faith which is already there through the Holy Spirit's work but it does nothing to convince unbelievers that Christianity is true. A more biblical approach is to focus upon the person and work of Jesus – the gospel of Christ.

ever more difficult there will be an increasing need to have an even greater confidence in God's sovereignty over history. The Book of Revelation gives a terrible picture of how human affairs will end, but this very same Book also shows that God triumphantly <u>accomplishes His will in the midst of those affairs.</u> The angels recognise this as they praise God in Heaven and so should we upon the Earth.

When viewed alongside Revelation 22:5, these two passages show that: -

1) The Lord and His Saints will reign forever in a new Creation

2) The Lord exercises His sovereignty over Creation, largely through natural processes

3) The Lord asserts His kingly authority through His judging of whole nations

BS13.4 Application

In response to God's *'Lordship'* believers would be wise to: -

1) Acknowledge this attribute in prayer

2) Be confident that God is in control of every aspect of life

3) Avoid believing that human rebellion against God can ever succeed

At the close of this study it's reasonable to conclude that God is an invincible King who will crush any opposition arrayed against Him

BS13.5 Conclusion

1) Divine *'sovereignty'* shows that God may deal with the sin of apostasy by using even global apostasy to accomplish His ends

2) At His death, Jesus demonstrated this attribute by choosing to overcome evil through the sheer goodness of His character

For further study please refer to the words *'King'* or *'Reign'* in any Bible Concordance or Dictionary

BS13.6 Epilogue

Oh sovereign King
How great are your ways
How masterful your rule
Who can compare with you?
Who can triumph over you?
Who can usurp your position on your heavenly throne?
Not one of us threatens your dignity
Not one of us can triumph over you
Not one of us can follow the way of rebellion
And even expect to escape your judgements.
You are beyond compare, oh Lord
For you are utterly complete in your sovereignty[120]

BS13.7 Questions

1) What effect should divine sovereignty have upon our prayer life?

2) Why do individuals and nations rebel against God, even though He is sovereign?

3) What are the likely short and long-term effects of rebelling against God?

4) How would you deal with someone who feels their life's in a mess and that God is far away?

BS14: TRANSCENDENCE

(Known also as *'Lofty Detachment'*)

BS14.1 Prelude

The wise man begins his prayers by heartily acknowledging the greatness of God but the foolish man thinks that by making many prayers he is doing the Almighty a favour

---

[120] This prayer was first made on Thursday, 17th February 2000. It expresses the way an appreciation of divine sovereignty leads to adoration.

BS14.2 Definition

This <u>barely shared</u> attribute of God's *'transcendence'* refers to His lofty detachment from Creation and His ability to enjoy an existence over and above it.

Divine lofty detachment is implied by the name **Elohim Marom** – meaning *'God most High.'* An example of this name being used in scripture occurs in Micah 6:6 which states *"Wherewith shall I come before the Lord and bow myself before the High God* (Elohim Marom)*? Shall I come before him with burnt offerings, with calves a year old?"* It demonstrates that God can, at times, seem very remote.

BS14.3 Bible Exposition

Two further Bible passages demonstrating the existence of this attribute are 2 Chronicles 2:6 and Matthew 6:9.

2 Chronicles 2:6
"And who is able to build Him a house, seeing the Heaven of Heavens cannot contain Him? Who am I then, that I should build Him a house, except only to burn sacrifices before Him?"

King Solomon is on the brink of building a Temple which will be characterised by its many elaborate sacrifices. Paradoxically, he sees the inherent limitations of this project but (motivated by a genuine desire to honour the Lord) he still goes ahead with it. Also acknowledged is the fact that God fills both this Universe and another unknown Universe which is His dwelling place. Scripture does support the view that more than one Cosmos exists. Yet in His transcendence the Lord goes beyond His Creation and stretches out for an unlimited distance. The effect of such a fact should generate a sense of humility within each one of us. We are to avoid any pagan notion that God is tied to one locality – He most certainly is not. His lofty detachment also enables us to see our own works from a realistic perspective. Like King Solomon, we are to accept that even our best works are only on a miniscule scale when compared to the works of God. Any significance they have is tied directly to our relationship with God. Hence, even the smallest works done in accordance with His will take on a huge significance. Thus a humble cleaner of public toilets who's following the Lord's will is in a far happier position than a proud Cardinal overlooking the building of a grand Cathedral in order to fulfil his lust for personal glory. In Christian ministry what matters is faithfulness, not worldly success.

Matthew 6:9
"After that manner you are to pray 'Our Father who art in Heaven, hallowed be your name.'"

These words represent a marvellous opening to the Lord's Prayer. The first divine attribute Jesus draws attention to isn't divine holiness, but divine transcendence. He seems to assume that focusing upon this attribute will instil the right attitude of worship. Christ's example confirms that it's often right to begin prayer by recognising the greatness of divine transcendence. He shows that we need to begin by focussing our attention upon God and not on ourselves. *'Me'* centred prayers are dangerous, precisely because they encourage the worship of *'self.'* All too often, our daily prayers can degenerate into *'wailing'* prayers which do nothing but vent a rather grumpy self-pity. In addition, it's helpful to see that divine transcendence allows scope for divine holiness. Through a lofty detachment from Creation the Lord is seen to be separate from all that is evil (even though He freely chose to identify with sin through Christ). Once again the presence of one divine attribute allows for the presence of another. God can be holy because He is transcendent.

When viewed alongside Micah 6:6, these two passages show that: -

1) God humbles people through revealing His own transcendence

2) The Lord dwells outside of His Creation

3) The Lord is separate from the evil found in Creation

BS14.4 Application

In response to God's *'lofty detachment'* believers would be wise to: -

1) Avoid thinking that impressive religious ceremonies do any favours for God

2) Acknowledge that God cannot be tied to one locality

3) Begin prayer by acknowledging divine transcendence

At the close of this study it's reasonable to conclude that God is able to both fill and go beyond His Creation

BS14.5 Conclusion

1) Divine *'transcendence'* shows that God may deal with the sin of apostasy by determinedly enforcing His standards even in the face of unrelenting spiritual and human opposition

2) At His Son's death God the Father demonstrated this attribute by removing His comforting presence from His Son as He suffered the penalty for our sin

For further study please refer to the words *'High'* or *'Most High'* in any Bible Concordance or Dictionary

BS14.6 Epilogue

Lord, do not be far from me
Or so high that you are beyond reach
I am exhausted
Renew me with a vision of yourself and
Cause me once again to be effective in your service[121]

14.7 Questions

1) What effect should divine transcendence have upon our prayer life?

2) What are the dangers of over-emphasising divine transcendence?

3) How can we ensure that our prayers and worship are *'God-centred'* rather than *'self-centred?'*

---

[121] This prayer was first made on Tuesday, 22nd February 2000. It expresses the need to receive a fresh vision of God during times of exhaustion and illness.

BS15: TRI-UNITY

(Known also as *Pluralistic Oneness*)

BS15.1 Prelude

The Trinity seems to be the most absurd of doctrines until the alternatives are considered

BS15.2 Definition

This barely shared attribute of God's *tri-unity* refers to His existence in three distinct Persons; Father, Son and Holy Spirit, who together enjoy an unlimited variety of attributes and constitute the three members of the Trinity.

Divine plurality is implied by the name **Elohim** – meaning *'awesome, majestic Gods.'* An example of this name being used in scripture occurs in Genesis 1:1 which states *"In the beginning God* (Elohim) *created the Heavens and the Earth."* It demonstrates that God did not create the Universe simply because He was lonely.

BS15.3 Bible Exposition

Two further Bible passages demonstrating the existence of this attribute are Isaiah 6:8 and Matthew 28:19.

Isaiah 6:8
"Also, I heard the voice of the Lord saying 'whom shall I send and who will go for us?' Then I said 'here am I – send me.'"

During a time of growing apostasy in the Kingdom of Judah, a discussion is taking place *'within'* the Lord and unless He was indulging in some elaborate playacting the dialogue indicates the presence of more than one distinct personality. (Also implied is the possibility that part of the prophetic office can involve the privilege of overhearing the internal dialogue of the Godhead.) A reasoned decision is being made over who should be called to carry out God's commands as a prophet. The Lord we follow not only commands, but also discusses and consults with those who are His friends. When the Lord actively seeks someone to follow Him into a particular line of work our response should be to listen and to volunteer. This passage also implies that it's possible to actually hear God's voice speaking. However, other scriptural passages like 1 Thessalonians 5:21 and 1 John 4:1 warn that careful tests are needed to establish that it is indeed God's voice we are hearing. The whole area of assessing spiritual occurrences is touched upon here. Nevertheless, once God's voice has been discerned it is to be obeyed.

Matthew 28:19
"Go you therefore and teach all nations, baptising them in the name of the Father and of the Son and of the Holy Ghost."

The three Persons who constitute the Trinity are revealed here as Jesus gives His disciples a commission to teach all nations and to baptise them. He also shows that, through baptism true believers are called into fellowship with all three Persons of the Trinity. Indeed, these Persons are so closely joined in love that where one Person is present the others are too. An indivisible bond draws them together. The verbal formula used in baptism is important because it helps decide whether the correct God is being followed. The problem with a *'Jesus only'* baptism is that it can place the candidate under the bondage of spirits who fuel a certain form of anti-trinitarianism.[122] It can also entice people into following *'another Jesus'* – one subtly different from the Jesus revealed in scripture. Baptismal formulas are important because they reflect the spiritual reality into which the baptismal candidate is being immersed. Hence, when a believer decides to be baptised care must be taken to ascertain exactly what they are being baptised into. Neglecting this question could possibly lead to the candidate's life being built upon a wrong spiritual foundation. Any water baptism should be shunned unless it is done in the name of the *'Father, Son and Holy Spirit.'*

When viewed alongside Genesis 1:1, these two passages show that:

1) The actual titles of God imply a sense of plurality

2) The internal dialogue, (as recorded in Isaiah 6:8) taking place within God allows scope for the doctrine of the Trinity

3) The baptismal formulas used by the Early Church each point to the doctrine of the Trinity

---

[122] From direct observation in an Afro-Caribbean Pentecostal setting (over the period of 1989-1999), the author has seen these spirits drive people into voodoo-like frenzies, making them receptive to even worse errors.

BS15.4 Application

In response to God's *'plurality'* believers would be wise to: -

1) Accept that it is possible to hear God's voice

2) Acknowledge the importance of Trinitarian baptism

3) <u>Avoid</u> non-Trinitarian forms of baptism

At the close of this study it's reasonable to conclude that God is a unity of three distinct Persons

15.5 Conclusion

1) Divine *'tri-unity'* shows that God may deal with the sin of apostasy by holding a consultation process involving all three members of the Trinity

2) At His death Jesus demonstrated this attribute by offering an effective sacrifice which could appease His Father's wrath against human sin whilst providing believers with an infinite number of blessings through the Holy Spirit

For further study please refer to the words *'Father,' 'Son'* or *'Holy Spirit'* in any Bible Concordance or Dictionary

BS15.6 Epilogue

Praise you Father
Praise you Jesus
Praise you Holy Spirit
For when I praise one of you
I praise all three because
You all constitute one God,
Forever – totally without end, Amen[123]

---

[123] This prayer was first made on Wednesday, 23rd February 2000. It expresses the wisdom of incorporating Trinitarian doctrine into worship.

BS15.7 Questions

1) What blessings are likely to follow from a robust belief in Trinitarian doctrine?

2) Why is it dangerous to receive a baptism which uses a *'Jesus only'* format?

3) How would you respond to the argument that the Trinity is purely a man-made idea, having no basis in scripture?

Summary

Su1: Each of the above 15 <u>barely shared</u> attributes may be summarised as follows: -

1) Divine absolute being: God's objective, free existence; it also means that He is the first cause of everything and could exist quite independently of His Creation

2) Divine adequacy: God's sovereign control and provision of circumstances to meet every type of human need and to bring happiness to all of His Creation

3) Divine glory: God's radiant splendour and justifiable fame which causes Him to be a fit object of human adoration

4) Divine immanence: God's active and caring presence everywhere and His total participation in everything He has made

5) Divine immutability: God's perpetual sameness, unalterable consistency and lack of any change in any of His attributes or His aims

6) Divine infinity: God's unlimited extent and boundless freedom from any external constraint – so there is never any end to Him

7) Divine omnipotence: God's control over every single part of Creation, even when it is in militant rebellion against His will

8) Divine omnipresence: God's ability to be everywhere at once, both inside and outside of the known Universe

9) Divine omniscience: God's ability to be aware of, to recall and to retain detailed information about everything, in and beyond all of His Creation

10) Divine wisdom: God's ability to devise perfect plans and to fulfil them in the best possible way

11) Divine perfection: God's wholeness, completeness and total freedom from every fault; no positive quality is absent from Him and no negative quality is present in Him

12) Divine self-sufficiency: God's ability to freely exist without the aid of His Creation and to effectively implement His plans in the face of severe opposition from both angelic and human beings

13) Divine sovereignty: God's ability to master and reign over the Creation He rightfully owns. He has the capacity to work through human free will, to fully master evil and to successfully implement all of His aims

14) Divine transcendence: God's lofty detachment from Creation and His ability to enjoy an existence over and above it

15) Divine tri-unity: God's existence as three distinct Persons; Father, Son and Holy Spirit, who together enjoy an unlimited variety of attributes and constitute the three members of the Trinity

<u>Su2:</u> In relation to the sin of apostasy: -

1) Divine absolute being: shows that God may deal with it by starting a new work outside of those Churches that refuse to obey His will

2) Divine adequacy: shows that God may deal with it by only blessing those who remain faithful to His scriptures

3) Divine glory: shows that God may deal with it by using the schemes perpetuated by wicked apostates to rebound to His, (rather than their own) glory

4) Divine immanence: shows that God may deal with it by recording all of the sins committed by apostates so that they can be condemned on the Day of Judgement

5) Divine immutability: shows that God may deal with it by completely refusing to compromise any of His moral standards

6) Divine infinity: shows that God may deal with it by ensuring that it produces everlasting loss for those who knowingly and persistently commit it

7) Divine omnipotence: shows that God may deal with it by suddenly removing apostates from positions of prominence

8) Divine omnipresence: shows that God may deal with it by exposing to public view the greed and secret schemes of apostates

9) Divine omniscience: shows that God may deal with it by recording every sin an apostate commits so theirs will be an utterly fair verdict on the Day of Judgement

10) Divine wisdom: shows that God may deal with it by giving loyal followers the wisdom needed to deal with particular apostate situations

11) Divine perfection: shows that God may deal with it by devising the perfect means to expose apostates for who they really are

12) Divine self-sufficiency: shows that God may deal with it by creating new church movements to replace those that have gone apostate

13) Divine sovereignty: shows that God may deal with it by using even global apostasy to accomplish His ends

14) Divine transcendence: shows that God may deal with it by determinedly enforcing His standards, in the face of unrelenting spiritual and human opposition

15) Divine tri-unity: shows that God may deal with it by holding a consultation process involving all members of the Trinity

Su3: During His death, Jesus demonstrated: -

1) Divine absolute being: by showing that God was free to solve the problem of sin in His own way, without any external constraint

2) Divine adequacy: by showing that He had adequately provided a perfect sacrifice to fully appease divine wrath against human sin

3) Divine glory: by showing that even the worst kind of suffering could gain long-term renown

4) Divine immanence: by caring for others whilst He Himself suffered terribly

5) Divine immutability: by being punished *'once and for all'* for sin – thus fulfilling God's plan of salvation and abolishing (making obsolete) the temporary sacrificial rules laid down by God in the Mosaic Law

6) Divine infinity: by producing an unlimited number of everlasting blessings – only a few of which can be enjoyed in this life

7) Divine omnipotence: by being sustained by divine power as God poured out His wrath upon Him

8) Divine omnipresence: by showing that God can play many different roles whilst manifesting His presence

9) Divine omniscience: by fulfilling the many detailed Bible prophecies foretelling this event

10) Divine wisdom: by demonstrating that God had devised the wisest way to deal with human sin – one that neither destroyed humankind nor compromised His divine attributes

11) Divine perfection: by offering a totally perfect sacrifice for sin which permanently abolished the need for any other sacrifices to appease God's wrath

12) Divine self-sufficiency: by being able to accomplish God's will in the face of human cruelty and opposition

13) Divine sovereignty: by choosing to overcome evil through the sheer goodness of His character

14) Divine transcendence: by removing His comforting presence from His Son as He suffered the penalty for our sin

15) Divine tri-unity: by offering an effective sacrifice which could appease His Father's wrath against human sin whilst providing believers with an infinite number of blessings through the Holy Spirit

C5:
THE OLDEST LIE

(A look at whether human beings can ever become like God)

Psalm 82:6-7

"I have said you are gods and all of you are children of The Most High. But you shall die like men and fall like one of the princes."

Thought Starter

"We must never use religion as an excuse to evade the gospel"

Definitions

1) Deification (*Divinisation*): The process whereby people believe they can become like God – often through the use of particular techniques. These may range from sophisticated forms of meditation through to crude magical practices. The intention is to *'awaken'* the *'divine inner self'* or *'potential deity,'* thereby becoming a mini-god or some other divine being like Christ.[124] Types of deification are: -

1.1 Full (*extreme*) Deification: The mistaken belief that the practitioner can become so like God that they possess all of His divine attributes. Any distinction between the practitioner and God ceases as they *'merge'* with the divine.

1.2 Partial (*moderate*) Deification: The mistaken belief that the practitioner can receive sufficient divine *'energy'* to recover the perfection and innocence originally lost by Mankind at *'The Fall,'* (Genesis 3). Some distinction between the practitioner and God remains.

2) Exaltation: The process wherein God blesses, honours, perfects and brings into a closer relationship with Himself those who would follow the Lord Jesus Christ. It begins here in this present life, reaching its final fulfilment in the afterlife. It does <u>not</u> lead to deification.

3) Friend of God: A spiritually regenerate person, known and loved by God in a deeply personal way. It results in a permanent, collaborative alliance (partnership) with God, shown in an affectionate and trusting relationship. It leads to an enhancement of human individuality.

4) Mysticism: A complex network of often distorted religious beliefs and devotional practices. These are all aimed at initiating devotees into mysterious spiritual *'secrets,'* not normally unavailable to the average person. Often characterized by extremely obscure language, its main aim is to attain some sort of *'union'* with the divine.

5) Mystic: A committed practitioner of mysticism

---

[124] The original Greek word for *'deification'* is *'theosis'* which specifically refers to *'the process of being made divine.'* It was extensively employed by early Christian writers and also by (mainly) Platonically-based Greek philosophers.

6) Platonism: An influential branch of Ancient Greek Philosophy which ranked the spiritual world on a far superior level to its counterpart, the physical world. In its later neo-platonic form, it also encouraged belief in full deification.

7) Religion: A strong belief in, and worship of, a supernatural power or person. It also represents humanity's attempts to engage with and earn the favour of that supernatural power or person. It is usually expressed in some form of ritual or moral code.

8) Revelation of Sin: An often painful divine exposure of personal sin[125] – designed to provoke a loss of confidence in one's own ability to reach God, or to merit His favour.

9) Righteousness: A right relationship with God through Jesus Christ. It is often expressed in daily life through a betterment of personal and moral conduct.

10) Sanctification: The lifelong process whereby sin is restrained and the Christian becomes more like Jesus in personal character; it is a by-product of exaltation.

11) Spiritual Humility: A self-effacing modesty and personal meekness, coupled with an honest realism about one's own capacity to do evil unless restrained by God. It is often expressed in a humble demeanour and a sense of genuine gratitude for all of God's mercy. Also present is a truly altruistic concern for the welfare of others. It leads to a faithful attempt to honour and obey God, once His will has been clearly discerned.

12) Spiritual Narcissism: An inordinate and uncontrollable love of self that leads to spiritual pride and belief in one's own divinity.

13) Spiritual Pride: A self-loving arrogance with a misplaced sense of personal superiority. A relationship with God is assumed to exist, when, in actual reality, it doesn't. Any sense of personal sin and accountability is missing – as is a willingness to accept a subordinate place in the created order. Spiritual pride is often expressed in a haughty, superior manner and a disdainful contempt of others. In its most extreme form it leads to rebellious attempts to overthrow and replace God.

---

[125] *'Sin'* is the inner corruption and self-centred rebelliousness which causes people to fall short of God's standards, as revealed in scripture.

14) Spirituality: The study and use of particular techniques (i.e. prayer and meditation) to relate to God (or some other form of supernatural reality). Both Christian and non-Christian forms of spirituality exist.[126]

15) The Free Spirit: A medieval religious movement with a number of diverse sects who believed in full deification and often practised amoral behaviour.

Prologue: The Self-Glorifiers

On the Judgment Day, *"When the Son of Man shall come in His glory, and all the holy angels with Him, then shall He sit upon the throne of His glory,"* (Matthew 25:31-32) and many who professed to follow His name tried to justify themselves in the following ways: -

"Lord, Lord, did we not keep all your commandments and obey all of the Law to earn your favour?"
"Lord, Lord, did we not prophesy and cast out devils in your name?" (Matthew 7:22)
"Lord, Lord, did we not give our bodies to be burnt as holy martyrs in order to earn your favour?" (1 Corinthians 13:3)
"Lord, Lord, did we not produce Creeds and devise Liturgies to earn your favour?"
"Lord, Lord, did we not scourge ourselves and wear hair shirts whilst sitting manacled to pillars to earn your favour?"
"Lord, Lord, did we not build splendid Basilicas and Cathedrals to earn your favour?"
"Lord, Lord, did we not take up Holy Orders and give up many pleasures to earn your favour?"
"Lord, Lord, did we not go on Crusades and fight unbelievers to earn your favour?"
"Lord, Lord, did we not try to make ourselves divine to earn your favour?"
"Lord, Lord, did we not pray and celebrate Mass each and every day to earn your favour?"

---

[126] Usually, the terms *'spirituality'* and *'mysticism'* are employed interchangeably whenever religious matters are discussed in the media. Strictly speaking, *'spirituality'* refers to those specific values, techniques and methods present within *'mysticism,'* all aimed at attaining union with the divine. By definition a *'mystic'* is a practitioner of *'spirituality.'* However, these two terms are hard to distinguish and much confusion surrounds them with even Atheistic forms of spirituality existing! *'Spirituality'* is an overused, *'catch all'* word referring to anything to do with the non-material world.

"Lord, Lord, did we not persecute and slay heretics to earn your favour?"

"Lord, Lord, did we not commission beautiful works of art and music to earn your favour?"

"Lord, Lord, did we not serve as ministers of an established Church to earn your favour?"

"Lord, Lord, did we not achieve high Church Office to earn your favour?"

"Lord, Lord, did we not write massive Bible Commentaries to earn your favour?"

"Lord, Lord, did we not hold many 'Revival Meetings' to earn your favour?"

"Lord, Lord, did we not go out onto the 'Mission Field' to convert poor heathen natives to earn your favour?"

"Lord, Lord, did we not die on the 'Mission Field' to earn your favour?"

"Lord, Lord, did we not help the poor and campaign for justice to earn your favour?"

"Lord, Lord, did we not strive to build a 'New World Order' to earn your favour?"

Only after these noisy protests had died away did an elderly lady quietly step forward and speak a few words; *"My Lord, I know that my life never added up to much and that when I was ending my days as a beggar woman some of the religious people here called me a smelly old hag and a lot of other things besides. I also admit that in my younger days I had to sell my body to live and my own family disowned me. So I can't see why you should ever let me into your Kingdom. But in my life I did, by your mercy, come to believe that you died for my sin and that you were a great Saviour. For that reason alone I believe you may give me a small place there even though I'm totally unworthy and can't boast of any achievements."*

In response, Jesus stood up to greet her, (Acts 7:55-56), gazing upon her with compassion and exclaiming, *"I shall clothe you in white and will preserve your name in the Book of Life, confessing it before my Father and His angels. Welcome into my Kingdom,"* (Revelation 3:5). *"As for those who tried to make themselves into mini-gods or bribe me with their so-called 'good works' (which they did for their own glory and not mine) I say, "I never knew you, depart from me you evildoers into the everlasting fire prepared for the devil and his angels,"* (Matthew 7:23 & 25:41)[127]

Such will be the fate of those who try to justify themselves before God rather than relying fully upon the justification which He alone provides through Christ's sacrificial death, (Luke 18:10-14).

5.1 A Deadly Ascent

To believe in the fatal lie of deification is to risk falling into the same sin (of spiritual pride) which ruined a powerful angelic being called Lucifer,[128] turning him into the devil we know today. Although initially enjoying a very close relationship with God, Lucifer had allowed himself to become infatuated with his own considerable beauty, knowledge and wisdom. This self-infatuation served to hugely inflate his ego, creating and sustaining a dangerously misplaced sense of self-reliance, (1 Corinthians 8:1b). This point is underlined by the following quote from Ezekiel 28:11-15, where the proud King of Tyre is used as a model or *'type'* of Lucifer;[129]

[11] The word of the Lord came to me, saying,

[12] "Son of man, take up a lamentation upon the king of Tyre, and say to him, Thus says the Lord God; you were full of wisdom and perfect in beauty

[13] You have been in Eden, the garden of God; every precious stone was your covering, the ruby, topaz and the diamond, the beryl, the onyx and the jasper, the sapphire, the emerald and the carbuncle, and gold: the workmanship of your jewelled mountings and of your settings was prepared for you in the day that you were created.

[14] You were the anointed cherub who covers with overshadowing wings; and I have set you so: You walked up and down the holy mountain of God; in the midst of the stones of fire.

---

[127] This fictitious story was written on Thursday, 9th July 2010 and is closely based upon Christ's teaching about the Judgment Day.
[128] The name *'Lucifer'* is used to designate the devil's identity before his expulsion from heaven; whilst the name *'Satan'* is used after that event. This does appear to follow a biblical precedent.
[129] This passage follows a common Jewish scribal practice of assuming that the behaviour of an earthly reality (*i.e.* the King of Tyre) reveals details about the behaviour of a spiritual reality (*i.e.* Lucifer).

¹⁵ You were perfect in your ways from the day that you were created, until iniquity and guilt was found in you."

The above quotation suggests that Lucifer had become so infatuated with his own beauty that his love came to be directed inward to *'self'* rather than outward to God. This encouraged an overweening pride which led him to commit the worst form of idolatry; the actual worship of *'self'*.[130] A vicious cycle was then set in motion, where pride fed *'self'* and *'self'* reinforced pride. Further evidence for this point is provided in the way Lucifer is addressed in Ezekiel 28:17a, *"Your heart was lifted up in pride because of your beauty, you have corrupted your wisdom for the sake of your bright splendour."* Through spiritual pride Lucifer came to hanker after deification (which he perhaps saw as his birthright). He wanted to be God and to receive the worship due to God alone.[131] Present here was an acute case of spiritual narcissism.

The following quote from Isaiah 14:12-15 further highlights these points. Its wording confirms that something far greater than human ambition was at play here: -

"¹² How you are fallen from heaven, O Lucifer, son of the morning! How you are cut down to the ground, you who did weaken the nations!

¹³⁻¹⁴   For you said in your heart,
- *I will ascend into heaven,*
- *I will exalt my throne above the stars [angels] of God:*
- *I will sit also upon the mount of the congregation, in the sides of the north:*
- *I will ascend above the heights of the clouds;*
- *I will be like the most High.*

---

[130] This form of idolatry acts as a basis for all other types of idolatry. It is usually the case that the worshippers of idols are really trying to enhance themselves, either by gaining some material blessing (like a good harvest of crops) or by receiving feelings of ecstasy and power which further heighten an inordinate pride in, and love of, *'self.'*

[131] This hankering after deity was still apparent during the wilderness temptations of Jesus when Satan offered Him all of the kingdoms of the world in exchange for His worship, (Matthew 4:9 and Luke 4:6). Shortly before Christ's return, Satan will entice the whole world to worship him through the anti-Christ (Revelation 13-14). His craving for worship appears to be insatiable; Satan is like a drug addict needing his latest fix. His fervent desire to become divine still remains his all-consuming obsession.

¹⁵Yet you shall be brought down to hell, to the innermost depths of the pit where the dead dwell."

The above five *'I wills'* (of Isaiah 14:13-14) confirm that Lucifer displayed a huge amount of self-will in his attempt to fulfil his all-consuming desire to be like God. Absolutely nothing else mattered and, regardless of the consequences, he simply had to be God. These utterly determined *'I wills'* display his thoroughgoing egocentricity and limitless sense of ambition. His malicious and proud self-will would explain why, unlike humans, Lucifer can never be redeemed. He was totally aware of what he was doing – that he was sinning against perfect knowledge, yet he continued along his self-chosen path. In doing this, he systematically resisted and blasphemed the Holy Spirit which (as Jesus Himself warned in Matthew 12:31-32) is the one sin that cannot be forgiven. Lucifer had doomed himself through his own self-defiance. This directly led to his own spiritual death and his eventual consignment to the deepest parts of hell, (Isaiah 14:15). The effect of this self-centred rebellion was that he forever cut himself off from the love of God. Pride had caused him to experience a massive and irrevocable fall from grace.

S5.1.1: An Angelic revolt

Lucifer's *'self-will'* also led him to launch an enormous angelic revolt that created pandemonium in the heavens. The fact that he managed to entice one-third of all of the angels to join him in this abortive rebellion testifies to his persuasive abilities, (Revelation 12:4).[132] Lucifer was a seducer of angels before he became a seducer of men.[133] Those *'fallen'* angels became devils, sharing in his full malignity, if not his power. Many of them still roam *'the waterless places'* on earth, seeking hapless victims to indwell,

---

[132] Maybe Lucifer did this by suggesting that the angels could become mini-gods themselves (thereby relinquishing their role as spiritual servants of the one true God). If this was the case then he was offering them the same bogus promise of deification that he still offers today.

[133] On a purely speculative note, it's possibly this angelic fall which explains why there appears to have been so much death and disorder in Creation before the presence of Mankind. Evil appears to have penetrated Creation at a very early stage of its existence. Genesis 3:1 would suggest that the serpent in the Garden of Eden (that led humanity into sin) was already a well-established figure; for how else could he be *'more subtle'* than any other creature if this was not the case? He will have needed a lengthy period of time to achieve this subtlety. This would appear to foreclose the possibility that Lucifer had suddenly swooped down to earth and assumed the guise of a serpent after the creation of Man. He appears to have been lurking in the undergrowth for some very considerable time.

(Matthew 12:43-48 and 1 Peter 5:8). Others were so powerful they had to be consigned to the depths of hell in order to be *'bound in custody'* until the Day of Judgement, (2 Peter 2:4). Were they ever to be released the result would be the kind of global destruction so vividly described in the Book of Revelation. It's hard not to conclude that these angelic psychopaths are being imprisoned for the protection of humanity. Evidence for this is suggested in Revelation 9 (which underlines the hideous nature of these beings). This passage shows them being allowed to go on the rampage for a limited period shortly before Christ's return. May none of those known to and loved by the writer actually see this!

With Lucifer there appears to have been a singular chain of events wherein: -
1) His own beauty, knowledge and wisdom engendered feelings of personal pride
2) He made a conscious decision to harbour and indulge those feelings
3) He began to become infatuated with himself rather than with God
4) This infatuation grew into an idolatrous worship of *self*, further fuelling any feelings of pride
5) He perhaps toyed with the question, *'Why can't I be like God?'*
6) Toying with the above question aroused feelings of jealousy and resentment against God
7) He consistently resisted any appeals to reason and blasphemed the Holy Spirit
8) A decision was made to violently seize the place of God in order to achieve *'deification'*
9) He tried to recruit other angelic beings, (possibly with promises of *'deification'*)
10) One-third of the angels were seduced by his promises
11) Lucifer led a massive angelic rebellion against God and became Satan, the great adversary
12) The revolt failed and Lucifer, along with all of his angels (who subsequently became demons) were cast out of heaven
13) Evil entered to spoil Creation; with the result that Satan now uses spurious promises of *'deification'* to entice human beings to re-enact his fall and to share in his eternal misery, (Genesis 3:5)

The above chain of events would suggest that Lucifer's main sin was his proud covetousness.[134] Where most human beings would

---

[134] *'Covetousness'* is an envious and excessive desire to acquire something that rightfully belongs to another person.

possibly covet their neighbour's wife or property (Exodus 20:17) Satan coveted all of the attributes of God, including God's ability to determine what was right or wrong, (Genesis 3:5). What Satan really wanted was to kick God off his throne and to take His place. When it came to sin the devil was certainly ambitious; he could *'think big.'* Although on a far grander scale, Lucifer's revolt against God was similar in nature to Absalom's revolt against his father David; present was the same pride in his own beauty, alongside his haughty distaste of authority, (2 Samuel 14:20-18:18). How Lucifer thought he could succeed in his revolt remains a matter of speculation but possibly he reckoned that if he could create a conflict between the attributes of divine holiness and divine love then God would lose His perfection and thereby become ripe for the taking. His rebellion was perhaps an attempt to set-up an internal conflict within God Himself as much as it was between God and some of his angels. If this was the strategy being pursued it shows immense cunning but also a huge underestimation of the fundamental harmony existing between all of the divine attributes. Blinded by his ambition, Lucifer had failed to observe that God's attributes are so well integrated that nothing can even slightly disturb their equilibrium. Not for the last time the devil had overreached himself (he was to make the same mistake in connection with the death of Jesus).

S5.1.2: A False freedom

All this would suggest that any spiritual exercise or technique designed to *'help contact the god/goddess within,'* *'ascend to godhood'* *'realize our divinity/deity,'* *'fulfil our divine potential,'* *'attain deification,'* *'gain cosmic awareness/consciousness,'* or *'climb the ladder of perfection,'*[135] are simply Satan's way of enticing people to re-enact exactly the same sin of pride which precipitated his own downfall. Hardly surprisingly, those who would presume to think they can become *'mini-gods'* often end-up behaving like devils, concerned only with fulfilling their own desires. They became thoroughly infatuated with *'self'* and are neither reachable by love nor reason. Being *'godlike'* they regard themselves as infallible and utterly incapable of making any mistakes. They become *'locked into'* this

---

[135] The precise jargon used is often very unclear and can vary greatly from group to group. Within Christian mystical circles, the term *'deity/divinity/god/goddess'* would be replaced by *'Christ'* or *'Jesus.'* Thus, unwary Christians are encouraged (often through such meditative techniques as contemplation and visualisation) to find *'the Christ within'* or *'the Christ self'* etc. However, this change of jargon does not make *'self-deification'* any more biblical or pleasing to God.

way of thinking and their same destructive behaviour patterns are played over and over again. This overwhelming sense of personal (and group) power may even engender a delight in cruelty.[136] Such behaviour patterns demonstrate that all attempts at deification simply lead to internal demonization. Those undergoing this process, instead of becoming godlike (and therefore benevolent) become more like the devil in their inner dispositions. Of such (thoroughly self-absorbed) people it may well be said: -

They think they are free
When in reality
They are the slaves of a cruel puppet master

They think they are above any law
When in reality
They are being crushed by 'The Law of sin and death'

They think they are enlightened
When in reality
They are becoming mentally darkened fools

They think they are knowledgeable
When in reality
They are expressing the most inane stupidity

They think they are ascending into a higher realm
When in reality
They are descending into the lowest regions of Hell

They think they are becoming divine
When in reality
They are becoming worse than the beasts

Woe to anyone who tries to be like God![137]

Should the reader think the author has been indulging in rhetorical exaggeration, support for the above outrageous claims can be found

---

[136] The leaders of various suicide cults would perhaps provide the best examples of this trait.
[137] Entitled *'In Reality'* this meditation was first drafted on Wednesday, 3rd March 2010 and was based upon earlier prose material.

in those who followed of the medieval *'Free Spirit'* heresy.[138] One lady belonging to that Movement actually boasted, *"When God created all things I created all things with him...I am more than God."*[139] Preoccupied with their own imagined deity such deluded individuals couldn't (or didn't want to) see that their highly valued *'special,'* esoteric knowledge was nothing more than dangerous nonsense. They also overlooked the inconvenient fact that their own inner obsession to become divine was simply a tool used by Satan to get them to suffer in his own eternal misery. His stance amply demonstrates the saying, *'misery likes company.'*[140] The popularity of such movements would suggest that Hell is full of deluded fools who thought they could be divine. Unfortunately, later examples will show that their *'deification'* error is enjoying a revival within certain parts of the Church. Movements like *'the Free Spirit'* aren't just a matter of historical interest.

An insight into God's response to such delusions is provided in the mocking words of Psalm 82:6-7. *"I have said you are Gods; and all of you are children of the most High. But instead you shall die like men and fall like one of the princes."* This satirical statement was directed against the corrupt judges and officials of Ancient Israel who, like their pagan counterparts, had come to think of themselves as *'mini-gods,'* far above any law or accountability. Verse seven ridicules this view by showing that such *'robber judges'* were not immune to the mortality facing all other members of the human race. They too would die. This passage lends weight to the view that the *'deification delusion'* hinders people from accepting their own fallibility and frailty as human beings. In pursuing this delusion they become locked in denial, convincing themselves that neither suffering nor illness have any objective reality.[141] In extreme cases, this may cause them to refuse proper medical attention or food. Such cases would indicate that, at the psychological level, an obsessive desire for *'self-deification'* may constitute a form of mental illness wherein a most desirable fantasy is mistaken for reality. Anything contradicting it is ignored, *'explained away'* or strongly rejected. Such people have created their own *'castles in the air'* and have begun living in them. A total disconnection from the normality of everyday life has taken

---

[138] An excellent analysis of this Movement is provided in chapters eight and nine of Norman Cohn's groundbreaking book, *'The Pursuit of the Millennium'* (first published in 1957).
[139] Quoted in Cohn p.176
[140] This raises the intriguing possibility that Satan cannot bear his own company. He would rather have millions abusing him in hell than be there utterly alone
[141] As can be seen in the Christian Science Cult

place, resulting in an inability to see reason. To go through life *'living in delusion'* is essentially *'living a lie,'* and this can result only in greater mental instability.

S5.1.3 Cultural Demonization

At the present time (2011) and on a wider societal level, the growing acceptance of *'spiritual deification techniques'* (especially amongst a generation of creative young people, some of whom will become the opinion-formers of the future) could easily lead to a further *'demonization'* of Western Culture.[142] In such a context, there will be no place for representatives of the one true God. Both Jewish and Christian communities will most likely come under immense pressure to *'accommodate'* (drastically dilute) their faith in order to make it *'fit'* into a thoroughly pagan *'social order.'* By way of a minor digression, it's worth warning that one feature of *'cultural demonization'* is the adoption of an *'elimination mentality'* in which it becomes socially acceptable to eliminate those deemed to be either a *'threat to'* or *'a burden upon'* society.[143] Once this mentality becomes widely adopted the proportion of the population deemed *'fit for elimination'* tends to grow. A momentum for mass extermination is therefore generated and an industry of death is created. Also raised is the *'who...who'* question which asks, *'Who decides who is going to be classified as fit for elimination?'* As the example of Nazi Germany showed such a mentality can create conditions in which the killing of millions is viewed as being normal with mass murder taking place in discreetly hidden locations and on a huge industrial scale.

The above point would suggest that the impact of *'cultural demonization'* is likely to affect not only Jews and Christians but also the elderly and infirm. As environmental and other pressures continue to mount, these vulnerable groups will increasingly be seen as *'unwanted burdens'* to be disposed of in as quick and efficient a manner as possible. As these words were being re-drafted (in February 2010) there was already mounting pressure within the UK to legalise *'assisted suicides'* which, in reality, is euthanasia by the

---

[142] This is a process whereby cultures become gradually dominated by overtly demonic influences. In the Western World this process appears to have been well underway since the mid-1960s, particularly seen in the rise of *'The Drug Culture.'*

[143] At the spiritual level, this is because the devil is by nature a murderer and *"was a murderer from the beginning,"* (John 8:44b). This means that as his grip on a society tightens, large-scale acts of murder will become a matter of routine. Satan will do anything to promote an *'elimination mentality.'* He delights to see the destruction of God's Creation.

back door. On one BBC Radio 4 Programme the words *'burden on society'* were used more than once in connection with the terminally ill[144] and on a *'straw poll'* (conducted on BBC Radio 4s *'Any Questions'*) a very large majority of the audience was in favour of assisted suicide if there could be safeguards.[145] They appeared completely oblivious to the possibility that they were giving their consent to the formation of a mass extermination society. As regards the UK and the USA, the writer wouldn't be at all surprised if the mass murder of millions lay around the corner. The populations within these countries are settling into a mentality willing to accept the large-scale killing of the elderly and disabled as long as it leaves their life-style intact. Like it or not they are developing an *'elimination mentality.'* Any further period of socio-economic and political breakdown could cause things to deteriorate rapidly. What is unacceptable today could easily become acceptable tomorrow. Thanks to modern industrial technology *'assembly line murder'* could all too easily take place, with robots rather than humans performing the task of killing and body disposal.[146] However, (and what may come as something of a shock) those having adopted and carried through such pagan values are likely to find themselves targets too. They will become the hapless victims of the very same values they espoused. Having adopted (or just quietly acquiesced and concurred with) pagan values they will find themselves suffering from the cruelties of those values. Theirs will be a merciless society, one having little or no regard for the finer, more feeling qualities of mercy and compassion. Their position will be akin to that of Communist Party loyalists, purged by Stalin once their use in building up his dictatorship had come to an end. The fate of the vulnerable will ultimately become their fate too. Lying ahead is a brutally savage future. Only those who truly know the Lord Jesus will be able to retain their humanity in the midst of it.

---

[144] *'The Moral Maze,'* Wednesday 3/2/2010
[145] *'Any Questions'* Friday 5/2/2010
[146] The advantages of using robotic technology would be obvious to any global totalitarian state. Problems of management and control would be avoided and such robots could be programmed by computer experts, far removed from any scenes of killing. (This would lessen empathy and the chances of developing a conscience.) It's also likely that any human remains could be re-cycled for environmental purposes, (*e.g.* for animal feed). This scenario is no more implausible than that which culminated in the industrial extermination of Europe's Jewish population. The germination of this diabolical event (which took place from 1933-1945) had its origins in *'The Eugenics Movement'* which arose in response to the rise of Social Darwinism in the late nineteenth century. One should never underestimate the speed at which evil can engulf whole societies.

This point was recognised by the Anglican Monk and liturgical expert Gregory Dix (1901-1952). In the conclusion to his excellent book *'The Shape of the Liturgy'* he made some very helpful observations concerning the issue of deification. Written at a time when the neo-paganism of Nazism was on the rampage they are worth quoting in full – not least because the warning they give is highly relevant for the twenty-first century: -

"The dream of the self-sufficiency of human power has haunted the hearts of all men since it was first whispered that, by slipping from under the trammels of the law of God, 'you shall be as Gods,' choosing your own good and evil," (Genesis 3:5). The shadows of that dream renew themselves continually in fresh shapes, even in the minds and wills of those who serve God's kingship. Where that kingship is unknown or consciously denied that dream rules men who are, in the apostle's terrible phrase 'free from righteousness,' (Romans 6:30). In its crudest form, in the politics of our day, the pagan dream of human power has turned once more into a nightmare, oppressing men's outward lives. That will pass, because it is too violent a disorder to be endured. But elsewhere and less vulgarly, as a mystique of technical and scientific mastery of man's environment, it is swiftly replacing the old materialism as the prevalent anti-Christianity of the twentieth century. In this subtler form it will more secretly, but even more oppress the human spirit.

In the Eucharist we Christians concentrate our motive and act out our theory of human living. Mankind are not to be as Gods, a competing horde of dying rivals to the Living God. We are creatures, fallen and redeemed, His dear recovered sons, who by his free love are made partakers of the Divine nature, (2 Peter 1:4). But our obedience and salvation are not of ourselves, even while we are mysteriously free to disobey and damn ourselves. We are dependent on Him even for our dependence. We are accepted sons in the Son, by the real sacrifice and acceptance of His body and blood, who though He were a Son, yet learned He obedience by the things which He suffered; and being made perfect, He became the author of eternal salvation unto all them that obey Him; called of God an High-priest after the order of Melchisedech, (Hebrews 5:9-10)"[147]

Dix rightly suggested that, the best remedy for any temptation to deification is to be fully devoted to Jesus. Where other faiths offer the

---

[147] Dix p.752

false hope that Man can become God through dint of his own efforts, Christianity offers the real hope that, out of love, God became man for our salvation. His highly pertinent observations also suggest that Western Christians will have to learn what it is like to witness in a culture that's both powerfully seductive and militantly hostile to the gospel. If true followers of Christ are to be effective witnesses they will need to know the extent to which they can and cannot be like God. Each regenerate Christian <u>may enjoy the *'largely'* and *'potentially'* shared divine attributes but what they can never possess, to any significant degree, are the *'barely shared'* attributes.</u> These will remain out of reach for all of eternity. This applies, no matter whether the Christian is a struggling new believer or the greatest saint who has ever lived. Some things can never be obtained, either in this life or the next. It really is no use greedily trying to possess all of God's divine attributes – doing this serves only to repeat Lucifer's original mistake. Instead, Christians may freely marvel in the fact that they can share in some of the very same attributes as their Maker. Theirs is a profound privilege.

Summary

The key points made in this Section were: -

1) To believe in self-deification is to risk falling into the same sin (of spiritual pride) which ruined a powerful angelic being called Lucifer (known as Satan or the Devil). This sin provoked him to want all of God's attributes

2) Lucifer's love became directed inward to *'self'* rather than outward toward God. This encouraged an overweening pride which led him to commit the worst form of idolatry; the actual worship of *'self.'*

3) Lucifer's all-consuming *'self-will'* led him to launch an enormous angelic revolt in which he seduced one-third of all of the angels into joining him

4) Human attempts at self-deification replicate the same sin of pride which caused Lucifer's downfall.

5) Those who believe they can become god-like in nature often end-up behaving like devils, concerned with their own desires. They become thoroughly infatuated with *'self,'* and are unreachable by neither love nor reason. An unhealthy self-infatuation predominates.

6) Growing belief in *'self-deification'* may lead to the *'demonization'* of Western Culture and the adoption of an *'elimination mentality'* wherein it becomes socially acceptable to eliminate Jews, Christians and indeed anyone deemed either a *'threat to'* or *'a burden upon'* society.

7) Western Christians will need to learn how to witness in a culture that's both powerfully seductive and militantly hostile to the gospel. For their witness to be effective, they will need to know the extent to which they can and cannot be like God. In particular, they must accept that, whilst they may enjoy the *'largely'* and *'potentially'* shared attributes of God, they can never possess (to any significant degree) those which are *'barely shared.'* They remain out of reach for all of eternity.

Questions

1) What is deification?

2) Why did Lucifer rebel against God? What were the results of this rebellion?

3) What are the attractions and dangers of believing in deification?

4) How should Christians respond to *'a progressive demonization of their culture?'*

5) Evaluate a mystical teaching which uses Luke 17:21 to claim that becoming a Christian involves discovering and getting in touch with one's *'inner spiritual light'* or *'hidden Christ.'* How does such teaching differ from the biblical view of salvation?

5.2 A Secure and Lasting Friendship

In the area of Christian spirituality, the term *'deification'* has wrought much confusion. To understand it more clearly the concept is best divided into two categories; its *'full'* (or extreme) form and its *'partial'* (or moderate) form. In its former (or full) sense it encourages the erroneous belief that an individual Christian can become so much like God that they are indistinguishable from Him. Through their determined use of such spiritual techniques as prayer and contemplation they believe they can *'ascend to godhood,'* experiencing all of God's divine attributes whilst sacrificing their own distinct human identity in the process. By attempting to make themselves *'divine'* they tend to cease viewing themselves as being merely human. This *'merging'* into the innermost being of God has (in their eyes) led them into believing they are mini-Gods. When they speak or act they believe they can do no wrong because they're convinced that it's God who is speaking or acting from within them. As infallible *'divine beings'* they place themselves above any law and have convinced themselves that they have no need for any organized doctrine to show them the truth. They negate scripture in favour of an imagined and *'fuller'* revelation of their own making. This *'full'* view of deification is especially prevalent within Eastern Religions.

Two chilling examples of this full use of *'deification'* were provided by a representative of the medieval *'Free Spirit'* heresy who claimed, *"The divine essence is my essence and my essence is the divine essence."* This was topped by the boast of another *'Free Spirit'* adherent, who went so far as to state, *"It is the same with me as with Christ, in every way and without exception. Just like him I am eternal life and wisdom, born of the Father in my divine nature; just like him, too, I am born in time and after the way of human beings; and so I am one with him, God and man. All that God has given him he has given me too, and to the same extent."*[148] Hardly surprisingly, both adherents believed they were above any form of law or morality.[149]

Alternatively, *'deification'* may be viewed in its *'partial'* (yet still mistaken) sense to mean a gradual and eventual regaining of the likeness of God, originally lost in *'The Fall.'* Here, Man does not merge into the essence of God, but becomes like Adam was before his fall from grace. Man shares in some of the divine attributes but not in all of them; with an element of distinction always present so that God remains uniquely *'other.'* If *'full deification'* portrays the believer as a bright comet crashing and melting into the sun, its *'partial'* counterpart portrays him/her as a planet orbiting near the sun and enjoying a great deal of its sunlight. Unlike the comet, the planet retains its distinct identity. However, further discussion will show that,

---

[148] These quotes are taken from Cohn (2004) p.173 and form part of an excellent analysis into the self-deification myth (Cohn pp.172-186).

[149] Like their Master, Satan, adherents of the *'Free Spirit'* heresy viewed themselves as being especially *'subtle in spirit,'* (Genesis 3:1). They used this term to distinguish themselves from *'the crude in spirit,'* which they viewed as being foolishly ignorant of their own inner divine potential.

even in this, its partial sense, the use of the term *'deification'* is grossly misleading. It completely overlooks the fact that a more biblical word exists to describe the whole process whereby Christians gradually receive some of the divine attributes and recover the sinless perfection which existed before *'The Fall.'*[150] This more biblical concept will be explored presently.

One example of this partial use of *'deification'* was provided by Bishop Athanasius (c.298-373AD) who (in a treatise *'On The Incarnation'*) stated that *"He* [Jesus] *indeed assumed humanity that we might become God,"* (Mowbray edition p.93). A more literalistic translation by Matthew (2003)[151] would suggest that Athanasius meant that Jesus became *'embedded in the flesh'* so that we might become *'embedded in God.'* Clearly, the terminology implies an extremely close union with God, but not necessarily full deification. Nonetheless, Athanasius would have been wiser to have used a clearer concept in place of the misleading phrase he took from Greek Philosophy.

Athanasius example shows that some degree of confusion and ambiguity has always existed in relation to Christian spirituality, right from its very inception. It's never been clear whether Christian writers have advocated *'full'* or *'partial'* deification or just a simple friendship with God. Generally, the world of Christian spirituality has been a menagerie of profound insight, biblical truth, human custom, psychological delusion and satanic deception.[152] This confusion has arisen, in part from the grafting of pagan thought-forms (most notably Greek philosophy) onto biblical teaching (largely Hebraic in origin). Now, in the twenty-first century, the only way to resolve this problem is to completely reject this alien *'tissue'* (the pagan thought forms)

---

[150] The writer assumes that such perfection is attainable only after death. During this life there always remains an element of sin, ready to ensnare the careless believer in its coils. Whilst exercising an itinerant teaching ministry during the early 1990s, the writer actually preached against the view that *'sinless perfection'* or *'entire sanctification'* is possible in this world. For both biblical and practical reasons, he believes such a view to be utterly unrealistic. It's a false belief which, if adopted, has the potential to be psychologically damaging.

[151] http://www.monachos.net/forum/showthread.php?1949-Athanasius-and-Theosis (accessed Wednesday 10th March 2010)

[152] Experience of Christian spirituality in a variety of church settings has led the writer to conclude that *'mystics'* tend to be either the most discerning or the most deceived of people. Also, in relation to the real Holy Spirit, they're again either open or extremely closed – with the latter possibly following *'another spirit'* altogether and not the Holy Spirit of scripture (2 Corinthians 11:4). In the area of religion, mystics don't do things by half and any conversations with them can be very fascinating or very frustrating.

and begin re-building Christian spirituality along Biblical first century Hebraic lines. In this area the influence of Greek philosophical thinking needs to be totally removed. As Paul's words in Acts 17:28 and Titus 1:12 demonstrate, scripture is well able to stand sturdily and resolutely on its own. Greek philosophy can be legitimately used to illustrate, but never to define the teaching of God's Word.

S5.2.1: A Lack of Biblical Support

The five bible passages which refer to deification are Genesis 3:5, 22-23 (where it's shown to be a temptation from Satan), Psalm 58:1 (which satirises it), Psalm 82 (which openly condemns it), John 10:34 (where irony is used to rebuke a misunderstanding of scripture)[153] and 2 Peter 1:4 which promises that believers will become *'partakers of the divine nature.'* However, the latter could simply mean that the believer shares in some of the attributes of God (the biblical position) or (if Gousmett 2008 is correct) they become *'partners of the deity'* (also an acceptable biblical concept). Although this interpretation of 2 Peter 1:4 raises some linguistic technicalities, it holds more closely to the correct biblical teaching that every believer is in a covenant relationship (partnership) with God.[154] This essentially Hebraic viewpoint is hugely different from the fundamentally pagan concept of *'deification'* which proffers the believer with the opportunity to become some form of deity or *'little god.'* Scripture has never promised this; but instead offers the chance to share in SOME of the divine attributes, the believer becoming an intelligent and covenant partner with God Himself. We are called to enjoy a loving partnership with God but not to embrace His full divinity. In this covenant relationship believers will exercise authority over angels and participate in the running of a perfect new Creation, (1 Corinthians 6:2-3a and Revelation 21:1-4).

The only possible conclusion to draw is that God's Word does not support belief in deification but presents it as a Satanically-inspired lie, encouraging delusions of grandeur and an amoral violence towards perceived enemies. As those with a recognized discernment ministry have pointed out; *"The Bible never says that God made man a god. That was Satan's seductive promise to Eve and it would have been meaningless if Adam and Eve had been created gods,"* (Hunt and McMahon 1986, p.85). It's only possible to use passages like

---

[153] See Hunt and McMahon pp.87-89
[154] www.earlychurch.org.uk/pdf/gousmett/appendix.pdf (retrieved Wednesday 10th March 2010)

Psalm 82, John 10:34 or 2 Peter 1:4 to defend this error by ripping them out of context and twisting their original meaning.[155] The fact that this has been done would confirm that the doctrine of deification represents an illegitimate addition to the teaching of God's Word, (Revelation 22:18). It's therefore hardly surprising that those who would propagate this heresy often unintentionally fulfil the words of Proverbs 30:6, which warn (in fairly strong terms), *"Do not add to God's Words lest he rebukes you and* [events and unfulfilled predictions] *show you to be a liar."*[156] Events in the real world openly belie those who would propagate such outlandish claims and prophecies, mistakenly viewing themselves as somehow being on a par with God and foolishly equating their own words with scripture.[157]

S5.2.2: The Origins of Deification

The full (extreme) and partial (moderate) forms of *'deification'* both share in the same root of Pagan Greek Philosophy. Their obscure, near-unintelligible and above all, grossly misleading meanings were seamlessly imported into Christianity by the Early Church Fathers, most of whom had received a Classical Education. Their fundamental mistake was to have viewed deification as a scriptural concept, when in actual fact it has no grounding in scripture at all. However, as Gousmett (2008) has repeatedly shown, *'deification'* as a descriptive term was frequently in use throughout much of Plato's Philosophical writings. As an everyday term it was accepted by the Early Church Fathers and continued to be propagated, at first by them and then by subsequent Christians throughout Church History. The abundance of citations provided by Gousmett would confirm that (not for the first time) Satan was using Greek Philosophy to sow his tares inside the Church, (Matthew 13:25). With great cunning, he was enticing the venerable *'Fathers'* into repeating the same original sin as Adam – that of accepting a bogus promise of *'deification,'* (Genesis 3:5). Satan's obvious success in doing this would perhaps explain much of the subsequent and long-term unhappy

---

[155] On p.84 Hunt and McMahon quote the American Writer Bill Volkman, who did just this.
[156] This can be seen in their regularly unfulfilled prophecies of revival and in the scandals attaching to some of their ministries
[157] One example being the notorious prophecy of Paul Cain who predicted that revival would break out in Britain in October 1990. The failure of this prophecy did much to discredit the Charismatic *'Signs and Wonders'* advocate John Wimber (1934-1997) who had (despite numerous warnings) supported Paul Cain's spurious prophetic ministry. In reality, Cain was never more than a spiritualist in prophetic clothing. He appeared to have a genius for telling isolated ministers what they wanted to hear.

developments scattered throughout Church History. At the very least, the result has been confusion and muddle and at worst an entry point for wholesale deception. This importation of deification, taken from Platonic Greek Philosophy and placed into the *'pot'* of Christian spirituality has thoroughly poisoned it, causing it to become a vast toxic waste dump, (2 Kings 4:38-41). This totally misleading concept has gradually spread its influence over a large geographical area, contaminating everything in its wake. Because its terminology has always sounded right and scriptural, those propagating it have continued to accept it as an authentically Christian concept. This Platonized form of spirituality has remained unchallenged right until this present time. It's been accepted for so very long that much of what passes for Christian spirituality is simply heading for absorption into a Neo-Pagan One World Order. This may well be the inevitable outcome of a Christianity which has inadvertently and incessantly tried to absorb and blend within itself a burdensome weight of Platonism too. As opposing thought forms they were NEVER meant to blend and even now Christianity needs to discard its Platonic baggage.

'Deification' as a concept is extremely wide-ranging and so easily misleads Christians from very different church traditions. Grasping its meaning is like trying to hold onto a slippery eel. Its advocates may convey the misleading impression that it's being used in its <u>partial</u> sense when in fact it's being used in its <u>fullest</u> (and worst) sense. Gousmett's citations show that some of the writers themselves weren't entirely sure which of the two meanings they were using. Such confusion cannot be of the Holy Spirit, (1 Corinthians 14:33). By allowing themselves to be seduced by this pagan intellectual system (Greek Philosophy), the Church Fathers had allowed themselves to be seduced by the very same temptation Satan had used in Genesis 3:5. (*"You shall be as Gods, knowing the difference between good and evil."*) The Church Fathers' teaching on *'deification'* represents yet another dire muddle for a future generation of Christians to clear up.[158] Whenever and wherever anything to do with deification has been allowed to gain a foothold the simple gospel of Jesus Christ has been lost. Those busying themselves in attempting to become divine <u>have forgotten that Jesus has already done everything needed to bring them into a relationship with God.</u> It's hard not to conclude that much of what passes for *Christian* mysticism today constitutes one enormous distraction,

---

[158] Other muddles have included anti-Semitism, their dismissive attitude toward women and their hierarchical approach to church governance

cleverly devised by Satan. As the authors wife remarked when checking this piece of writing, *"this whole concept of deification represents another of Satan's alluring, anything but Christ (ABC) strategies."*[159] The Christian Church needs to come to terms with the fact that much of what has passed for its *'so-called spirituality'* has been totally misleading. A candid re-assessment of how best to live out the Christian life (at both the individual and community level) is long overdue. There's much rebuilding to be done in the area of spirituality (as well as in the vital area of doctrine). Where necessary, the old structures (previous ways of doing things) must be allowed to drop away in favour of a true re-building of the Christian Faith. What the Church cannot afford to do is to continue living on yesterday's nonsense.

One example of the resultant muddle left behind by the Church Fathers is provided in the following quote, taken from Ware p.28: -
"By virtue of this distinction between the divine essence and the divine energies, we are able to affirm the possibility of a direct or mystical union between man and God – what the Greek Fathers term the theosis of man, his deification – but at the same time we exclude any pantheistic identification of the two: for man participates in the energies of God, not in the essence. There is union, but not fusion or confusion. Although oned with the divine or annihilated, but between him and God there continues always to exist an 'I – Thou relationship' of person to person."

Here, the impression emerges of a well-intentioned author attempting to moderate the harmful effects of a seriously flawed concept. However, what remains again is yet further confused ambiguity – with any clear meaning simply not in evidence. This problem of ambiguity is again present in another of the major sources Ware uses *'The Philokalia'* (an anthology of Eastern Orthodox spiritual writings, dating from the fourth to sixteenth centuries.)[160] It can be seen in the following quote, taken from the first volume of this work: -

"He took upon Himself, becoming what we are, so that we become what He is. The Logos became man, so that man becomes Logos."[161]

---

[159] She said this in May 2010
[160] In fairness, *'The Philokalia'* has some very helpful things to say about spiritual discernment
[161] Philokalia p.155

"The intellect manifests itself in the soul, and nature is the body. The soul is divinized through the intellect, but the nature of the body makes the soul grow slack."[162]

"God...has created all things that man may be saved and deified."[163]

Presented is another offering of turgid muddle! Is a person being *'made like God'* in the sense of receiving His divine *'energies'* or is he being *'made like God'* in his inner and personal nature, (in which case full deification is being referred to)? Surely the sooner the full (and worst) concept of *'deification'* is discarded the better; getting rid of it should become a priority. The cruellest thing about *'deification'* has been its subtle enticement of Christians (over the ages) into pursuing an unattainable ideal. Devout believers, who should have been climbing the ladder Christ had graciously let down for them, have condemned themselves to laboriously clambering-up a self-placed, worm-eaten ladder, [164] ending in a wispy nothingness in the clouds. This misguided seeking for deification has led many Christians into thinking they've received *'something from God'* when, in reality, it's been nothing but a product of their own imagination. Deification has <u>always</u> been a fraudulent concept, often resulting in personal frustration, delusion and even despair. An example is provided in a medieval *'Free Spirit'* tract, wherein a Sister Catherine falls into a deep trance before emerging with the conviction, *"I am made eternal in my eternal blessedness. Christ has made me his equal and I can never lose this condition."*[165] Yet this claim seems modest compared to other female devotees who claimed that they had become greater than God and had such command over the Holy Trinity that they could *'ride it as in a saddle.'*[166] Having placed themselves above Him in status they no longer felt any need of God. Their nonsensical statements revealed that Satan was going out of his way to mock the most dearly held beliefs of the Christian Faith. They also show that deification is attractive because it appeals to human pride. It has a strong *'feel good'* factor about it.

---

[162] Ibid p.349
[163] Ibid p.355
[164] We have no need to climb any ladder of perfection to merit a *'mystical union'* with God. Instead, we receive this *'union'* as a free gift from Christ and only then do we begin to grow spiritually. It's a case of *'a union with God producing a growth in holiness'* rather than *'a growth in holiness meriting a union with God.'*
[165] Cohn p.175
[166] Ibid

Over the long term, the effect of this seriously flawed and unattainable concept has been to reduce Christianity to nothing more than a religious performance. Evidence for this can be seen in the Russian Orthodox Saint, Serafim of Sarov (1759-1833), who advised *"Achieve stillness and thousands around you will find salvation."*[167] The immediate problem here is the failure to perceive that such stillness is <u>not</u> something to be <u>striven after.</u> It is a precious (free) gift to be <u>received</u> by forgiven sinners who, in the spiritual area, can achieve nothing for themselves. Jesus made this point very clear when he left His troubled disciples with the gift of peace, (John 14:25f). He stated quite emphatically *"My peace I give to you,"* (John 14:27b). He did <u>not</u> say *"achieve my peace in order to save souls."* There's the added point that Serafim's concept of peace (what he terms as *'stillness'*) may well have differed entirely from the Biblical notion of peace. The mystical tradition he belonged to would suggest that he was commending a mindless passivity rather than the active wellbeing of the Hebraic understanding of peace. Serafim's background makes it likely that he would have drawn heavily upon the teachings compiled in *'The Philokalia.'*[168]

The evidence provided in such an influential anthology as *'The Philokalia'* would suggest that belief in some form of *'personal deification'* has always been present as an undercurrent within Christian spirituality. As the *'Free Spirit'* heresy has shown the concept of deification has tended to remain discreetly in the background until suddenly bursting forth in utterly bizarre forms during times of great instability, (as in the late Middle Ages and the Reformation era.)[169] It also resurfaced later in the emotional, revivalist forms of Protestantism. The Methodist faith healer John G. Lake (1870-1935) stated, *"Man is not a separate creation detached from God; he is part of God Himself... God intends us to be gods,"*[170] More recently, it has become apparent in the *Word of Faith Movement,* with Kenneth Copeland[171] proclaiming, *"You don't have a*

---

[167] Quoted in MacCulloch (2009) p.546
[168] According to MacCulloch p.546 this work had been translated into the Slavonic by 1793
[169] It was a definite feature in some of the millennial cults of these periods. Cohn's account of the Munster Uprising 1534-5 (in the thirteenth chapter of his book) is especially instructive in this regard
[170] Quoted in Morrison 1994, p.468
[171] When watching a video of Kenneth Copeland unleashing the Toronto Deception at Lakeland, Florida in 1993, the writer was reminded of one of those malign ventriloquist dolls who somehow manage to *'take over'* their owner. Rarely have the powers of darkness been so starkly evidenced; yet judging by their reactions most of the

God in you, you are one"[172] and *"God's reason for creating Adam was His desire to reproduce Himself....he* [Adam] *was not a little like God, he was not almost like God, he was not subordinate to God even."*[173] More blatant than even this was the *father* of the *Word of Faith Movement,* Kenneth Hagin (1917-2003) who stated, *"Man... was created on terms of equality with God and he could stand in God's presence without any consciousness of inferiority.... God has made us as much like Himself as possible.... He made us the same class of being that He is Himself... Man lived in the realm of God, he lived on terms equal with God.... the believer is called Christ... that's who we are; we're Christ."*[174]

These above quotations (taken from some of the most damaging ministries in Evangelical Christianity) confirm that the whole concept of *'deification'* has been (and still is) wide open to abuse. Its innate ambiguity has made it a readily accessible plaything of charlatans who've twisted and verbally manipulated it to mean whatever they've wished it to be. Gullible and undiscerning Christians have been hoodwinked over the ages. However, any so called *'ascent'* into *Godhead* has really only ever been a *'descent'* into the worst forms of badness, madness and even demonization. Those seeking to become divine have often not been very nice individuals – certainly not the sort of person from whom sensible Christians would wish to receive *'ministry.'*

Belief in the concept of *'deification'* has been especially marked in those Churches where Christians have departed from Biblical teaching, opting instead for a preferred *'cultural idol.'* In Ancient Greco-Roman culture one such idol was Greek Philosophy (especially Platonism); whereas now in contemporary Western Culture the current idol is *'Consumer Materialism.'* By nature idolatry is a self-centred activity and this makes it easier for people to entertain over-inflated opinions of themselves and therefore more ready to succumb to the temptation of *'self-deification.'* Having turned away from God, their remaining option has been to make a mini-god of themselves. With no higher object to worship *'self'* has become ruler of all. The devotion which should have been directed toward the one true God has become twisted inward toward *'self.'*

---

audience on the video clearly regarded Copeland as a real man of God. He was treated as some form of charismatic celebrity.
[172] Ibid
[173] Quoted in Hanegraaff p.108
[174] Ibid

Those who would *'deify'* themselves end-up becoming *'lovers of self'* rather than *'lovers of God,'* (2 Timothy 3:2a). An inflated sense of personal entitlement prompts them to become *'lovers of money,'* who greedily purchase the most expensive items in order to *'puff up'* an imaginary status. Hence, belief in *'self-deification'* can strengthen an idolatrous attachment to *'Consumer Materialism.'* The result is the *'Prosperity Preacher'* living in his mansion, complete with air conditioned dog kennels and large golf course. However, the proud, self-reliant attitude of such charlatans is often masked by a cloak of false humility, (2 Corinthians 10:15 & Colossians 2:18-23) – having the *'outward appearance'* of religion but lacking any real spiritual power. Mankind's deepest religious instincts have become perverted – with Man taking centre stage and God being pushed out to the peripheral. In his fallen condition, Man wants to knock God off His throne and take all of His glory. Such spiritual self-centredness would help explain why *'religion'* lies at the centre of much (but not all) evil in human affairs. At its best religion represents Man's attempt to find God and at its worst Man's attempt to <u>become</u> God.

S5.2.3: Conflicting Lines of Reasoning

When looking more closely at Man's relationship to God, two conflicting lines of reasoning jockey for position. The first is Scripturally-based (opposed to the concept of deification) and the second is Platonically-based (and in favour of personal deification): -

Biblical Line of Reasoning	Platonic Line of Reasoning
1. Creation was made by a good Creator	1. Creation was made by an inferior semi-God
2. Creation is basically very good	2. Creation is basically evil
3. Creation is to be enjoyed	3. Creation must be escaped from
4. Salvation is through faith in Jesus	4. Salvation is through mystical enlightenment
5. Salvation involves the resurrection of the body	5. Salvation involves *'freeing'* the soul from ignorance
6. Salvation enhances human individuality	6. Salvation obliterates human individuality
7. Salvation leads to *'partnership with God'*	7. Salvation leads to *'self-deification'*
8. Salvation produces an eternal, loving friendship with God	8. Salvation produces a merging of the *'inner-self into the divine'*

9. Believers can receive <u>some</u> divine attributes as a free gift of grace	**9.** Believers need to work hard to gain all of the divine attributes
10. A distinction between God and Man remains	**10.** A merger occurs between God and Man

What the above Table shows is that *'deification'* derives from a Platonic line of reasoning. This constitutes a part of Greek Philosophy which is a whole network of thinking diametrically opposed to God's Word at every level. The two can never be reconciled and attempts to find compromise between them are futile. Especially noteworthy is its concept of salvation; where divine revelation takes a holistic view of salvation (viewing it as a blessing, involving body, mind and spirit) the man-made philosophy of Platonism views it in hyper-spiritual terms (the *freeing* of the human spirit from the *'inferior realm'* of matter). Importing the Platonic concept of deification into Christianity has been the equivalent of having injected a slow-acting poison into a healthy human body. This is precisely what has taken place within much of Eastern Christianity over the centuries.[175] Western Christians, even now (in their acceptance of unscriptural ways of thinking through deceptions like the *'Word of Faith Movement'*) are repeating this very same mistake. All Copeland and Hagin have done has been to repeat, in albeit very crude terms, much of the teaching of earlier (platonically-based) Christian spiritual writings. It really is the same old poison, minus the Platonic philosophical wrapping.

One further reason why *'deification'* can be such a blasphemous notion is that it assumes that God created creatures so worthless that the only fitting solution was to merge them into His own divine essence. What is implied here is that the Almighty made something of a blunder when He created us as distinct individuals. In response to this one can only exclaim *'poor old God – don't worry, we all make mistakes!'* Completely ignored is the teaching of Genesis 1:31 which stresses that everything God made was originally *'very good.'* It's this original goodness which makes the distinct aspects of our personality worth preserving for all of eternity.[176] Also, the gospel of Christ offers something far better than an absorption into the divine. Christians have eternal life and <u>part of that life involves an enhancement of our God-given individuality</u> which, in the New

---

[175] This was demonstrated by the way it was unable to withstand Islam
[176] Sin entered the world at *'The Fall.'* Only by accepting Christ's work upon the cross can we ever be viewed as *'good'* by God.

Creation, will remain forever – with sin being the only (and major) element having been totally removed from it. In short, far from being merged into God's essence, our individuality will have been perfected through God's grace and <u>not</u> through our own self-effort. We will not have become *'mini-gods'* but will have continued always to be *'sinners saved by grace.'* Perfection is a blessing which only comes to a Christian after they die but it's something they can look forward to with eager anticipation.

It should now be apparent that the term *'deification'* should <u>never</u> have been used at all. If early Christian writers had remained true to biblical terminology then the Church of today would now be in a far healthier condition. It simply <u>never pays to mix pagan concepts with direct biblical teaching.</u> As a body of writers, the Church Fathers were far too enamoured with Greek Philosophy for their own (or anyone else's) good.[177] They left behind a tremendous muddle which Christians are only now beginning to untangle. Moreover, in today's climate of mass spiritual deception the continued use of such a pagan term as *'deification'* gives every appearance of evil, (1 Thessalonians 5:22). By blurring the crucial distinction between biblical and non-biblical (Platonic) thought-forms such terminology reduces Christianity to being just another mystical cult. Biblical thought-forms (through the use of clear scriptural terminology) need to be rediscovered and put into everyday practise. Doing this should help unravel this most confusing of legacies.

S5.2.4: A Biblical Alternative

If the term *'deification'* should be discarded from the life of the Church (and it should) which descriptive term (if any) should be used in its place? One candidate is the Biblical word *'sanctification'*. However, strictly speaking, sanctification refers to the lifelong process whereby sin is restrained and the believer becomes more like Jesus in personal character. The emphasis is very much upon the restraint of sin and the promotion of personal holiness. The term is a correct one but it isn't sufficiently broad enough to describe the

---

[177] This problem partly arose because of the Churches estrangement from its Jewish base. Once detached from its Hebraic roots the only obvious alternative was to re-root itself into its surrounding Greco-Roman culture. Without the Synagogue, *'The Fathers'* had only the Greek Academy to turn to. Tertullian (c.160-220AD) in his *'Apology'* (published in defence of Christianity) was alone in discerning that this development had the potential to create major problems. However, his stance against the philosophical influences emanating from *'Athens'* was completely atypical of his day – his was a lone voice which sadly went unheeded.

process whereby Christians are *"transformed from one degree of glory to another,"* (2 Corinthians 3:18b.) A far better word is *'exaltation'* which allows greater scope for believers to be blessed by God with no reference at all to *'personal deification.'* It also has the definite advantage of being found in such biblical passages as Joshua 13:7, 4:14; 1 Samuel 2:1, I Kings 14:7, Psalm 75:10, 89:17,148:14; Proverbs 4:8, 11:11a; Ezekiel 21:6 Luke 1:52, 2 Corinthians 11:7 and I Peter 5:6. Reference to the wider setting of each of these passages would show that the term is used in connection with the growth in holiness and daily blessing of God's people. It also covers the process in which we come to share some of the divine attributes. In short, where *'sanctification'* refers to one specific area of blessing (growth in personal holiness), *'exaltation'* refers to all the areas in which a Christian is blest, in both this life and the next. *'Exaltation'* includes *'sanctification'* but it's not the equivalent of *'sanctification.'* It is a far wider application.

Through the process of *'exaltation'* Christians are (or will be) blessed: -
- **Spiritually,** with a new capacity to worship God the Father, Son and Holy Spirit
- **Emotionally,** with a new, altruistic *'other-centred'* attitude of self-giving love
- **Mentally,** with a renewed mind, able to understand God's ways
- **Creatively,** with a heightened imagination and originality
- **Personally,** with an ability to grow in individual holiness
- **Physically,** with a new resurrection body that will live forever
- **Relationally,** with a new friendship and ability to engage with God at a deeply personal level
- **Socially,** with a new status, greater than that of angels
- **Eternally,** with a new life that will last forever

In this context, exaltation is a *'holistic'* process wherein God blesses, honours, perfects and befriends (brings into a close relationship with Himself) those who would follow the Lord Jesus Christ. Beneficial changes take place, affecting every aspect of the human personality, *'Exaltation'* begins in the *'here and now,'* reaching its final fulfilment in the afterlife, (1 Corinthians 13:12). The blessings experienced now are only a dim foreshadow of those awaiting us in eternity. *'Exaltation'* entails the reception of some (but not all) of the known attributes of God.

'Exaltation' will also be evidenced in *the New Creation,* where Christians will actually rule over angels (1 Corinthians 6:2-3a and Revelation 20:4a). This will be possible because we'll be so free from sin that nothing will hinder our relationship with God, whose unlimited love will be poured into us. Yet paradoxically, the effect of this love will be not to destroy our individual identity, nor to *'merge us with the divine essence'* but to enable us to relate to God in a deeply personal way forever. Our individuality will be enhanced and made perfect in the Lord Jesus Christ. We will not be exalted into deity – but into a joyful personal friendship and partnership with Almighty God. Daniel 12:3 provides a tantalizingly brief glimpse of what this could mean when it promises that the wise *"shall shine as the brightness of the firmament and they that turn many to righteousness as the stars, forever and ever."* Therefore, the prospect of enjoying a loving relationship with the Father, Son and Holy Spirit is something which should excite every true child of God. We may not become a mini-god but we do become intimate friends with God; exactly how will be shown in the next and final Section of this Chapter.

Summary

The key points made in this Section were: -

1) In the area of Christian spirituality the term *'deification'* has wrought much confusion because: -
1.1 It is an ambiguous and wholly incorrect concept, whether viewed in its *'full'* or its *'partial'* sense
1.2 Leading writers on the topic weren't themselves always clear as to its meaning
1.3 It's often been associated with clumsy and misleading teaching
1.4 It mixes Biblical with Pagan influences
1.5 It feeds and puffs up personal pride
1.6 It encourages exaggerated and boastful claims from deceitful ministries
1.7 Any other terminology associated with it seems only to add further to the confusion

2) God's Word does not support belief in deification but presents it as a Satanically-inspired lie, encouraging only delusions of grandeur and immoral or even violent behaviour.

3) The whole notion of *'deification'* derives from Greek Philosophy and was imported into Christianity by the Early Church Fathers, most of whom had received a Classical Education.

4) Belief in *'deification'* has always been a powerful (though subtle) undercurrent within Christian spirituality.

5) Belief in *'deification'* is particularly apparent within apostate Churches where Christians have departed from Biblical teaching and have chosen instead to follow some form of *'cultural idol.'*

6) Belief in *'deification'* belongs to a whole network of thinking opposed to God's Word. It assumes that God created creatures so worthless that the only fitting solution was to merge them into His own *'divine essence.'*

7) The term *'deification'* should be replaced by the more Biblical term *'exaltation,'* wherein God blesses, honours; perfects and brings the believer into a closer relationship with Himself. This process of *'exaltation'* is characterized by: -
7.1 Beneficial changes taking place at every level of a believer's personality
7.2 Enjoyment of some but <u>not</u> all of the divine attributes
7.3 A joyful and exciting friendship with God
7.4 An elevated status, wherein believers will rule over angels

Questions

1) Explain how belief in *'deification'* has wrought much confusion in the life of the Church.

2) What are the differences between *'deification'* and *'exaltation?'*

3) Why are Christians sometimes deceived by *'deification'* and how can this be corrected?

4) How would you answer the following question; *'Did Jesus affirm the concept of 'deification' in quoting Psalm 82 when debating with His religious enemies,' (John 10: 22-39)*?

5.3 Becoming a Friend of God

Having exposed the folly of deification, a meaningful and clearly defined alternative needs to replace it. The solution lies in the simple yet profound notion of becoming a friend (and maintaining a life-long friendship) with God. However, the following five (seemingly insurmountable) barriers appear to stand implacably in the way of such a friendship: -

1) Limited capacity – by nature Man is a limited creature, incapable of relating to an unlimited Being, whose characteristics far surpass his own at every level, (Isaiah 55:8)

2) Sin – this lies at the heart of every human being. It causes Man to turn away from God and to defy His laws; opting to follow the self-centred road to eternal destruction. Mankind would prefer to continually entertain incorrect and even ridiculous ideas about God rather than admit to being inherently sinful and in need of salvation, (Genesis 3:8-13)

3) God's justified outrage against sin – this provokes God to withdraw His blessings and to inflict His perfectly fair judgements in order to forcibly remove sin, (Romans 1:18)

4) Living in a Fallen Creation – Mankind must continually battle with all of the worlds distracting troubles and pressures which frequently prevent even believers from giving God the full attention He deserves, (Genesis 3:16-19)[178]

5) Satan and his Demons – yes, Satan really does exist and, along with his demons, seeks to exploit every distraction in order to continually steer Humanity away from God, (Mark 1:23-25)[179]

Any one of these barriers would prevent a person from being able to achieve a relationship with God and none can be removed through human effort alone. Each barrier can only ever be effectively dealt with when the Holy Spirit freely chooses to apply the benefits of Christ's crucifixion and resurrection in a particular human life. Without the intervention of God the Holy Spirit each one of the above barriers would remain firmly in place.

Moreover, each one of the above barriers leads inexorably to the same conclusion that, when it comes to relating to God in any positive and meaningful way, *'we do not' 'we cannot,'* and above all, *'we will not.'* Instead, we prefer to follow any and everything else. A

---

[178] This is particularly the case with those struggling to survive on a day-to-day basis
[179] The distraction of *'deification'* being a case in point

selection of bible passages pointing to the utterly ruined condition of humanity include Job 14:4, Psalms 5:4, 51:4-5, Ecclesiastes 7:20-29, Isaiah 48:22, 57:21, 64:6 Jeremiah 15:9-10, Mark 7:15, 20-23, Luke 19:10, John 3:19,Romans 3:10-20, 1 Corinthians 12:2, 2 Corinthians 4:3-4, Ephesians 2:1-3, 12, 4:17-18 and 1 John 3:4. These all show that, without divine intervention, not one person upon earth would, of their own volition, ever choose to be a friend of God. This is because the whole of human nature agitates, squirms and cries out against this possibility. This antagonism is so excessive that humanity could be said to be suffering from *'allergy' to God* syndrome, reacting to Him as badly as any hay fever sufferer would to grass pollen. Hence, when a noisy atheist boasts of his unbelief in God, all He's doing is parading his utter unwillingness to relate to Him. He denies Him because he <u>wants</u> to deny Him. This boastful non-belief reveals more about the atheist's own spiritual state than whether God does or does not exist. Nothing makes an atheist more uncomfortable than a good dose of Christian doctrine, presented in a calm and reasonable manner.[180]

Amongst religious people the main psychological *'stumbling stone'* preventing a true relationship with God is that of self-justification. Its often to be found in a well-disguised personal pride (which Christ Himself exposed as hypocritical during His earthly ministry, Psalm 118:22-23, Isaiah 28:28:16, Matthew 21:42-43, Romans 9:30f). As seen in the example of the Pharisees, religious people waste a great deal of their time in trying to establish their own self-made righteousness. By relying upon their own self-effort, they fail to receive the all-encompassing righteousness freely given through Christ's sacrificial death and resurrection. This desire for self-justification remains the great curse of all religions, not just Christianity. It's likely that Hell is full of tormented souls who damned themselves by trying to earn a right relationship with God through their own self-effort. It's a sobering thought that there may well be far more religious people in hell than there are Atheists! Any attempt to challenge this self-righteousness tends only to meet with a furtive evasiveness or an indignant *'how dare you!'* response. Sadly, there remain those so full of their own self-righteousness that they feel in no need of correction. From their perspective, their way of thinking is the right way and that's that. Only the gracious working of the Holy Spirit could ever deliver these people from the deeply ingrained sin of self-justification.

---

[180] This comment is based upon discussions with atheists at various cultural events from 2008-2010.

On an imaginative and totally speculative note one wonders whether the medieval Italian poet Dante (1265-1321) would have reserved a place in his *'Inferno'* for those trying to put themselves right with God through their own personal efforts. In true medieval fashion he may well have chosen to vividly portray them as determined zealots perpetually climbing excessively long ladders and, upon reaching the top, falling down into a pit full of snakes, refuse and other nasty things. Devils would then haul them out and use pitchforks to force them to climb the very same ladders again. Represented here is a striking and possibly overly-graphic portrayal of the utter futility of personal self-justification. But perhaps Hell does hold a special place of torment for those who would continually try to justify themselves before God. They will have learnt, too late, that their much vaunted *'ladders of perfection'* had been nothing more than *'ladders of corruption,'* leading only to their own eternal condemnation.

Each one of the previously mentioned five barriers represents a near water-tight reason for Mankind <u>never</u> to get to know God in any meaningful, let alone friendly way. *'So how can any of these barriers ever be breached?'* The answer lies in a two-pronged approach; BECOMING A FRIEND OF GOD INVOLVES BOTH A LOSS OF FAITH AND A GAINING OF FAITH. WE NEED TO LOSE FAITH IN OURSELVES AND PLACE OUR FAITH IN CHRIST AS SAVIOUR AND FRIEND. IT REPRESENTS A TOTAL SHIFT FROM US TO GOD. Friendship with God is conditional upon us firstly acknowledging our own abject helplessness and alienation from Him. DISBELIEF IN SELF MUST PRECEDE A REAL BELIEF IN GOD. Christ's words in Matthew 5:3 reiterate this point; *"Blessed are the poor in spirit for theirs is the Kingdom of Heaven."* This personal acknowledgement of spiritual bankruptcy, causing a loss of faith in *'self'* can only ever come about following a work inside the human heart by the Holy Spirit. As the writer's wife noted[181] *"It's the work of the Holy Spirit which directly causes this sense of inner helplessness, whereby we cry out to be saved."* Left to ourselves, we would never allow God to come near us, preferring instead to remain locked forever in denial or slothful apathy. Particularly apt is the statement in Zechariah 4:6 which states, *"Not by might, nor by power, but by my Spirit, says the Lord of Hosts."* Divine grace is needed before we can ever begin to make a favourable response to God; without it we would remain forever trapped in our sin.

---

[181] This was a comment made by my wife in July 2010, written in the margin of a draft copy

This point was supported by Randles (1994) who (after quoting John 3:13) argued that *"God has to intervene, to condescend and save us by His grace. He enters our condition. We are too weak, bankrupt, and empty to save ourselves. We need God. He doesn't need us. One mystery (the lie) exalts us while the other (the truth) humbles us."* Randles made this wise observation whilst arguing against *'the lie'* of deification. He took the view that it appealed to the all too human love of power and control.[182]

Does this all sound too simplistic – surely getting to know God requires some form of religious ritual at the very least? Thankfully *'no,'* for there's absolutely NOTHING that we can ever do which would grant us a right relationship with God – it is Christ's death and resurrection forever, nothing more, nothing less, which forms the solid bedrock upon which rests every Christian life. Ritual plays only a secondary role in helping to mature a relationship with God that has already begun through divine grace. It cannot create that relationship.[183]

S5.3.1: Losing Faith in Ourselves

Becoming a friend of God involves a total loss of faith in our own ability to reach out to Him. It means a complete shedding of the delusion that we can ever merit God's favour by our own self-effort or by looking for a mysterious *'inner spiritual light'* to guide us to Him. What we need to accept is that, in our unregenerate condition, there really is no *'inner light'* within us,[184] but instead, an impenetrable darkness and a hateful antagonism toward God, forever separating us from His love. Seeking an elusive *'inner light'* is the equivalent of looking for warmth from a methane ice lake. From the moment of our conception, sin has been an integral part of our make-up; we are spiritually lacking, unable to see, hear, feel or connect to the living God. Instead, what is present within us is an overwhelming drive to rebel against Him. Our inner moral-spiritual compass is broken – continually set to guide us away from Him, pointing in every direction except the right one.

---

[182] Randles p.51

[183] This point most certainly applies to the rituals recorded in *'The Leeds Liturgy'*

[184] The implication here is that professing Christian organizations like the Quakers (who believe in an *'inner light'*) are living and practising their faith in a state of delusion. Given this flawed spiritual framework it's easy to see how Quakerism has slipped into a *'believe what you like'* mentality and moved off into an interfaith direction too.

Our *'inner waywardness'* is all too readily seen in a whole range of supposedly Christian Web Sites, each advocating what, in effect, is a form of eastern spirituality. Often characterized by a rarefied language,[185] their emphasis tends to be very much upon *'authenticating oneself'* or obtaining *'self-realization'* by getting into contact with the god (or goddess) within. This is supposedly achieved by tapping into one's *'latent creativity'* or through engaging in a lengthy process of psychotherapy or indulging in imaginative forms of play.[186] The aim is to obtain *'personal wholeness'* or *'integration.'* Very little, if anything is said about the need to repent of one's sins and to receive a life-changing relationship with God through Jesus Christ. Instead, the emphasis is wholly upon self-fulfilment. Equally absent is any systematic application of scripture, which is usurped instead by a whole array of spiritual and psychological techniques. These may include meditative practices drawn from Jungian Psychology,[187] Buddhism and Hinduism.

Conveniently ignored is the fact that in our *'fallen'* condition, our response (if any) to the concept of God is mostly one of revulsion or leaden apathy which, in some cases, may be moderated by a superficial intellectual interest. We have no desire to obey His commandments unless we perceive some form of selfish gain in them. Hence, a person may outwardly avoid committing particular sins (*i.e.* adultery) only because of the fear of unpleasant consequences (like being horse-whipped by an angry husband.) However, this sin may still be committed every night in their dreams. It's a case of obeying God's law for the wrong reasons. Although such nominal obedience may prevent some of the troubles caused by outward acts of sin (and at a social level that's better than nothing) it can never please God nor make us acceptable to Him. It's a case of sin repressed rather than sin removed.

---

[185] A cynic would state that such language was specifically designed to entice gullible members of the middle classes to part with their money.

[186] In one case, the proposed method consisted of exploring fairy tales in order to create our own *'personal tale'* to assist us in our *'life journey.'* Upon reading this nonsense the writer couldn't help but exclaim, *"Well, they're certainly away with the fairies!"* It was a matter of having to laugh otherwise he would have cried.

[187] The Swiss psychiatrist Carl Jung (1875-1961) was steeped in the occult. He owed some of his teachings to an evil spirit mimicking the early second century Gnostic Teacher, Basilides. Sadly, the writer has come across so-called Christian Ministries which rely heavily upon a Jungian approach in pastoral matters. Personally, the writer couldn't think of a more toxic influence. Jung was also known for his repeated extra-marital affairs with women, some of whom had been his patients.

Being selfishly motivated means that we try to relate to God through our own good deeds, religious practices or attempts at self-improvement. All of this is done in a vain attempt to please Him and to *'earn our way to Heaven.'* These self-serving efforts represent broken bridges, attempting to reach an all-seeing God whose utter holiness means that His response <u>will always be one of complete rejection.</u> These futile attempts to justify ourselves simply mask the fact that, at every single level of our being, we are thoroughly estranged from our Maker. We can <u>never</u> merit (nor earn) His favour because our relationship toward Him is one of unremitting antagonism. This point is highlighted in the following meditation, entitled, *'Lost':* -

In terms of inner spirituality
We cannot communicate with God
In terms of subconscious instinct
We violently recoil from God
In terms of creative imagination
We manufacture idols to replace God
In terms of passionate desire
We strongly disdain God
In terms of deeply felt emotions
We fervently dislike God
In terms of personal motivation
We lack any inner drive to follow God
In terms of rational intellect
We are unable to understand God
In terms of individual volition
We wilfully choose to reject God
In terms of language construction
We frequently mock God
In terms of interactive sociability
We prefer to ignore God
In terms of religious devotion
We try to justify ourselves before God
In terms of outward application
We use any activity to avoid God
In terms of personal relationships
We are the enemies of God
In terms of eternal destiny
We will remain forever separated from God[188]

---

[188] *'Lost'* was originally drafted from some prose and was written in early May 2010.

The above grim meditation shows that, as fallen human beings, we lack both the ability and the desire to know and love the one true God as revealed in scripture. Every fibre of our being rebels against Him and we disdainfully toss His laws aside, preferring instead to follow our own flawed values. Left to ourselves, the possibility of redemption doesn't even remotely exist. Our plight is aptly summarised in the following witty, yet meaningful *'memory-jogger'*: -

We are revolting sinners
Who are both revolted by and
Endlessly in revolt against God
Who, in His holiness
Finds us utterly revolting!

This extremely silly saying demonstrates that we need a radical overhaul of our entire being. Our old corrupt nature needs to be replaced completely otherwise our eternal doom is inevitable. It will be a case of *'Hell is our fate because we don't have God as our mate.'* Such a radical replacement can only ever be initiated and achieved by God. We have no capacity whatsoever within ourselves to do this; it really is a matter of grace – as my wife likes to say; *"Its grace at the beginning, grace in the middle and grace at the end."* Miraculous divine intervention is the only solution to provide this brand new nature and to rescue us from Hell.

As the next sub-section will explain, Christ's death upon the cross is that specific miraculous intervention. His death and resurrection are the means whereby we can be completely forgiven and graciously offered a new regenerate nature (which then immediately begins to counter the effects of our hereditary rebelliousness). To fully appropriate these benefits the Holy Spirit first works in our hearts to cause us to become aware of the utter dreadfulness of our own inner nature. Before this we were *'dead in our trespasses and sins,'* (Ephesians 2:1b) unaware of our inner rebelliousness and utter depravity before God. We were without hope and *'without God in this world.'* (Ephesians 2:12b).This paring away of our inner nature takes place either gradually or suddenly but always with the aim of driving us to repentance. We become aware of the heartfelt conviction and emotionally distressing realization that we are indeed lost sinners, rightly under God's wrath and whose deserved destination is hell. This whole process of stark inner illumination can be psychologically mortifying[189] and may take place either before or after a profession of faith in Jesus Christ.[190] However, such a trauma <u>needs to take place</u> because we are resolutely stubborn and utterly incapable of changing our own fundamental nature.[191] We need to become fully aware of the horror of our sinful condition before being willing to accept a remedy. In His loving severity God smashes the idols in our hearts so that we can begin to want Christ.[192] A clear and unambiguous revelation of sin is needed to cause us to lose faith in ourselves and to begin to gain faith by looking to Jesus for our salvation. Such a revelation can be a horrific and sobering experience, which thankfully may have the beneficial effect of destroying that fatal self-reliance wherein we smugly presumed that *'we were alright as we are'* or *'we could get to God by our own efforts.'* The bad news of sin goes hand in hand with the good news of salvation. As the writer's wife has noted; *"For a robust Christian*

---

[189] In my case, it took place on Friday, 22nd October 1976 in a polytechnic library in Newcastle-Upon-Tyne, England. This was just over a year after my sudden conversion to Christ in a Christian Union prayer meeting on Saturday, 18th October 1975.

[190] With me, the mortification was so great that I staggered out from the above-mentioned library in a state of shock. I was too numbed to cry. For the next three days, I hovered on the brink of insanity and didn't know what I was doing or saying. Yet, through it all, there was a mysterious inner strength that just about kept me together. I didn't make a full recovery until March of the following year. An awareness of my lost condition had been triggered by my having read Erickson's *'Young Luther'* where I'd seen striking similarities between his personality and my own. I'd experienced a very traumatic summer when, as a voluntary social worker, I'd been working amongst drug addicts (including a white witch and heroin user) in Notting Hill, London. Also, I'd been physically attacked by an evil spirit on Holy Island on Monday, 6th September 1976, (followed by severe poltergeist activity in the same location two evenings later.) Only God's grace had brought me through such an awful time. Now, in April 2011 I still remember it all as if it were only yesterday.

[191] This isn't to deny that, under God's common grace people may *'improve themselves'* by acquiring new skills, better habits and even more *'positive'* ways of thinking. However, they are still incapable of altering by *'one single degree'* their fundamental problem of inner sinfulness which directly causes rebellion and alienation from God. In evangelism, it may sometimes be appropriate to deal with the more distracting outward problems caused by a specific personal sin (like alcohol abuse) before even beginning to deal with the fundamental problem of inborn sinfulness by sharing the gospel. The Salvation Army understood this when following a policy of *'first getting a drunkard sober and then preaching the gospel to him.'* Conversely, there are certainly times where the opposite approach is the one most needed. In such cases, the fundamental problem of sin has first to be dealt with before there can be any alleviation of outward symptoms. The Holy Spirit's wisdom is required to discern which of these approaches is the most appropriate to a particular situation, (James 1:5).

[192] He also begins to unravel the confusion in our minds so that we can begin to perceive Christ

life the one must always precede the other."¹⁹³ Christians need to grasp the concept that the Holy Spirit is both a destroyer and a creator of faith. He destroys whatever faith we have placed in ourselves so that we can have faith in His Son, Jesus Christ. <u>Radical disbelief must occur before true belief.</u> Our role is to cooperate with this process and not to resist it; yet even such a limited co-operation is possible only because the Holy Spirit has already begun exposing the sin in our hearts. It's only AFTER He has stirred on our conscience that we become aware that we need to make a personal stark choice regarding Christ – whether to follow Him or remain in our sin. Without this inner and stirring work of exposing our sin we would forever remain resolutely on our own, <u>always</u> preferring to choose the other option than that provided by Christ. Our inner restlessness and turmoil can only ever be stilled by Christ's forgiveness. Hence, our inner will is not so much like impervious stone¹⁹⁴ but rather like a wild horse, bucking and kicking to throw off its rider unless first tamed (or *'broken in'*) by God the Holy Spirit. Only then does the concept of free will come into play. It really is a case of accepting or rejecting Christ – it's as simple as that. It is the Holy Spirits work upon our innermost conscience that makes any preaching of the gospel a meaningful exercise.

This need to lose faith in oneself is highlighted in the following parable, entitled; *'Touching the Clouds'.*¹⁹⁵

On a pleasantly warm day a man looked up to the sky, really wishing he could touch the clouds floating so high above his head. In fact so obsessed was he that he tried using a step ladder and searching out his arms as far as he could. However, the clouds still remained far out above him. Then he tried using a succession of ever taller ladders – resulting in nothing but frustration. Finally, he grabbed hold of the tallest ladder he could find – so tall in fact that his friends had to steady it at the bottom. Up and up and up the ladder he climbed, higher and higher until, sweating and exhausted, he neared the top.

---

[193] Made in an editorial comment on Monday, 2ⁿᵈ August 2010
[194] This somewhat inadequate analogy (of our wills being as hard as impervious stone) has been overused by Calvinists when defending the doctrine of predestination (which teaches that God chooses to select only a few people for salvation).
[195] It was first drafted in early December 2009, when in correspondence with a very pleasant and devout Roman Catholic who had mystical leanings. Having held a conversation with him (on the evening of Saturday, 1ˢᵗ August 2009) he'd described himself as an *'Eastern Orthodox Neo-Platonist.'* My short and rather blunt reply was, *'Well, you're stuffed!'* After my sudden outburst he graciously gave me a rather wan smile and we spent the remainder of the evening amicably discussing literature.

Once there he again stretched out his arms but still the clouds evaded him, appearing no closer than before. Suddenly, the ladder snapped in two and the man tumbled down to earth, his fall thankfully broken by a large mound of manure. His many friends looked on with consternation (and half-hidden smiles) as he emerged from the pungent heap, looking rather bemused.

A few days later this same man, by now very disconsolate and bruised, decided to take a pleasant walk along a meandering river bank. Suddenly the weather changed and a mist rapidly descended. With no effort at all on his part he found himself completely enveloped in a cloud. He could touch and feel the moisture on His skin as he smiled to himself – realizing that that all of his previous efforts had been totally unnecessary.[196]

Implicit in this parable is the suggestion that Church History has been dominated by a prolonged struggle between two conflicting views of salvation.[197] One is the *'Man-centred'* view which minimises the role of the Almighty, emphasising Man's attempt to bribe his way to Heaven through his own good works, correct performance of ritual or by climbing some mystical *'ladder of perfection.'* However, in complete contrast to this stands the *'God-centred'* view which honours and maximises the role of the Almighty by showing that the entrance to His Kingdom is only ever possible through a miraculous work of divine grace, wrought in the human heart and mind. Entrance to heaven is not earned but received (like the descending mist in the parable) as a free gift from God. Should the first view prevail the Church is wholly apostate and totally out of step with the teaching of scripture. However, should the second view prevail the Church is being faithful to biblical teaching and may even be enjoying a revival. A stark contrast exists between a religious Christian who attempts to justify himself before God and a truly regenerate Christian who is secure in the belief that Christ has (through His work upon the cross) already justified him, with the result that all of his past, present and future sins have been totally forgiven. Holding to the latter belief can do much to engender a healthy peace of mind.

---

[196] Ironically, after preparing this parable, the writer managed to touch some clouds during an arduous climb up Ben Nevis with his youngest son on Tuesday, 10th August 2010. It was a *'once in a lifetime experience'* with the emphasis being on the word *'once!'* (Located outside Fort William, Scotland, Ben Nevis stands at 4,504 feet and is Britain's highest mountain. In the original Gaelic, it perhaps meant *'Terrible Mountain.'*)

[197] This conflict was particularly intense during The Reformation Era (1517-1660) and The Evangelical Revival (1738-1860)

To re-cap, the very first step in becoming a friend of God is to lose faith in ourselves, in any idolatrous substitute for Him and in our own capacity to please God by our own self-effort (whether big or small). We need to realize that, in His infinite holiness, God will <u>never</u> accept us *'just as we are,'* mired in our own sin.[198] To believe that is to be deceived. God's stance toward unregenerate sinners is one of total rejection and this must be so if His holiness is to be upheld and the moral order of Creation preserved.[199] Far from *'accepting us just as we are'* He *'rejects us just as we are'* <u>until we place our faith in Christ.</u> Vital though this first step of *'losing faith in ourselves'* is, it can never, by itself, redeem us. To remain stuck in this position (of having lost faith in oneself) leads only to an embittered and despairing loss of hope; the next (and most decisively important) step is to receive and retain a real faith in God and His Son, Jesus Christ. *"It must <u>always</u> be a case of us turning away from ourselves <u>and</u> subsequently <u>turning to</u> Christ. Without the Holy Spirit working in our hearts we would consistently and continually turn inward to self. The Holy Spirit <u>always leads us to Christ</u> and it's at this point that we either accept or reject Him."*[200]

S.5.3.2: Receiving Faith in Christ

Strictly speaking, the term *'gaining faith'* is misleading. This is because it implies a striving to obtain something from God through our own efforts. In reality, all we can do as empty-handed sinners is to humbly RECEIVE the faith that God freely offers to us. It's only ever possible to approach God as a destitute beggar, hoping to receive a mercy we do not deserve. By this stage, it's possible to further qualify the earlier statement by asserting that BECOMING A FRIEND OF GOD INVOLVES BOTH A COMPLETE LOSS OF FAITH IN OURSELVES AND A HUMBLE RECEPTION OF A SAVING FAITH IN CHRIST, THROUGH THE AGENCY OF THE HOLY SPIRIT. Thanks to the secret operations of divine grace, the faith which had once been directed inward, attempting to feed one's own imagined spiritual potential is now directed outward toward God and His Son, Jesus Christ. Through this process we become God-

---

[198] Refuted here is the erroneous cliché that *'God accepts/affirms/loves/takes us just as we are.'*

[199] There's the added point that if divine holiness is not upheld then God would cease to be perfect and therefore cease to be divine and therefore unable to control the evil in Creation. Such a feeble deity couldn't be respected.

[200] The writer's wife, in an inserted comment, Wednesday, 21st July 2010, underlining in the original

centred rather than self-centred. To receive God's gift of saving faith we need to choose to place our entire confidence in the fact that: -

Motivated by an incredible love
God freely chose
A particular moment in human history
To send his only begotten Son
To become a perfect Jewish man
In order to offer
A perfect sacrifice for our sins
Accomplishing what we could <u>never</u> do
And opening the way for us to enjoy
A wonderful personal relationship
With God as our Father and Friend

In short, the only remedy for the human predicament is Jesus Christ. *"There is no other name under heaven, given among men, through which we are saved,"* (Acts 4:12b). To believe otherwise is to risk committing spiritual suicide. Its either Jesus or eternal damnation; the choice is as stark as that.

However, when we do believe in Christ, we find that His work upon the cross ensures that <u>all of our sins are completely forgiven and the way cleared for the Holy Spirit to regenerate our hearts and to give us a new God-centred nature.</u> The result is that we are *'born again from above,'* (John 3:3). The hitherto dead spiritual side of us comes alive as if a light bulb were suddenly switched on. We find ourselves relating to God directly and, over time, we grow increasingly sensitive to His will. Through this spiritual *'re-birth,'* we become *a 'new creation,'* (2 Corinthians 5:17a), and our naturally self-centred will begins to freely co-operate with God, (John 8:32). In short, having faith in Jesus Christ involves us believing in the gospel narrative as outlined in John 3:16-18. This famous passage reveals that: -

"God so loved the world that He gave his only begotten Son, that whosoever believes in Him should not perish, but receives everlasting life. For God sent not his Son into the world to condemn the world; but that the world through Him might be saved. He who believes on Him is not condemned: but he who does not believe is condemned already, because he has not believed in the name of the only begotten Son of God."

If we believe that the above narrative is true and applies to us then we have also received the faith God has given us. It's as simple as that! *'Believing faith'* is equated with *'belief in the gospel story'* as told in scripture. We trust in its content, believing that Jesus is our Lord and saviour who died for our sins before rising bodily from the dead three days later. Through this faith we are given a new God-centred nature, the characteristics of which are summed up in the following meditation, entitled *'Found'*: -

In terms of inner spirituality
We receive the guidance of God
In terms of subconscious instinct
We hunger after God
In terms of creative imagination
We submit our fantasies to God
In terms of passionate desire
We are strongly attracted to God
In terms of deeply felt emotions
We fervently love God
In terms of personal motivation
We have an inner drive to follow God
In terms of rational intellect
We are able to understand God
In terms of language construction
We frequently praise God
In terms of individual volition
We willingly accept God
In terms of interactive sociability
We personally engage with God
In terms of religious devotion
We praise Jesus for justifying us before God
In terms of outward application
We centre our activities upon God
In terms of personal relationships
We are friends with God
In terms of eternal destiny
We will remain forever united to God[201]

Belief in the gospel message doesn't mean that we become perfect overnight (or even over the course of an entire lifetime) but it does give us the opportunity to grow into the positive qualities outlined in

---

[201] This meditation was produced at the same time as *'Lost'* and was originally meant to follow it.

the above meditation. We need no longer be self-centred, conditioned by our flawed heredity or sin-ridden environments; instead we are adopted children of God, enjoying the freedom to love and serve Him. Thanks to the intervention of divine grace, free will becomes a glorious reality. Above all, we are delivered from the frustrating nightmare of trying to please God through our own efforts. Thus we can see that Christ died, not only to save us from sin, but to save us from dead religiosity[202] and the cruel bondage it can bring.[203]

However, receiving the gift of faith involves far more than an intellectual assent or a positive emotional response to the gospel message (although good and valid in themselves). What it really amounts to is a <u>wholehearted belief in the gospel narrative and a humble dependence upon the Lord Jesus Christ as our only source of salvation.</u> The Christian could be likened to someone in a blazing building, reading the instructions in a safety manual and then following them in order to make a safe escape. This analogy suggests that faith must be followed by faithful obedience if it's to be effective in changing lives. Consequently, through faith we must learn TO TRUST JESUS ENOUGH TO DEPEND UPON HIM ENTIRELY FOR EVERYTHING, FOR THE REST OF OUR LIVES. Through this faith, WE ALSO TRUST HIM ENOUGH TO OBEY HIM ENTIRELY, IN EVERYTHING. So faith leads quite naturally to a dependent, faithful obedience (faithfulness) which helps us to grow into the people we would have been if there had been no sin. Where the world equates freedom with a self-centred autonomy, Christianity equates it with a Christ-centred obedience to God's will. Present are two conflicting ideas of freedom. The world will constantly deny that true freedom is to be found in the service of the God of Scripture. However, as already stated, being busy in the work of God helps

---

[202] In this discussion, the term *'religion'* is equated with any futile attempt to relate to God (or to some other supposed spiritual reality) through our own self-effort.

[203] Atheists are not altogether wrong to point out that religion is indeed a source of many evils. This is because its *'works orientated'* approach to salvation imposes a tremendous burden upon people, who are expected (often by tyrannical leaders) to obey impossible standards. Man-made religions make the path to God appear very hard and uncertain because of their reliance upon rules, elaborate rituals and/or mind-emptying meditative techniques. This constant striving may generate acute psychological frustrations and inner tensions which sometimes find release through acts of violence *i.e.* a pogrom against a despised minority who act as a convenient scapegoat for these frustrations. Essentially, religion is about human performance, designed to earn divine favour. In contrast, the gospel involves accepting that, <u>through Jesus Christ, God has done everything needed in order to bring us into a relationship with Himself.</u> There is <u>nothing</u> we can do to improve upon this work.

curb sin and frees us up to be the people we ought to be. We are liberated from sin and released into grace.

Especially during times of affliction Christians must cling to Jesus as never before. Their situation may well be likened to that of storm-tossed sailors clinging onto a well supplied life raft in a shark-infested sea in the dead of night. Theirs is a complete dependence upon Him for everything, including the need to make difficult decisions in response to the stresses of living in a fallen world. We may depend upon Him to give us the wisdom needed to make the right decisions that bring honour to Him and benefit others, (James 1:5). This confirms the earlier point that faith quite naturally leads to faithfulness. Indeed, these characteristics are so closely intertwined that where one is present the other is also.[204] They are mutually and inseparably bonded.[205] Moreover, as we depend upon Christ we find that He in turn is utterly dependable in fulfilling all of the unconditional promises of Scripture. He limits temptation or grants the wisdom needed to take a difficult decision, (1 Corinthians 10:13 & James 1:5). He also judges false teachers by giving them over to the folly of their ways, (Jude 4-16). His utter trustworthiness engenders the confidence to turn prayer from being a ritualistic or meditative practice into a time when we can directly encounter and enjoy the presence of our Maker. We listen to and speak with Him in a deeply intimate way.

---

[204] In the original Hebrew and Greek the biblical words for *'faith'* and *'faithfulness'* are used interchangeably

[205] One problem with *'easy decision'* evangelism was that it tried to separate the two qualities of *'faith'* and *'faithfulness'* by suggesting that it was possible to *'accept Jesus as saviour'* by faith and then to decide at a later date whether or not to *'obey Him as Lord'* which would (so displaying *'faithfulness'* to His will). Motivated by a desire to make Christianity popular and relevant such evangelism resulted in many superficial professions of faith that simply didn't last. Emanating from America, this essentially man-centred form of evangelism was often encountered by the writer during his Pentecostal days in the late 1970s. At worst, it led people into mistakenly thinking they were Christians when they weren't. Also, it adopted worldly ways of handling things, *i.e.* emotional pressure and business selling techniques in place of the Holy Spirit's work of bringing people to Christ. The result was that any *'conversions'* were spurious with no real inward life-changes ever taking place. Some of those brought into the Church in this way later became heretical leaders, championing such deceptions as the Toronto Experience. The superficial preaching associated with this type of evangelism encouraged the notion that *"God loves me just as I am and that's enough for me – I can live as I like."* Since the 1950's the long term effect of this wholly erroneous stance has been a collapse in doctrinal and behavioural standards. As a Muslim once said to me in late 2001, *"Christians seem to think they can believe and behave in any way they like and still call themselves a Christian. There's no discipline."* The writer could only agree with that observation.

Furthermore, the Holy Spirit's work of regenerating our hearts ensures a complete reversal of priorities. This point is demonstrated in the following meditation, entitled *'Reversing Humanity'*: -

Where once we believed in ourselves and not in God
Now we believe in God and not in ourselves
Where once we displayed pride and we scorned humility
Now we display humility and scorn pride
Where once we followed lies and despised the truth
Now we follow the truth and despise lies
Where once we had Satan as our father and not God
Now we have God as our Father and not Satan
Where once we loved sin and hated Jesus
Now we love Jesus and hate sin
Where once we relied upon self-help and not on God's help
Now we rely upon God's help and not on self-help
Where once we followed demons and not the Holy Spirit
Now we follow the Holy Spirit and not demons
Where once we rejoiced in vice and rejected virtue
Now we rejoice in virtue and reject vice
Where once we trusted in our 'spiritual potential' and not divine grace
Now we trust in divine grace and not our 'spiritual potential'
Where once we happily disobeyed God's laws
Now we are happy to obey them
Where once we were rebels and not followers
Now we are followers and not rebels
Where once we were religious and not righteous
Now we are righteous and not religious
Where once we were heading for Hell and not Heaven
Now we are heading for Heaven and not Hell

All these 'reversals' occur because of God's almighty power, Alleluia!

One further paradox is that Christ's sacrificial death upon the cross represented a divine *'crossing out'* of <u>all</u> religious and non-religious *'alternatives.'* When nailed to the cross Jesus showed an unbelieving world that He was the <u>ONLY</u> way to knowing God and to receiving His salvation, (John 14:6). The crucifixion represented God's great *'no'* to all man-made religious and philosophical systems, showing them to be a lie (or at best a half truth).[206] They were completely

---

[206] The mockery Christ endured from religious people during His Passion shows how man-made religiosity is so sharply antagonistic to God. It rejects the real way of salvation in favour of its own false man-made religious edifice.

delegitimized (robbed of any rightful authority and claim to obedience). This, in part, explains why representatives of every other belief system will unite together to conspire against Christians, no matter how much these representatives may despise and hate one another.[207] This is because they are aware (albeit in a vague yet instinctive way) that the presence of faithful Christian believers challenges and even threatens the validity of their own belief systems. Their position within the particular system (alongside any political or socio-economic privileges associated with it) is suddenly exposed and called into question. When it comes to worldly belief systems Christianity can be the most subversive of faiths; receiving Jesus into one's life denies the validity of every other belief system. It says a definite *'yes'* to God and a just as definite *'no'* to any supposed alternative. When it comes to believing in gods outside of the biblical revelation Christians can be the most stubborn of atheists.[208] Such a stance is unlikely to be tolerated in a world increasingly committed to pursuing an interfaith agenda.[209]

Christ's death was also a divine retort, a definite *'no'* to all spiritual self-help books.[210] His death did not take place as part of some plan

---

[207] A contemporary example is the tacit alliance between Secular Leftists and Militant Islamists, both united in their wish to eradicate both Israel and Christianity. The writer came across one web site where there was clear collaboration between American white supremacists and radical Muslims. Their strained attempts to be polite to one another were wryly amusing.

[208] Roman persecutors of the Early Church understood this point all too well, singling Christians out as *'atheists'* because of their disbelief in the old gods.

[209] Should a *'Global Order'* be built upon this agenda then the inevitable result will be an attempt to eradicate Biblical Christianity from the face of the earth because of its unwillingness to conform. This is simply because Christianity stands alone – Christ being the ONLY means of salvation – there is no other way. Consequently, there can never be a uniting of true Christianity with other religions. A respect for other ways of life and the many and varied cultures in the world *'yes,'* but the adoption of non-Christian religions associated with those cultures, *'no.'* A revived Biblical Christianity will never wish to accept the legitimacy of a *'One World Religion.'* Intoxicated by a lust for power, the leaders of such a *'Global Order'* will have no other option but to try and destroy bible-based forms of Christianity if they wish to pursue a policy of uniting the world's population under the banner of a *'One World Religion.'* Christians will return to the perilous position they occupied within the early Roman Empire, (which also included martyrdom). This is not to deny that a false (possibly nominal) form of Christianity may well appear to do very well under a New Global Order – even assuming the status of an *'official'* religion. If this happens it could be the deception that would *'lead astray the elect if this were possible,'* (Matthew 24:24).

[210] When dealing with secular issues, the better type of *'self-help'* books can certainly be of use, for the children of this world are often shrewder in their dealings with people than are the children of light, (Luke 16:8b). As long as the advice given broadly conforms to scriptural values and norms it may be accepted. However, a great deal of junk does exist in this area and many so-called self-help books are best left unread.

to enable an individual to fulfil his or her own *'spiritual potential.'* Far from it, Christianity views people as being *'dead in trespasses and sins'* before a new life is discovered in Christ. Fully applicable are the words of Paul in Ephesians 2:1, *"And you He has made alive who were dead through trespasses and sins."* By dying in abject helplessness Jesus exposed the folly of human pride and refuted the hollow promise that we can *"become gods, knowing the difference between good and evil,"* (Genesis 3:5). Instead, (as has often been stated) what we can definitely enjoy is eternal friendship with God. Truly, *'we shall be known as He is known,'* (1 Corinthians 13:12) and our rejoicing in divine goodness will never cease. So, because (and only because) of Christ's work upon the Cross: -

We come to know God as our friend
By losing faith in ourselves and
By exercising a saving faith in Christ
Through the work of the Holy Spirit

This *'saving faith'* <u>always points us to Christ</u> in whom we place our complete confidence, knowing He has dealt fully with our sin. As we continue to faithfully believe this we are liberated to enjoy freedom from sin's tyranny and from the bondage of man-made religiosity. In the end, it boils down to applying the promise of Romans 10:9, which states, *"If you confess with your mouth that Jesus is Lord and believe in your heart that God raised Him from the dead, you <u>shall</u> be saved."*

S5.3.3: Application

Should the reader wish to apply the points made in this chapter he/she may find the following prayer useful, either spoken out loud or silently: -

Dear God
Relying upon your strength alone
I renounce anything that goes against your will
I abandon faith in my own ability
To please you or to merit your favour
Through either good deeds or religious activities
I renounce as false any idea
That lying dormant within me
Is an 'inner light' or 'spark'
That can relate to you.

In particular, I reject as being thoroughly deceptive
The delusion that I can become divine
Or share in all of your attributes;
Instead, I am a lost sinner
Whose relationship with you is dominated by
Antagonism, misunderstanding and rejection;
Your perfection means that
You will not accept me 'just as I am'
In this state of sin
I am separated from your love and
Am heading for a lost eternity –
Where, with the devil and his angels (Matthew 25:41)
I shall endure the full fury of your righteous anger
In a never-ending Hell

Yet, dear God
You have not abandoned me to sin
But you sent your only Son to die on my behalf
Offering a perfect sacrifice which
Allowed my many sins to be forgiven

Depending once again upon your strength
I affirm my belief in the Gospel narrative
As told in your scripture

In response to this
I willingly invite Jesus into my life
To be my Saviour, Lord and God
He has the full right to be obeyed in everything

Please forgive all of my sin and
Take up residence in my heart and mind;
You are very welcome

I also ask you, dear God
To send your Holy Spirit
To regenerate my dead spirit
And to give me a new nature
That can relate to you as Father
Rather than as Judge

In response to your love,
I commend myself to your daily care

I commit my life to you
I pledge my loyalty to you
Thank you Jesus for allowing me
To become a true friend of God, Amen

Summary

The key points made in this Section were: -

1) The following five barriers prevent human beings from enjoying friendship with God: -
1.1 Limited ability
1.2 Personal sin
1.3 God's rejection of sin
1.4 The distractions of living in a fallen Creation
1.5 Satan and his demons

2) Getting to know God as a friend involves losing faith in ourselves and gaining faith in Christ

3) Losing faith in ourselves involves: -
3.1 Shedding the delusion that we can merit God's favour by our own self-effort
3.2 No longer believing that, within ourselves, lies an inner *'spiritual light,'* able to relate to the divine
3.3 Honestly admitting our complete incapacity to please God
3.4 Realizing that, at every level of our being, we are thoroughly antagonistic to our Maker
3.5 Acknowledging that our ingrained sinful nature needs a miraculous remedy

4) Christ's death upon the cross ensured forgiveness for our sin and a new regenerate nature to counter its ill-effect in our lives. However, to appropriate such benefits the Holy Spirit may give us a discomfiting revelation of our own personal inner corruption, either before or after a profession of faith in Christ.

5) Receiving a *'saving faith'* in Christ involves: -
5.1 Exercising a freedom of choice to believe (or not) that God sent His Son to die for our sin
5.2 Trusting that Christ's death and resurrection secured the complete forgiveness of our sins

5.3 The once dead spiritual side of us now coming alive, enabling us to communicate with God
5.4 Receiving a new God-centred nature
5.5 The freeing of our wills from the bondage of sin
5.6 Fully committing our lives to Him

6) Where the world equates freedom with a self-centred autonomy, Christianity equates freedom with a Christ-centred obedience to God's will.

7) Christ's sacrificial death upon the cross confirmed that God has: -
7.1 Rejected all man-made religions and philosophies
7.2 Humbled human pride
7.3 Exposed the false promise of deification
7.4 Designated His Son as the ONLY means of salvation; no other alternative is valid
7.5 Shown that faith and faithfulness are indivisible

Questions

1) What prevents people from knowing God?

2) Why do we need *'to lose faith in ourselves'* in order to become a friend of God? Explain why such a loss of faith can be psychologically traumatic.

3) Explain how it's possible to place a saving faith in Christ. Outline the benefits of this faith.

4) Comment on the statement; *'True freedom is to be found only through obedience to Christ.'* How does this view of freedom differ from that offered by the World?

5) Is Romans 10:9 a good text to use when sharing the gospel with an honest enquirer from a non-Christian background? How is its meaning best explained?

OVERVIEW

At the close of this study, it seems reasonable to conclude that: -
- The divine attributes and names of God reveal important details concerning His character
- God responds to the sin of apostasy in ways which reflect His character
- God's known attributes were put on public display during Christ's Crucifixion

Knowing more about God's character feeds a healthy speculation – believers gradually learn more of what God is really like and the ways in which He relates to this world. Such knowledge can only further stretch the mind and encourage correct thinking along biblical lines. A greater understanding of God's attributes also inspires worship and practical action in the service of others. All manner of *'good fruits'* invariably result. (Some are found listed in **Appendix 1**).

A Good Basis

Knowing what God is like provides a good basis for effective Christian living. The attributes should always inspire celebration and a thoughtful speculation, encouraging believers to apply biblical teaching in their everyday lives.[211] Familiarity with these noble attributes should form an essential foundation to the Christian life and not just an *'optional extra'* to it. The most constructive way to respond to their existence is to adopt the following five-stage progression: -

Examination – using only scripture to examine God and His attributes

Speculation – using scripture and human reasoning to speculate what God is doing in the *'here and now'*

Contemplation – using scripture and a thoughtful silence to contemplate the nature of God[212]

---

[211] The assumption is that God is best served when the believer possesses a clear picture of who He really is. As the accelerating decline of Western Christianity has shown, muddled thinking leads only to muddled worship and muddled living.

[212] Such contemplation represents an application of Psalm 46:10a. This bible-based meditation is not to be confused with its eastern counterpart – the latter seeks to empty the mind and encourage a state of spiritual passivity. The effect of this is to open up the mind to malign spiritual agencies

Celebration – using scripture and any helpful worship resources to celebrate God
Application – using scripture and common sense wisdom to apply the knowledge of God in daily life
(These stages can be summarised under the heading of *'ESCCA.'*)

In this context, it's perhaps wise to heed the following exhortation, entitled *'Let'*: -

Let the character of God be shown in your lives
Let His holiness be shown in your conduct
Let His love be shown in your deeds
Let His Holy-Love permeate every area of your being[213]

God's many and varied attributes should also act as a focal point for specific acts of worship. As **Section 28** of *'The Leeds Liturgy'* has demonstrated, one attribute could be acknowledged each week.[214] Also, at the beginning of each year a congregation could run through all of the attributes, with the worship leader calling out the name and the congregation reverently responding with the definition. This would greatly assist in any individual and corporate contemplation of the divine nature. Participants would receive a clear reminder of who God is and of what He's like. *'The 52 Attributes of God'* was never intended solely as an object of academic study. It was always meant to be naturally integrated into private and public worship – so spilling over into everyday life. It's only at such times that God's attributes take on a real and tangible role. They were never meant to be *'closeted away'* and *'aired'* each Sunday. His attributes are a wonderful resource for which we can be hugely thankful each and every day of the week.

The ease with which it's possible to convert a theology of divine attributes into liturgical form is demonstrated in the following example which draws on material from the bullet point list on **p.249** of this book. (In this example *'P1'* stands for *'Presiding Participant'* or *'worship leader'* and *'P2'* for *'Other People'* or *'Congregation.'*)

P1: Rejoice! Through the process of *'exaltation'* we receive many blessings

---

[213] This meditation was written on Saturday, 30th October 2004. The main theme is the need to reflect God's character in every area of our lives.
[214] *'The Leeds Liturgy'* **Sections 15** and **28:1** (December 2010 edition)

P2: Spiritually, we are blest with a new capacity to worship God the Father, Son and Holy Spirit

P1: Emotionally, we are blest with a new attitude of self-giving love towards others

P2: Mentally, we are blest with a renewed mind, now enabled to understand God's ways

P1: Creatively, we are blest with a heightened imagination and problem solving ability

P2: Personally, we are blest with a growth in individual holiness

P1: Physically, we are blest with a perfect new resurrection body, designed for a new Creation

P2: Relationally, we are blest with a new friendship and an ability to engage with God at a deeply personal level

P1: Socially, we are blest with a new status, greater than that of the angels

P2: Eternally, we are blest with a new life that will last forever

The above example demonstrates that liturgies can legitimately be used as a vehicle whereby Christians may interact with Biblical doctrines they would otherwise find forbidding if confined to reading theological textbooks alone. Using a liturgy can make the teaching of scripture both pertinent and real.[215]

In order to progress in the areas outlined by **'ESCCA,'** it's helpful to remember that each divine name listed in **Appendix 2** reveals something about the character and practical work of God; a clearer idea of His various roles is portrayed by His names. He is shown to be both majestic and awesome and actively involved in promoting the welfare of His people. His greatness does not distance Him from them, but allows for an even closer relationship. Although these divine names can be used in private and public worship they must never be viewed as: -

---

[215] A detailed (and thoroughly biblical) defence of the use of liturgies in Christian worship is made in the article *'Why Liturgies?'* A copy of this article has been placed on the writer's web site and can also be found in **Appendix 1** of *'The Leeds Liturgy.'*

- Endless mantras (repetitive, mindless chants)
- Superstitious charms to ward-off evil spirits, invoke angelic powers or to manipulate the supernatural
- A means of smuggling in (usually anti-Trinitarian) false doctrine[216]

When used wisely, these Biblical names of God can account for much blessing in prayer, bringing the believer nearer to the source of their faith. At the very least, they focus our attention upon God our Creator.

An Impossible Division

With regard to *'deification'* both the discussion in the previous chapter and the analysis of **Appendix 3** show that, whilst people may share <u>some</u> divine characteristics (attributes) they can <u>never</u> enjoy all of them. *'Partial Deification'* is possible but *'Complete Deification'* is not. To deny this limitation is to heed the serpent's enticing lie, *'you shall be as gods,'* (Genesis 3:5c.) However, even the term *'Partial Deification'* is itself misleading; a better and more descriptive word would be *'exaltation,'* wherein God is seen as graciously edifying those who would faithfully serve Him. Through this process of *'exaltation'* regenerate Christian believers may increasingly display the *'potentially shared'* as well as the *'largely shared'* attributes of God. Using the word *'exaltation'* in place of *'deification'* has the advantage of acknowledging the all-important distinction between God the <u>Creator</u> and His <u>created</u> human beings.

However, should God be continually regarded as having little or nothing in common with people then He tends, inevitably, to be viewed as someone far removed from His Creation. The notion that such a God could reveal or communicate His will would also seem incongruous. Such a view by-passes the teaching of Genesis 1:26-27 which shows that *'Man'* was created in *'God's image'* or *'likeness,'* – thus suggesting that God created Man to share in some of His attributes and making possible a personal relationship between the two parties.

Furthermore, it's worth stressing that <u>all of the divine attributes are equally present in God to an unlimited degree.</u> Consequently, it's misleading to assume that some attributes are <u>more</u> prevalent in

---

[216] This appears to be the case with *'The Sacred Name Movement'* in America which lays great stress upon using the Hebrew names for *'God'* and *'Jesus.'*

God than others. My book *'The Phantom Conflict'* will demonstrate that considerable dangers arise when attributes like holiness and love are viewed as being somehow greater than any other divine attributes. This leads only to an imbalance in both the corporate and individual lives of God's people. Attention should be paid to the wise caution of Grudem (1994) who stated, *"We would not want to say that these attributes are only characteristic of some part of God, but rather they are characteristic of God himself and therefore characteristic of all of God."*[217] He then proceeded to demonstrate that *"God's being is not a collection of attributes added together;"* nor do His attributes represent *"additions to His real Being."*[218] Rather, they are qualities that permeate the whole being of God to an unlimited degree. This means that, where one attribute is present, so too are all the others. Therefore, such divine character traits as holiness and love (or wrath and mercy) are to be seen as wholly inseparable.

The same also applies to the *'barely-shared'* attributes like *'divine immanence'* and *'divine transcendence.'* God is simultaneously everywhere within Creation, but He also occupies a countless number of *'heights'* which lie above and beyond the created order. There is no limit to how far He can go, travel into infinity and God will still be there undiminished in His power, glory and love. We can truly praise Him *'in the heights,'* (Psalm 148:1).

All of this would suggest that any attempt to divide God's attributes is like trying to divide the heat and light of the sun – it just can't be done! Instead, the very best solution is to allow these attributes to inspire both celebration and holy living. Our *'knowledge of the Holy'* is always to be applied in our daily lives. To be more aware of His attributes can surely only enhance the Christian life. They lend greater clarity concerning many things, including wisdom, truth and love.

Psychologically, a relationship with God enables His Holy Spirit to throw His light into the secret recesses of our personalities. Areas of sin are exposed and are either skimmed away or at least contained. On a more positive note, we begin to see that we've been given gifts that can be used to help others in our local church and community setting. We're no longer in darkness about our innermost sinful self. By *'knowing God'* we can also come to know ourselves and learn to

---

[217] Systematic Theology p.178
[218] Ibid, pp.178-9

trust Him as our Lord, Saviour and guide. Greater personal maturity is assuredly one of the positive results of this process.

The Harmony of Attributes

In the end, it's possible to conclude that God is able to harmoniously combine many apparently opposite attributes because: -
- Being all-loving, He has the motive to prevent any inner conflict
- Being all-powerful, He has the power to prevent any inner conflict
- Being all-perfect, He cannot, by His very nature have any conflict within Himself

(God may well have other, still unknown attributes which directly sustain the harmony present between each of the known attributes.)

Clearly, God is not at war within Himself. Any apparent hostility between His different attributes exists only within the minds of unbelievers or those immature in the faith. The basic harmony between all of the attributes was demonstrated at the crucifixion where they were clearly and publicly displayed. It is a gross mistake to view the crucifixion as a desperate attempt by God to reconcile apparently opposing divine attributes like justice and mercy. In brief, a perfect harmony exists between all of God's attributes.

Overall, any celebration of the divine attributes should inspire: -
1) Quiet thoughtfulness, as God's true nature is revealed perhaps for the first time
2) A sense of awe and heartfelt reverence for God
3) Humility and a greater sense of dependence upon God
4) Heartfelt worship, due to a fresh appreciation of who God is
5) Greater confidence that God can and does answer prayer
6) A sense of security and quiet calm because of the greatness of God – knowing that He is in control of everything
7) Obedience, because God is not to be trifled with, in either attitude or action
8) Evangelism, because a correct view of God is held and can therefore be proclaimed
9) A love for God – which is the most appropriate response to God's love for us
10) A willingness to serve others, because God cares about every aspect of people's lives

It's hoped that having completed *'The 52 Attributes of God'* the reader will feel inspired to continue in the knowledge and love of God (as displayed in all of His divine characteristics). Should this knowledge be lacking, it can be received through placing one's faith in Jesus Christ and the work He did on the cross. What the Christian author A. W. Tozer called *'The Knowledge of the Holy'* is freely available to all those who genuinely want it. When it does become available, the reader will discover that the divine attributes represent a life-changing reality rather than a piece of abstract theology.

Questions

1) Why should greater knowledge of the divine attributes form an integral part of public worship?

2) Why is it dangerous to emphasise one divine attribute at the expense of others?

3) How is it possible to show *'the character of God'* in our lives?

4) How can we tell whether people have allowed God's *'Holy-Love'* to influence their lives?

5) What's the most appropriate response to a young Christian claiming to love God but finding biblical doctrine *'boring and irrelevant?'*

APPENDICES
TABLES AND BIBLE SUMMARIES

"Humility is usually an older person's virtue. Young people are often too full of themselves to see the need for it."[219]

---

[219] The author, Thursday 13 January 2000

A1: BIBLICAL SUMMARY

Shaded rows with bold lettering denote those passages commented upon by the writer either in this book or its sequel *'The Phantom Conflict.'*

The scriptures teach that divine oneness (or unity): -

#	Description	Book	Ref
1	Was revealed to Moses	Ex	3:14
2	**Excludes the possibility of following other Gods**		**20:3**
3	Is shown by the title *'The Lord'*	Le	16:8
4	Is proclaimed in the first *'Creedal statement'* of scripture	De	6:4
5	Is highlighted by the singular *'I am He'*		32:39
6	Emphasises God's uniqueness	1K	8:23
7	Should exclude consultation with other gods	2K	2:16
8	Can be recognised by more enlightened pagans		5:15
9	Is mocked by Godless pagans	2C	32:15
10	Inspires prayer and worship	Ne	9:6
11	Was highlighted by the Lord's dialogue with Satan	Job	1:7
12	Is denied by fools	Ps	14:1
13	Encourages a joyful unity amongst believers		133:1
14	Encourages a sense of reverence	Ec	12:13
15	Excludes polytheism (the belief in many Gods)	Is	43:10
16	Denies the very existence of the gods followed by other religions		44:6
17	Excludes deification (the belief that people can ascend to Godhood)	Ezk	28:9
18	Implies there can only ever be one Saviour	Ho	13:4
19	Indicates that God is *the Lord of* [angelic] *hosts*	Mal	4:3

#	Description	Book	Ref
20	Was publicly confirmed by Jesus Christ	Mk	12:29
21	**Implies that worship is to be *'in spirit and in truth'***	**Jn**	**4:24**
22	Shows that, *'it is one God who shall justify by faith'*	Rom	3:30
23	Prompts Christians to *'keep the unity of the Spirit in the bond of peace'*	Ep	4:3
24	Is expressly shown by the title; *'one God'*		6
25	Promotes *'the unity of faith'*		13
26	Encourages those believers engaged in spiritual warfare		6:10
27	Highlights the need for *'one mediator between God and Man'*	1Tim	2:5
28	Guards against spiritual complacency	Jam	2:19
29	Is a cause for angelic celebration	Rev	4:11

For further Bible references to the divine *oneness* of God please refer to a Concordance and look up the words, *'God,' 'against God,' 'High God'* and the title *'Lord'*

The scriptures teach that divine holiness (or purity): -

1	Keeps God separate and distant from humanity	Ex	3:5
2	Destroys those people who try to approach God by their own efforts		19:21
3	Prevents both people & priests from ascending to God		24
4	Requires that someone in a *'Priestly Office'* make atonement for sin	Lev	17:32
5	Is proclaimed by God		21:8
6	Warns that Gods holy name is not to be profaned		22:2
7	**Motivates the divine jealousy that punishes sin**	**Jos**	**24:19**
8	Demonstrates that, *'There is none as holy as the Lord'*	1S	2:2
9	Brings awareness of the gulf existing between a *'holy God'* and humanity		6:20
10	Encourages worshipping Jews to *'glory in His holy name'*	1Ch	16:10
11	Incites worshipping Jews to *'give thanks to* [His] *holy name'*		35
12	Prompts the Lord to save David, *'His anointed King,'* from trouble	Ps	20:6
13	Can be acknowledged during times of great suffering and rejection		22:3
14	Provokes a joyful trust in His Holy Name		33:21
15	**Should inspire people to praise Gods *'Great and terrible name'***		**99:3**
16	Can promote an exultant worship, *'for He is holy'*		5
17	**Highlights the fact that *'The Lord our God is holy'***		**9**
18	Enables people to *'Bless His holy Name'*		103:1
19	Realises the hope of redemption from evil		111:9
20	Confirms that *'The Lord is holy in all His works'*		145:17
21	Exhorts *'all flesh* [to] *bless His holy Name forever'*		21
22	Proclaims that *'the knowledge of the holy* [Lord] *is understanding'*	Pr	9:9
23	Exposes human ignorance on spiritual matters		30:3
24	Expresses itself in righteous judgements	Is	5:16
25	**Provokes endless angelic worship directed toward God Himself**		**6:3**
26	Is displayed by Gods almighty power		52:10
27	Can indwell those of *'a contrite and humble spirit'*		57:10
28	Confronts the idolatry of those who rebel against Gods holy name	Ezk	20:39
29	Leads God to oppose those who discredit His name amongst the heathen		36:20
30	Allows God to take pity on His people		21
31	Provokes compassion for a wayward people		22
32	Means that both Jews and Gentiles will know that God is holy		39:7
33	Means that Israel will no longer defile Gods holy Name		43:7
34	Means that to defile Gods holy name is to provoke divine anger		8
35	Is defiled by both social injustice and sexual immorality	Am	2:7

36 Causes Christians to know when to refrain from being *'holier than thou'*	Mt	7:6
37 Secures the goodness of God	**Mk**	**10:18**
38 Allowed Mary to declare *'Holy is His Name'*	Lu	1:49
39 Causes Jesus to pray to His *'Holy Father'* for the safety of His disciples	Joh	17:11
40 Is displayed by the outpouring of Gods Holy Spirit	Acts	2:4
41 Is highlighted by the Spirit of holiness	Rom	1:4
42 Is to be reflected in the lives of congregational elders and deacons	Ti	1:8
43 Exhorts people to build themselves up in their *'most holy faith'*	Jude	20
44 Is continually celebrated by the highest-ranking angels in heaven	**Rev**	**4:8**

For further Bible references please refer to a Concordance and look up the words, *'Holy Ghost,' 'Holy Spirit,' 'Holy Name,'* and *'Holy One of Israel'*

The scriptures teach that divine love (or compassion): -

1 Motivated Gods selection of the Israelites to be His people	De	7:7
2 Bestows many blessings		7:13
3 Will lead to the eventual restoration of Israel into a place of blessing		30:3
4 Inspires prayer	1K	8:50
5 Turns away divine anger from a disobedient people	**2K**	**13:23**
6 Inspires God to deliver people from a variety of perils	Ps	91:14
7 Leads to a godly reverence		103:18
8 Causes God to comfort Israel	Is	43:4
9 Is shown by Gods pity for afflicted people		**63:9**
10 Never fails	La	3:22
11 Is revealed in Gods pity for His people Israel	Joel	2:18
12 Is revealed in Gods pity for the pagans of Nineveh	Jon	4:11
13 Will subdue our iniquities by working in our hearts	Mic	7:19
14 Prompts God to rejoice over His people with singing	**Zep**	**3:17**

15 Was expressed in the care given by Jesus to needy individuals	Mt		9:22
16 Was expressed in the care given by Jesus to a needy multitude			15:32
17 Motivated Jesus to heal the blind and the lame			21:14
18 Motivated Jesus to warn His disciples against deception			24:4
19 Motivated Jesus to cast out demons	Mk		1:34
20 Motivated Jesus to heal the deaf and dumb			7:37
21 Is to be expressed in humble service			10:43
22 Was highlighted by the parable of the prodigal son	Lu		15:20
23 Was shown by God the Father in sending His Son, Jesus, into the World	Joh		3:16
24 Rebukes religious people who do not have Gods love in them			5:42
25 Emphasises the responsibility of all believers to abide in God's love			15:10
26 Can be poured into the hearts of believers	**Rom**		**5:5**
27 Was shown in the manner in which Jesus died for sinners			:8
28 Allows nothing to separate it from believers			8:34
29 Is selectively revealed to believers			9:15
30 Can inspire the wording of specific prayers	2Co		13:14
31 Directs our hearts into *the love of God*	2Th		3:5
32 Was manifested through Jesus Christ	Ti		3:4
33 *'Can have compassion on the ignorant'* who are unaware of the truth	Heb		5:2
34 Can be demonstrated through the love Christians show for one another	1Pet		3:8
35 Is shown by those who *'keep His word'*	1Joh		2:5
36 Had its ultimate manifestation in the death of Jesus			3:16
37 Should prompt Christians to show compassion for the poor			:17
38 By definition, is one of the attributes of God			**4:8**
39 Was proven by God sending His Son *'into the World so that we may live'* in Him			:9
40 Gives Christians a responsibility to *'love one another'*			4:12
41 Leads believers to keep Gods commandments			5:3
42 Exhorts Christians to keep themselves *'in the love of God'*	**Jude**		**:21**
43 Highlights the need for compassion to be shown in disagreements			:22
44 Emphasises that Jesus should be the *'first love'* of every Church	Rev		2:4

For further Bible references please refer to a Concordance and look up the words, *'compassion,' 'loving' 'kindness'* and *'mercy'*

The scriptures teach that Gods almighty power: -

1 Was proclaimed by the Lord Himself	Ge	17:1
2 Shows that nothing is too hard for God		18:14
3 Causes people to be 'fruitful and multiply'		28:3
4 Created whole Nations		35:11
5 Enables God to appear to people		48:3
6 Gives people the many different 'blessings of heaven'		49:25
7 Was revealed to Moses		6:3
8 Can be experienced in a vision	Nu	24:4
9 Can be acknowledged during times of personal failure	Ru	1:20
10 May be mistakenly perceived as a source of affliction by suffering people		:21
11 Can be mistakenly feared by ill and depressed people	Job	6:4
12 Means that God is to be *feared* (held in reverent awe)		:14
13 Is never misused to pervert justice		8:3
14 Should inspire people to seek God		:6
15 Is needed if people are to find God in their lives		11:7
16 Creates a hunger to know God		13:3
17 Makes it impossible for people to win any dispute with God		15:25
18 Can be doubted during times of affliction		21:15
19 May be manifested in divine anger		:20
20 Can make God seem remote from human affairs		22:3
21 Is questioned by doubters		:17
22 Gives an incentive to repentance		22:23
23 Defends people and may bring financial prosperity		:25
24 Uses affliction to soften people's hearts		23:16
25 Is not always acknowledged		24:1
26 Can be a source of vexation to the distressed		27:2
27 Inspires heated debate		:10
28 Leads to a desire to teach others about God		:11
29 Overthrows wicked oppressors		:13
30 Means that 'the voice of the Lord is powerful'		29:4
31 Raises questions		:5
32 Is sorely missed when it seems absent		31:2
33 Gives understanding of spiritual things		31:35
34 Excludes any possibility that God 'should commit iniquity'		34:10
35 Excludes any possibility that God 'should pervert judgement'		:12
36 Means that God 'will not hear vanity' in a person's prayer life		35:13
37 Is beyond human comprehension		37:23
38 Rebukes those who persistently argue with God		40:2
39 Scatters Kings	Ps	68:4
40 Provides a place of shelter for those who trust in God		91:1
41 Brings anguish to the godless	Is	13:6
42 Is openly proclaimed through divine prophecy	Je	32:27
43 Can be emphasised in a dramatic manner	Ezk	1:24
44 Enables God to speak to humanity		10:5

45 Can bring destruction	Joel	1:15
46 Will, during the Day of Judgement, forcibly remove *'all that do wickedly'*	Mal	4:1

47 Is manifested in the scriptures	Mt	12:24
48 Can amaze people	Lu	9:43
49 Was acknowledged by Jesus when on trial for His life		22:69
50 Was displayed by the Holy Spirit who gave the disciples power to witness	Acts	1:8
51 Was claimed by an evil sorcerer		8:10
52 Is shown when salvation takes place through the *'Gospel of Christ'*	Rom	1:16
53 Is revealed in *'the preaching of the cross'*	1Co	1:18
54 Is shown to those who are called by God		24
55 Makes true faith possible		2:5
56 Sustains a ministry in the midst of great suffering or persecution	2Co	6:7
57 Allows God to act as a Father to His people		6:18
58 Strengthens weak saints during times of affliction		13:4
59 Enables persecuted Christians to accept affliction	2Tim	1:8
60 Is shown in the convicting power of God's Word, the Scriptures	Heb	4:12
61 Can be restrained by divine patience shown toward sinners	1Pet	2:9
62 Is linked to other divine attributes, including eternal existence	Rev	1:8
63 Is a source of heavenly thanksgiving		11:17
64 Inspires singing in Heaven		15:3
65 Gives *'true and righteous judgements'*		7
66 Is opposed by Satan's demons		16:14
67 Will be expressed when Christ rules the nations with *'a rod of iron'*		19:15
68 Will be fully displayed in the *'New Jerusalem'*		21:22

For further Bible references please refer to a Concordance and look up the words, *'mighty,' 'power,' 'strength'* or *'thy strength.'*

Highlighted in these summaries is the fact that holiness and love are two equally important characteristics of God, neither of which should be ignored. Both attributes markedly influence God's conduct toward the human race

A2: THE EIGHTY-EIGHT NAMES OF GOD

Divine Name	Meaning of Divine Name	Reference	
1. Adhonai teshu athi	Oh Lord, my salvation	Ps	38:22
2. Adon	Lord, Master or Judge	Ge	18:32
3. Adonai	My almighty Ruler and Judge	Ex	4:1
4. Agape*	Compassionate, self-giving God of love	1Jn	4:8
5. Apokalupsis	Sudden disclosure or dramatic revelation	Re	1:1
6. Apseudes Theos*	Never-lying God (or the God that cannot lie)	Ti	1:2
7. Christos*	The anointed Saviour	Mt	16:16
8. Echad	Complex or compound oneness	De	6:4
9. El	High God, first Deity, or pre-eminent Lord	Nu	23:19
10. El abhikha	The God of your fathers	Ge	49:25
11. El elohe haruchoth lekhol basar	God of the angels and God of all flesh	Nu	16:22
12. El elohe-Yisrael	God, the God (or Creator) of Israel	Ge	33:20
13. El elyon	God most High	Ps	78:56
14. El olam	The everlasting God, or God from everlasting	Ge	21:33
15. El chai	The living God	Ho	1:10
16. El de oth	God of knowledge	1Sa	2:3
17. El em unah	God of faithfulness	De	32:4
18. El emeth	God of truth, or faithful God	Ps	31:5
19. El gadol venora	The great and terrible God	De	7:21
20. El gemuloth	God of recompense	Je	51:56
21. El gibbor	The mighty God	Is	9:6
22. El hakkabhodh	God of glory or God the glorious	Ps	29:3
23. El neqamoth	God of vengeance	Ps	94:1
24. El ohenu	Our God	2Ki	18:22
25. El rachum vechannum	Compassionate (merciful) and gracious God	Ex	34:6
26. El roi	God all-seeing or the God who sees	Ge	16:13
27. El shaddai	God almighty, or God all-powerful	Ge	17:1
28. El simchath gili	God, my exceeding joy	Ps	43:4
29. El ya aqobh	The God of Jacob	Ps	146:5
30. El yesuhrun	God of Jeshurun (Israel)	De	33:26
31. El yeshu athi	God is my Salvation	Is	12:2
32. El Yhwh vayya er lanu	God is the Lord who shows us the light	Ps	118:27
33. El yisra el	God of Israel	1Ch	4:10
34. Elah	Majestic God	Ez	4:24
35. Eli	My God	Ps	22:1
36. Eli attah	You are my God	Is	44:17
37. Eli malki	My God and King	Ps	68:24
38. Eli tsuri	God my rock	Ps	18:2

39. Eloah	The awesome, majestic, righteous God	De	32:6
40. Eloah selichoth	God of forgiveness	Neh	9:17
41. Elohe Amen	God of truth	Is	65:16
42. Elohe ma uzzi	God in whom I take refuge	Ps	43:2
43. Elohe mesrachoq	God who is not distant or afar off	Jer	23:23
44. Elohe mishpat	God of justice or of judgement	Mal	2:17
45. Elohe thehilathi	God of my praise	Ps	109:1
46. Elohim (Plural of Eloah)	Awesome, majestic, righteous Gods	Ge	1:1
47. Elohim chai	Living God (or Gods)	Is	37:17
48. Elohim gadhol	Great God (or Gods)	Ps	95:3
49. Elohim marom	God on high	Mic	6:6
50. Elohim mistatter	Hiding God (or Gods)	Is	45:15
51. Elohim neeman	Faithful God (or Gods)	De	7:9
52. Elohim nose	Forgiving God (or Gods)	Ps	99:8
53. Elohim noqem	Avenging God (or Gods)	Na	1:2
54. Elohim qanna	Jealous God (or Gods)	Ex	20:5
55. Elohim qedhoshim	Holy God (or Gods)	Jos	24:19
56. Elohim qerobhim	God (or Gods) who is near	De	4:7
57. Elohim rachum	Merciful (or compassionate) God (or Gods)	De	4:31
58. Elohim rachum vechannun	Merciful and gracious God (or Gods)	Ex	34:6
59. Elohim tsaddiq	Righteous God (Gods)	Ps	7:9
60. Elohim tsaddiq umoshia	The righteous God (or Gods) and Saviour	Is	45:21
61. Elohim zo em	Angry, indignant God (or Gods)	Ps	7:11
62. Emmanuel	God with us	Is	7:14
63. Ha el yeshu athenu	God is our salvation	Ps	68:19
64. Kurios*	Lord, Sir or revered Master	Rev	22:5
65. Logos	Creative Word (or Intelligent Reason)	Jn	1:1
66. Pneuma*	Spirit or breath	Jn	4:24
67. Soter*	A Saviour who actively delivers from peril	Lu	2:11
68. Theodidaktos*	God-taught or God-teaching	1Th	4:9
69. Theos Soter*	God our Saviour or preserver	Ti	3:4
70. Theios*	Godhead or that which is divine	Acts	17:29
71. Theos*	God to be worshipped	Mt	12:4
72. Theotes*	Godhead, Divinity or Deity	Rom	1:20
73. Tsur	A rock	De	32:15
74. Yeshua (Jesus)	The Lord is my Saviour (or salvation)	Joh	6:43
75. Yhwh (pronounced Yahweh)	Absolute, self-existent, enduring Lord God and Master	Ex	15:2
76. Yhwh El Gemolah	The Lord Most High or God our recompense	Je	51:56

77. Yhwh Elohim	The Lord, the mighty One (or Ones)	Jud	5:3
78. Yhwh Maccaddeshem	The Lord your sanctifier (or giver of purity)	Ex	31:13
79. Yhwh Nakeh	The Lord who smites	Ezk	7:9
80. Yhwh Sabbaoth	The Lord of (angelic and human) hosts	1sa	1:3
81. Yhwh Tsebha oth	The Lord of vast (angelic and human) hosts	Is	48:2
82. Yhwh-Nissi	The Lord is my banner or refuge	Ex	17:15
83. Yhwh-Raah	The Lord is my shepherd	Ps	23:1
84. Yhwh-Rapha	The Lord your healer	Ex	15:26
85. Yhwh-Shalom	The Lord is peace or complete wholeness	Jud	6:24
86. Yhwh-Shammah	The Lord is there	Ezk	48:35
87. Yhwh-tsidkenu	The Lord is our righteousness	Je	23:6
88. Yhwh-Yireh	The Lord provider (or who provides)	Ge	22:14

An asterisk (*) denotes all Greek transliterations. No asterisk means that the transliteration is from the original Hebrew or Aramaic (as in the case of *'Elah'*). For further Biblical references please refer to a Young's Concordance.

In the Old Testament, the word *'El'* is employed 250 times, the word *'Eloah'* 57 times (41 times during Job's dialogues with his friends), *'Elohim'* 2,570 times and *'Yahweh,'* over 7000 times. All of these names are often used interchangeably. The prophecies of Balaam in Numbers 23-24 provide one example of such an interchangeable usage.

'Elah' is an Aramaic version of *'Elohim'*. In turn, this name is the plural of *'El.'* Its frequent usage leaves scope for the doctrine of the Trinity. However *'Yahweh,'* unlike the other terms, is only ever used in connection with the one true *'God of Israel.'* In scripture, it is never used in connection with other gods.

Finally, the name *'Yisrael'* means *"One who strives and rules as a prince with God."* It was given to the patriarch Jacob in Genesis 32.28 & 35.10. This name also implies that Jacob was a person through whom God showed His strength in a very special way.

A3: DIFFERENT VIEWS OF DEIFICATION

The Autonomous (Non-Deification) View

God **(G)** and Man **(M)** have their own distinct identities, with no inter-relationship between the two **(Ø)**. They both exist in their own separate spheres and possess different attributes **(A1** and **A2)**. However, in contrast to Man whose particular attributes are limited in number and warped by sin **($A1^{ns}$)**, God has an unlimited number of perfect attributes **($A2\infty$)**. This autonomous view believes that no real connection exists between God and people. It was prevalent amongst the Deists of the eighteenth century Enlightenment and was held by thinkers like the French Philosopher Voltaire (1694-1778). At best, the Deity is regarded with some sort of vague reverence.

The logical outcome of this position is a practical atheism which encourages people to lead lives without reference to God. They feel free to do *'what is right in their own eyes,'* (Judges 21:25). Under this model, no kind of deification is possible. It is represented by the simple formula: -

$M(A1^{ns})$ Ø $G(A2\infty)$

The Dissolution (Complete Deification) View

Man is seen as dissolving (or merging) into God (sometimes known as *'The One'* or *'The Infinite'*) like a drop of water in the ocean; his human characteristics become meaningless. Through the practice **(⊃)** of spiritual techniques **(ST)** like Eastern Meditation, Man **(M)** ascends **(↑)** into deity – but in so doing loses all his distinctly human attributes **(↓A1)** and individual personality **(↓I)**, so that in the end he becomes nothing **(0)**. Prevalent in Eastern Religions like Hinduism, the Dissolution View believes that, in order to become completely divine, people need to overcome ignorance and *'realize their divine potential by getting in touch with own inner God.'*

The logical outcome of this position is a worship *of 'self'* **(WM)** which encourages people to believe that they are above any moral law **(>L)**. Under this model, full deification is assumed to be possible – albeit at the expense of losing everything that makes one distinctly human. It is represented by the more complex formula: -

$M(A1^{ns}) \supset SP \Rightarrow \uparrow G(A2\infty) \Rightarrow \downarrow A1 \supset \downarrow I \Rightarrow 0 \Rightarrow WM > L$

The Linkage (Partial Deification) View

Man has some attributes which he largely shares with God **(LS)** despite the presence of human sin and a hostile separation from God **(HØ)**. Upon becoming a believer in Christ any division with God becomes far less pronounced. Both believer and God are linked together **(∩)** in a relationship of love. A growth in grace ensures that, over time, the believer has an <u>increasing number of traits</u> in common with God, yet <u>each party retain their distinct identities.</u> Further reducing any division is the way a Christian is filled with God's Holy Spirit. The effect of this is to enhance their individuality <u>but not to make him (or her) divine.</u> He (or she) is closely linked to God (<u>but is not absorbed by Him</u>) and, over time, comes to enjoy the *'potentially shared'* **(PS)** divine attributes. There is also a reduction in sin **(↓S)** as God's Spirit begins to influence more areas of their personality. However, there are still many attributes which remain *'barely shared'* **(BS)** and <u>will always (both now and in eternity) belong only to God.</u> This *'linkage view'* is the one taught in scripture. Highlighted is the extent to which people can become like God.

The logical outcome of this position is an intelligent relationship with God and a growth in personal holiness. This encourages practical action to help other people. In Christianity, there's no separation between the spiritual and the practical. Under this model only *'exaltation'* is possible. It is represented by a multi-layered formula in which the top line **(L1)** represents a person's condition before they enter a relationship with God through Jesus Christ whilst the middle line **(L2)** represents their condition once such a relationship has been established. The bottom line **(L3)** shows what their relationship will be in eternity where there's no sin and a perfect union **(U)** with God is enjoyed.

Throughout out this process a person's individuality increases rather than diminishes **(↑I)**. At the end, no area of sin is left **(/0S)**.

L1: $M(A^{ns} \supset LS - PSBS) \ HØ \ G = (A^\infty \supset LS + PS + BS)$

$$\Downarrow$$

L2: $M(A^{ns} \supset LS + PS - BS) \cap G = (A^\infty \supset LS + PS + BS) \Rightarrow \uparrow A1 \supset \uparrow I \downarrow S$

$$\Downarrow$$

L3: $M(A^{ns} \supset LS + PS - BS) \ U \ G = (A^\infty \supset LS + PS + BS) \Rightarrow \uparrow A1 \supset \uparrow I/0S$

SELECTIVE BIBLIOGRAPHY

Caution

All readers are expected to use their own discernment when consulting or otherwise employing the sources listed in this Bibliography or mentioned elsewhere in this publication. Listing in the Bibliography does not mean that the author (Raymond Creed) necessarily endorses either the content or style of these sources – nor is he responsible for the conduct or financial/legal affairs of any organization associated with them. The quotation or citation of a source in this work should not be taken as a recommendation of its quality unless the author's previous comments strongly suggest otherwise.

S1: Book List

Adair John (1998)
Puritans:
Religion and Politics in Seventeenth Century England and America
Sutton Publishing
ISBN: 0-7509-2117-X

Athanasius (1979)
Incarnation:
The Treatise De Incarnation Verbei Dei
Mowbrays
SBN: 264-65313-0

Bavinck Herman (1979)[220]
The Doctrine of God
The Banner of Truth Trust
ISBN: 085151-255-0

Brierley Peter Dr (2000)
The Tide Is Running Out
Christian Research
ISBN: 1-85321-137-0

---

[220] Unless otherwise stated, the dates in brackets refer to the date of the particular edition consulted and not necessarily the original date of authorship.

Brierley Peter Dr (2006)
Pulling Out of the Nosedive
Christian Research
ISBN: 978-1-85321-168-3

Brown G. Callum (2001)
The Death of Christian Britain
Routledge
ISBN: 0-414-24184-7

Charnock Stephen (2000, Originally Published 1682)
The Existence and Attributes of God
Baker Books
ISBN: 0-8010-1112-4

Cohn Norman (1957, 2004 edn)
The Pursuit of the Millennium
Secker & Warburg

Dix Gregory Dom (1960 – first published 1945)
The Shape of the Liturgy
Dacre Press, Adam & Charles Black

Glover Peter (1997)
The Signs and Wonders Movement Exposed
Day One Publications
ISBN: 0902-548-751

Grudem Wayne (1994)
Systematic Theology: An Introduction to Biblical Doctrine
Inter-Varsity Press & Zondervan Publishing House
ISBN: 0-85110-652-8

Hanegraaf Hank (1993)
Christianity in Crisis
Harvest House Publishers
ISBN: 0-89081-9769

Hunt Dave McMahon (1986)
The Seduction of Christianity:
Spiritual Discernment in the Last Days
Harvest House Publishers
ISBN: 0-89081-441-4

Jenkins Philip (2006)
The New Face of Christianity: Believing the Bible in the Global South
Oxford University Press
ISBN: 0-19-530065-3

Jukes Andrew (2000)
The Names of God
Kregel Publications
ISBN: 0-8254-2958-7

MacCulloch Diarmaid (2009)
A History of Christianity:
The First Three Thousand Years
Allen Lane ISBN: 978-0-713-99869

McDonald Elizabeth (1996)
Alpha: New Life or New Lifestyle?
St Matthew Publications
ISBN: 0:9524672-6-7

Morrison, Alan (1994)
The Serpent and the Cross: Religious Corruption in an Evil Age
K & M Books
ISBN: 0-9523041-0-4

Nader Mikhaiel (1995)
Slaying In the Spirit: The Telling Wonder
Southward Press
ISBN: 0-646-12574-5

Packer J. I. (1978)
Knowing God
Hodder and Stoughton
ISBN: 0-340-1913-7

Pink W. Arthur (2001)
The Attributes of God
Baker Book House Company
ISBN: 0-8010-6989-0

Randles Bill Pastor (1994)
Making War in the Heavenlies:
A Different Look at Spiritual Warfare
Self-Published

Sparrow Giles (2006)
Cosmos: A Field Guide
Quercus
ISBN: 1-905204-29-9

Tozer A. W. (1976)
The Knowledge of the Holy
Send the Light Trust

Ware Kallistos (1981)
The Orthodox Way
Mowbray
ISBN: 0-264-66578-3

S2: Reference Works

Augustine of Hippo (1991)
Saint Augustine: Volume V, Writings against the Pelagians
T & T Clark and Eerdmans Publishing, USA
ISBN: 0-567-09394-8 & 0-8028-8102-5

Brierley Peter Dr - Editor (2003)
UK Handbook, Religious Trends 4
Christian Research
ISBN: 1-85321-149-4

Brierley Peter Dr - Editor (2005)
UK Handbook, Religious Trends 5
Christian Research
ISBN: 1-85321-160-5

Douglas D. J. - Editor (1978)
The New International Dictionary of the Christian Church
The Paternoster Press Ltd
(By arrangement with Zondervan Corporation)
USA ISBN: 0-85364-221-4

Ferguson B. Sinclair & Wright F David (1988)
New Dictionary of Theology
Inter-Varsity Press
ISBN: 0-855110-636-6

Fisher-Park George (1927)
History of Christian Doctrine
Edinburgh T & T Clark

Lane Tony (1992)
The Lion Book of Christian Thought
Lion Publishing PLC
ISBN: 0-7324-0575-0

Palmer G. E. H. Sherrard Philip and Ware Kallistos (1983)
The Philokalia: The Complete Text (volume one)
Faber & Faber
ISBN: 0-571-13013-5

S3: Media Sources

Buerk Michael (Chairperson)
The Moral Maze,
Radio 4, Wednesday 3/2/2010

Dimbleby Jonathan (Chairperson)
Any Questions
Radio 4, Friday 5/2/2010

Wroe Martin (2006)
Publish and Get Instant Gratification with the ITunes of Literature
Sunday Times News Review p.4.3
13.8.2006

S4: Other Information Sources

These have included various private contacts whose names cannot be disclosed for reasons of confidentially. Also, video footage of some Television Programmes dating from the mid-1990s concerning the Toronto Experience

Gousmett Chris (2008) *Theosis and the transformation of the Body*
www.earlychurch.org.uk/pdf/gousmett/appendix.pdf

Matthew *Deacon* (2003) Forum Contribution
http://www.monachos.net/forum/showthread.php?1949-Athanasius-and-Theosis

OTHER TITLES BY THE AUTHOR

NOTICE

For information on the ordering and pricing of these titles please visit
http://stores.lulu.com/rebuildchristianity or
http://stores.lulu.com/store.php?fAcctID=976144

For information on their contents and for sample extracts please visit the author's website at
www.rebuildchristianity.com/LS1.htm

For other publications by the author please visit
www.rebuildchristianity.com

For contact details please visit
www.rebuildchristianity.com/LS5.htm#co

Soft cover versions of these titles should be available through Amazon and other International Distributors.

In the event of any difficulty with these *'links'* please search using the *'Book Title'* and the name *'Raymond Creed.'* Doing this should access a relevant site.

FACING THE UNTHINKABLE

'*Facing the Unthinkable*' dramatically portrays the likely emotional and psychological reactions of a beleaguered number of Jewish people at the very point when they turn to their true Messiah. Their state of near-total despair will suddenly change to one of exuberant joy. Following their recognition and acceptance of the Messiah all of the bible prophecies concerning the restoration of Israel will begin to be fulfilled.

'*Facing the Unthinkable*' provides hope for the Messianic Jewish Community and for those Christians with a genuine interest in the Jewish people. It helps rebuild Christianity by emphasising its links to both Israel and Judaism.

Great care is taken to address the following questions: -
1) How will the Jewish people come to believe in their true Messiah?
2) How will they react when they encounter Him?
3) How will the world react to this unexpected development?

This book breaks new ground in its creative expression of the spiritual and psychological aspects likely to be experienced when the true Messiah is recognised. It's assumed that both the nation of Israel and the whole of humanity itself will be on the brink of annihilation before this unique event happens. G-d will have allowed much suffering to have taken place to show man's abject failure in his attempt to create a New World Order. The promise of a better and fairer world will have been cruelly exposed and falsified.

'*Facing the Unthinkable*' is an invaluable resource for those engaged in any form of Jewish work or who have a sympathetic interest in the State of Israel. It may be regarded as an independent work or as a successor volume to '*The Leeds Liturgy.*'

To purchase a download, hard or soft cover edition please visit: -

http://stores.lulu.com/rebuildchristianity or

http://stores.lulu.com/store.php?fAcctID=976144

Soft cover editions may also be available through Amazon and other International Distributors.

THE LEEDS LITURGY

'The Leeds Liturgy' encourages Christians to worship God *"in spirit and in truth"* (John 4:24). In terms of doctrine, it aspires to be the truest and most accurate book outside of scripture. Its pages contain *'The Leeds Creed'* which is the most comprehensive creedal *'Statement of Faith'* in Christianity to date, (Acts 20:27). This *'statement'* integrates bible-based insights from every Christian Tradition and provides a comprehensive summary of those doctrines needed for salvation and for effective Christian living. Also included are revised versions of the Apostles, Nicene and Athanasian Creeds.

'The Leeds Liturgy' aims to: -
1) Provide a legacy of truth for present and future believers
2) Testify to the one true Gospel that *"Jesus Christ came into the world to save sinners,"* (I Timothy 1:15b)
3) Portray doctrine in a fresh, interactive and understandable way
4) Promote an exuberant style of worship
5) Declare the *whole counsel [full teaching]* of God to a Church that currently seems to value everything else <u>but</u> the teaching of Scripture
6) Enable believers (largely due to its provision of sound doctrinal teaching) to better withstand persecution and hardship
7) Bring Jew and Gentile together in joint worship of the one true God of Israel
8) Nurture the community life of Messianic Jewish and Christian groups
9) Offer a distinctive way of presenting timeless truths to a sinful world
10) Enable believers to interact with bible teaching (either individually or in a group setting)

'The Leeds Liturgy' proclaims the Gospel by pointing to Christ as the only means whereby eternal life is received. His full deity and full humanity are equally emphasised – as is the Trinitarian relationship between Himself, His Father and the Holy Spirit. Christians are encouraged to relate to These Persons through the material provided in this resource. It attempts to be a vehicle with the innate capacity to be used by the Holy Spirit, who eagerly wants to lead Christians into all truth, (John 16:13a). It highlights the fact that, in order to place our faith in God, we must first of all lose faith in ourselves.

'The Leeds Liturgy' closes with two articles exploring the biblical roots of Liturgies and Creeds. These could be of particular interest to students working in the field of liturgical studies. Its successor volume, *'Facing the Unthinkable'* provides a dramatic anticipation of how Israel will recognize the true messiah during a period of great affliction.

To purchase a download, hard or soft cover edition please visit: -

http://stores.lulu.com/rebuildchristianity or

http://stores.lulu.com/store.php?fAcctID=976144

Soft cover versions may also be available through Amazon and other International Distributors.

THE PHANTOM CONFLICT

'The Phantom Conflict' endeavours to rebuild Christianity by showing how a balanced emphasis between divine holiness and divine love is a necessary prerequisite for healthy Christian living. The problem of Christian idolatry is also tackled.

Great care is taken to address the following questions: -
1) How does divine holiness relate to divine love?
2) How is it possible to avoid incorrect views of God?
3) How is it possible to avoid idolatry?

'The Phantom Conflict,' assumes that correct ideas of God are a vital precondition to spiritual fruitfulness. It argues that to exaggerate divine holiness at the expense of divine love (or vice-versa) produces a warped and ineffective version of Christianity. At one extreme it becomes a religion of fear and at the other a religion of flippancy. Both deviations harm their adherents and discredit the gospel.

This book should prove particularly useful to religious ministers (of all denominational backgrounds), local church elders, Christian teachers, evangelists and theological students. The Messianic Jewish community and those wishing to delve deeper into theology would also benefit.

'The Phantom Conflict' serves as a practical and interactive teaching tool, being divided into easily accessible sections, all undergirded by ancient Jewish methods of bible interpretation (*'Midrash'*). It may be regarded as an independent work or as a successor volume to *'The 52 Attributes of God.'*

To purchase a download, hard or soft cover edition please visit: -

http://stores.lulu.com/rebuildchristianity or

http://stores.lulu.com/store.php?fAcctID=976144

Soft cover editions may also be available through Amazon and other International Distributors.

NOTES

www.ingramcontent.com/pod-product-compliance
Lightning Source LLC
Chambersburg PA
CBHW030239170426
43202CB00007B/47